THE BEAUTY OF JUDAISM ON FILM

ALSO BY MIKE KING:

Enigma's Coda
(Stochastic Press, 2016)

Quakernomics: An Ethical Capitalism
(Anthem Press, 2014)

Luminous: The Spiritual Life on Film
(McFarland & Company, 2014)

The Angel of Har Megiddo: A novel of the US-Israel-Palestine conflict
(Stochastic Press, 2012)

Postsecularism: The Hidden Challenge to Religious Extremism
(James Clarke & Co., 2009)

The American Cinema of Excess: Extremes of the National Mind on Film
(Stochastic Press, 2016 / McFarland & Company, 2009)

Secularism: The Hidden Origins of Disbelief
(James Clarke & Co., 2007)

Othe writings are archived at www.jnani.org/mrking/writings

THE BEAUTY OF JUDAISM ON FILM

Mike King

Stochastic Press

Text copyright © 2017 Mike King

All rights reserved. No part of this book may be reproduced or transmitted in any form or by any means, electronic or mechanical, including photocopying, recording, or by an information storage and retrieval system – except by a reviewer who may quote brief passages in a review – without permission in writing from the author.

mike@jnani.org

Version 1.0 © 2017

This book is also available in Kindle format.

ISBN-13: 978-0-9956480-2-9

ISBN-10: 0995648026

London: Stochastic Press

CONTENTS

Introduction 1
   Judaism and Film 1
   Judaism v. Jewishness 2
   Writings on Judaism and Film 3
   Filmmaking and Secularism 5
   Gershom Scholem's vision of Judaism 6
   Martin Buber's vision of Hasidism 10
   Plotinus's vision of Beauty 11
   Kierkegaard's vision of Faith 12
   Selecting Religious Films 15
   Terminology 16
1. Essential Judaism 17
   Preamble 17
   The Chosen 17
   Ushpizin 28
   The Quarrel 33
   Summary 37
2. Musical Judaism 38
   Preamble 38
   Yentl 38
      An Ethical Assessment 43
   Fiddler on the Roof 44
   The Jazz Singer 47
      The Jazz Singer (1927) 48
      The Jazz Singer (1980) 49
   Summary 52
3. Mystical Judaism 53
   Preamble 53
   Kabbalah Films 53
      Preamble 53
      Bee Season 54
      Pi 59
      A Stranger Among Us 63
   Dybbuk Films 70
      Preamble 70
      A Serious Man 71
      The Possession 73

The Dybbuk	74
Summary	82
4. Crazed Judaism	**84**
Preamble	84
Secular Craziness	86
The Believer	86
Song of Songs	94
Time Of Favor	98
Supernatural Craziness	101
Der Golem	101
Simon Magus	105
The Jewish Millennium	107
Summary	109
5. Secular Judaism	**110**
Preamble	110
Woody Allen's *Crimes and Misdemeanors*	111
Introduction to Woody Allen	111
Introducing *Crimes and Misdemeanors*	113
The Seder Meal	116
Critiques of Woody Allen	118
Other Dialogues across the Divide	119
Holy Rollers	120
Little Jerusalem	121
Summary	122
6. Holocaust Judaism	**124**
Preamble	124
The Believer	126
The Diary of Anne Frank	128
Left Luggage	131
The Pawnbroker	133
The Quarrel	135
The Devil's Arithmetic	138
Summary	138
7. Israel Judaism	**140**
Preamble	140
Israel History	141
Preamble	141
Masada	141
Exodus	144
Kippur and *Waltz with Bashir*	145
Jerusalem Judaism	148
Preamble	148

  The Body 149
  Ushpizin and *Kadosh* 150
  My Father My Lord 152
 Shifting Tides 156
  Preamble 157
  Live and Become 158
 Summary 162
8. Gendered Judaism 164
 Preamble 164
 Kadosh 164
 A Price Above Rubies 169
 Arranged 172
 Eyes Wide Open 174
 Trembling Before G-d 176
 Women in Judaism 178
 Summary 180
9. Family Judaism 181
 Preamble 181
 Festivals and celebrations 182
 Weddings 183
 Sexual Relations 185
 The Shabbat 187
 Summary 190
Conclusions: The Beauty of Judaism on Film 192
Appendix: Glossary of Judaic Terms 194
Appendix: Ten Best Judaism Films 198
Filmography 199
Bibliography 201
References 203

Introduction

Judaism and Film

I imagine that religion for the non-religious might appear like a mysterious box. One turns it over and round and finally spots in small letters: OPENING INSTRUCTIONS. Underneath, in even smaller letters, is the legend: SEE INSIDE FOR OPENING INSTRUCTIONS. In other words it is very hard for the non-religious – for those with secular minds – to peer into the box of religion. Within that box there are of course more boxes marked "Buddhism," "Christianity," "Hinduism," "Shinto," "Judaism," and so on. One may stand within the larger box – that is, one may be sympathetic to and understanding of religion in general – but might still grapple with the opening instructions on some of the smaller boxes. But there are some openings perhaps to all these boxes, and I happen to believe that film is one of them.

It may sound strange to talk about the beauty of religion, even more so if the beauty here is not in the first instance an aesthetic one. And it may be more puzzling still to seek this beauty in film. And why Judaism anyway? But to answer these questions in reverse order, I could have chosen any religion, but happened to decide on Judaism for this particular book because my previous work on religion and film threw up so many interesting cases of something profoundly religious conveyed in that medium about this religion, and I can only describe what I saw as something "beautiful." However, as film is undoubtedly a visual medium, we return to the question of what beauty we are seeking exactly. Here I will draw on the "Ennead on Beauty" by Plotinus, a classical text known to generations of those taught in Western art colleges, a text that has nothing to do with Judaism. It has instead a universal application to all the religions, suggesting that something of the method developed in this book could be applied to filmic representations of other faiths.

Although a I had a Jewish grandfather, he had Bolshevik and Gnostic beliefs, and I have no more loyalty to Judaism than any other religion, and probably less actual knowledge of it than, say, Buddhism. But I am a keen observer of the world's major and minor religions, love all that is authentic in them, and do believe that there are something like forty films from which

Introduction

one can glimpse something of the inner beauty of Judaism. It is a compelling vision when taken as the sum of these glimpses, and I hope that this book conveys it. One could do the same with Buddhism or Christianity, but not with Islam, for example, because Islamic cultures do not seem to throw up the same kind of cinema.

But what Judaism am I hoping to reconstruct through film, given that I am not a Jew or a scholar of this religion? In the first instance it is the Judaism of the mystics, and more specifically the Judaism as I understand if from Gershom Scholem's famous book: *Major Trends in Jewish Mysticism*. Of course, I am familiar with the Hebrew Bible, and some modern works by great Jewish theologians, including Martin Buber and Emmanuel Levinas, but it is Scholem's account that links my investigation to the work by Plotinus I mentioned above. I also draw on a text called *Basic Judaism*, by a Milton Steinberg, who was for some time the rabbi of the Park Avenue Synagogue in New York. My aim in this book is not however to give a systematic account of Judaism, as Steinberg sets out to do, or to traverse its long history using the device of Scholem. Rather, it is the films themselves that have shaped the structure of this book, and there is nothing I can do if it leaves an incomplete or lopsided view of Judaism. That can always be rectified by reading a textbook.

Mysticism has a beauty, when properly understood, and I think that Plotinus did properly understand it. But just to complete the picture of how religious beauty is different to mere aesthetic beauty I also draw a little on Kierkegaard, who makes a sharp and useful distinction between the two.

Judaism v. Jewishness

A comprehensive list of films dealing with Jewish topics probably runs into the hundreds or even thousands, but the aim here is to provide a glimpse into Judaism as a religion, not as a culture. Hence I have largely excluded from my search films which deal with Jewishness, the experience of being a Jew, the history of the Jews, and even the Holocaust, major subject that it is, if the film does not also make the Jewish religion central to its theme. Of course we can sometimes know the shape of a thing by its absence, and the loss of faith can tell us things about faith. However the mere incomprehension of faith is not the same thing, so I have to flag up right here that I consider the films of Woody Allen for example to contain little or nothing of the beauty of Judaism *as a religion*, though as a series of meditations on Jewishness, on the other hand, they are perhaps unparalleled. Having said that, a scene in his film *Crimes and Misdemeanors* (a film examined in the chapter on Secular Judaism) contains a useful remark about the protagonist's father, suggesting that his Judaic faith was a gift like

Introduction

"an ear for music or the talent to draw." A Jew who is thoroughly secularized, or one who we might refer to as an Enlightenment Jew, may be totally "unmusical" to Judaism, and to any religion for that matter, indeed perhaps the terms "musical" and "unmusical" hint at my approach here. The great sociologist Max Weber wrote that he was unmusical to religion, though compared to some atheists today he is remarkably sensitive to the subject in his writings. Rousseau also wrote about one who did not "vibrate" to religion,[1] explaining that he thought the difficulty of trying to explain the source of religion within personal experience was like trying to convince the deaf of the existence of sound. Religion, then, is something subtle that can be misheard or misperceived by those not attuned to it, and a mishearing or misconceiving of Judaism as a religion by a Jew may well be no more informative than that by a non-Jew.

But what in essence is Judaism? Steinberg says: "The simultaneous love of G-d[a] and man: here is Judaism's first postulate and final inference, its point of departure and its destination, the root of it and its fruitage." [2] This is a good an introductory sentence as any, but in the course of this book we will build up something of a mosaic of Judaism's deeper character, little fragments that flesh out this simple definition, bearing in mind too that a hundred scholars of Judaism would probably have given a hundred different definitions of the religion's essence. An additional key characteristic that Steinberg flags up early in his book, and is worth mentioning now, is that Judaism is a *book* religion. [3] As we will see, much hinges on this idea, including that Judaism therefore became "portable." Also important for the understanding of Judaism is the idea, broached by religious scholar Karen Armstrong, that it is more a religion of orthopraxy – meaning conformity of practice – than a religion of orthodoxy – meaning conformity of belief. [4]

Writings on Judaism and Film

Judaism on film has been touched on by many scholars of religious cinema. In *Over the Top Judaism* by Elliot B. Gertel we find a sustained lament for clumsy, inappropriate or secularist visions of Judaism in film and television. Gertel's warnings over how badly Judaism can be represented in the moving image are important, but, even with such caveats in mind it is possible, I believe, to be a little forgiving of error and to find in many films positive and informative portrayals of Judaism. I also suggest that it is the

---

[a] This spelling and other conventions used throughout this book are explained in the section on terminology at the end of the Introduction.

Introduction

cumulative picture that matters more than individual lapses of accuracy. At the end of *Luminous: The Spiritual Life on Film* I wrote:

> No reduced set of films covers enough ground to adequately portray the spiritual life in the round. Instead, it is better to declare that the spiritual life on film is a matter of gathering up a host of smaller clues, rather than a single great revelation. [5]

Gertel's rather pessimistic theme is taken up by the American cultural conservative and critic Michael Medved in a short chapter called "Jabbing the Jews" in his book *Hollywood vs. America*. He thinks that rabbis are ridiculed less in cinema than Christian clergy but concludes: "this has less to do with the high concentration of Jews in the movie industry than with the prevailing perception that Judaism is all but irrelevant as a religious system." [6] Needless to say I disagree with this.

Other than in Gertel's book the theme of Judaism on film is usually lost in surveys which are on the lookout for Jewishness in film. For example *The New Jew in Film* by Nathan Abrams pursues the thesis that the Jew has become "normalized" in film in more recent offerings – instead of Jewish characters stereotyped as "Jew-as-thief," or "Jew-as-liar" we now have "Jew-as-typical-American." The film *The Big Lebowski* by the Coen brothers is taken as a key example of this normalization, where the Jewish character is a slightly deranged Vietnam veteran who maintains his religious identity – including naming his dog Maimonides – yet otherwise exhibits all the stereotypical traits of the gun-toting individualistic paranoid white American male.[7] The cover of Abrams's book even depicts a scene with this character at a bowling alley, but the distance from any real interest in Judaism is reinforced by the fact that the character is not even Jewish by birth but by conversion. If Shakespeare created one of the most negative stereotypes of the Jew in Shylock, then the journey from that cultural low point – in regard to Jews that is – to American normalization is not, it seems, that much to celebrate after all. The "New Jew" in film is merely a classic American archetype with quaint eccentricities derived from Jewish observance, the meaning of which is assumed to signify no more than the brand choice of whisky, motorcycle or gun.

Abrams does have a chapter on religion in his book, which begins:

> Given the volume of research dedicated to analyzing the Jewish contribution to film, both in front of and behind the camera, it is surprising to note that to date not much work has been done on *Judaism*, overshadowed by a

tendency to focus on the *image* of the Jew/ess or on the Holocaust in film.[8]

The image of the Jew or Jewess in cinema is not our concern here. In an age where religion is largely an embarrassment to media-savvy cultural producers such as the Coen brothers, we cannot learn much about Judaism from questions about Jewish stereotyping. The prejudices of non-Jewish society will not help us; neither will the converse, i.e. Jewish self-preoccupation, enlighten us to the real meaning of Judaism. Hence books which further examine the role of the Jew on screen, such as *The "Jew" in Cinema: From "The Golem" to "Don't Touch My Holocaust,"* or which celebrate Jewish film-making such as *The 50 Greatest Jewish Movies: A Critic's Ranking of the Very Best* are mostly dealing with very different priorities. However, where these books or other critical writings analyze Judaism on film here and there, I shall draw on them.

Filmmaking and Secularism

If, as Medved claims, there is a high concentration of Jews in Hollywood, why are there not more films that attempt a genuine portrayal of Judaism? I have considered such questions in my two earlier books, *Secularism*, and *Postsecularism*, and was much drawn to the argument of Professor David Martin at the London School of Economics that the locus of cultural production is in an intellectual and metropolitan centre drawn to atheism, while the audience represents a religious periphery, or at least a periphery much less certain of the irrelevance of religion.[9] This "centre-periphery" theory would hold that Jewish film directors such as the Coen brothers are culturally inclined to skepticism, even if, as Medved insists, the majority of Americans are not.

In my book *Luminous* I pointed out that atheism as a cultural assumption seems to travel with the movie-camera wherever film making has spread to non-Western cultures.[10] I also pointed out that films of genuine religious significance are often an accident of the director's general trajectory, so in some ways all of this means that the hunt for good films about Judaism is not an easy one, but rather a matter of the unexpected and surprising.

Some people understand the term "secularism" to mean a doctrine of separation of church and state, where, to use more ancient terms, temporal authorities deal with matters of this world – the saeculum – and ecclesiastical authorities deal with matters of the next. To them a secular society, perhaps like that of India, implies that government is in the name of all the people regardless of their religion, while in America the separation

Introduction

of church and state is guaranteed by the establishment clause of the First Amendment. But I use the terms "secular" and "secularism" in my work to mean something a little different: to mean a non-religious or anti-religious sensibility and a belief system promoting that outlook. In the context of Judaism secular Jews are therefore non-practicing Jews, even if they maintain some of the outward rituals of their tradition. It is not quite the same as atheism, however, because to reject the idea of G-d one has to have some reason to entertain it in the first place.

While it is clear that film-making is undertaken in a largely secular context, cinema is such a huge activity in terms of volume that there are still many films made which are sympathetic to religion, or at least to the moral structures that religion teaches. The British directors Michael Powell and Emeric Pressburger were a famous team responsible for many successful films, some of which, like *A Matter of Life and Death* and *Black Narcissus*, have spiritual or religious themes. Powell and Pressburger's production company was called "The Archers" and Pressburger once set out a manifesto for it which includes this remarkable statement: "At any time, and particularly at the present, the self-respect of all collaborators, from star to prop-man, is sustained, or diminished, by the theme and purpose of the film they are working on." [11] I interpret this to mean that if the theme is an ugly one, for example of violent revenge, or in general involving a glorification of violence, then all those working on it are diminished. They are made smaller to the extent that they participate in something which is the antithesis of love. On the other hand, and the two films just mentioned show this quality, if a film has a strong moral structure – if it has a moral beauty – all those involved in its making are added unto. The word used by the directors was "sustained" which is telling: it implies that we need such sustenance. Now, if this is true for those who made the film, it must be just as true for those who watch it. The ten best Judaism films that I extract from the longer list discussed in this book have, I believe, that quality of providing such spiritual sustenance, over and above the insights into Judaism that they convey, while the longer list as a whole rounds out that sustenance.

Gershom Scholem's vision of Judaism

I mentioned earlier that I draw on Scholem's *Major Trends in Jewish Mysticism*. But why chose this as a key portrait of Judaism? Firstly, as a text on mysticism, it allows us a way into the religion that makes some parallels with other traditions possible, for example with the mysticism of Plotinus, or with Christian mysticism. Secondly, Scholem's history of Jewish mysticism portrays Judaism itself as an entity undergoing continuous evolution. And thirdly, Scholem himself was a key Jewish figure of the twentieth century, spanning the secular and religious worlds, the European and the Israeli, and old and the new. He helped found the Hebrew University of Jerusalem, was a friend of Walter Benjamin, and was an intellectual sparring partner to Martin Buber. Above all he was a serious thinker, and we will find many clues in his work as to the nature of Judaism and how to approach its portrayal in film.

Scholem considers that mystics are not so much a rebellious group persecuted by the mainstream but rather "faithful adherents of the great religions."[12] We understand from him that mystics in Judaism were not persecuted for heresy as we find in Islam and Christianity, however, but were instead largely accepted both as fostering a deeper understanding of the faith and as the source of fresh thinking. However, Scholem is also clear that Jewish mystics have a particular character unlike those of other religions, for example in not normally seeking "union" with G-d. Indeed it is the gulf between man and G-d that is the wellspring of mystical thought in Judaism. Scholem says:

> Man becomes aware of a fundamental duality, of a vast gulf which can be crossed by nothing but the *voice*; the voice of G-d, directing and law-giving in His revelation, and the voice of man in prayer.[13]

This idea, that it is the *voice* that bridges the gulf between humanity and G-d, illuminates much of Judaism. As Scholem says, it indicates on the one hand the voice of G-d as He interacts with the people of Israel, directing them and constructing their holy Law, and on the other the voice of the Jews in prayer. Steinberg reinforces the point when he writes quite simply: "Prayer is the bridge between man and G-d."[14] Above all this idea points to language as the key to Judaism – indeed I know of no other religion so obsessed by language in general, or where its mysticism can so properly be described as "language-mysticism". In an essay called "Reification of Language in Jewish Mysticism" the scholar Moshe Idel explains this special place of language in the Jewish tradition:

> In creation and in ritual, the Hebrew language was considered by Jewish mystics as playing a role much more important than the common communicative one that language regularly plays. It was the main instrument of the creation of the world, and it is the vessel that is prepared by man to contain the divine light that is attracted therein in order to experience an act of union or communion.[15]

Introduction

What this means for Judaism on film it that we are not, as in some other religions, peering into a religion that is silent and inward in all its manifestations. On the contrary Judaism is often very vocal; for example when Tevye in *Fiddler on the Roof* has a problem he communicates this verbally to his G-d. To some ears it might sound like complaining, but a clue lies in the meaning of the word "Israel": some suggest that it is "the struggle with G-d." It is this element of struggle – quite foreign as part of the religious impulse in Buddhism for example – that is key to much of the spiritual drama in the films we will examine, from the endearing humor of Tevye to an extreme in the film *The Believer* where the Jewish protagonist becomes a rabid and violent anti-Semite in personal anguish over his faith.

If the emphasis on language and the vocal dialogue between Jew and G-d is one defining feature of Judaism, then its rejection of Nature as a site of the sacred is another. Much of the Hebrew Bible can be read as a determined journey away from the Nature- and Goddess-religions of earlier and neighboring cultures, epitomized in the condemnation of all that is "idolatry." As Scholem describes this fundamental feature of Judaism:

> Religion's supreme function is to destroy the dream-harmony of Man, Universe and G-d, to isolate man from the other elements of the dream state of his mythical and primitive consciousness.... the scene of religion is no longer Nature, but the moral and religious action of man and the community of men, whose interplay brings about history as, in a sense, the stage on which the drama of man's relation to G-d unfolds.[16]

The nature of Judaism as a drama between man and G-d is the basis on which this book suggests again that cinema is particularly suited to exploring Judaism. As pointed out earlier the films discussed here will not assemble anything like a comprehensive or systematic portrait of Judaism, instead we find two major clusters of filmmaking, one centered on Hasidic Jews in New York and another on the "Haredi" or ultra-Orthodox of Jerusalem. A third much smaller group covers the Jews of the middle-European "shtetls" or small towns, while the remainder have a variety of settings, most of which focus on Ashkenazi Jews, i.e. those of Eastern European origin. Only one film is about Sephardic Jews and only one about Jews from North Africa. None of this yields for example a history parallel to that of Scholem's history of mysticism, nor a survey of the division of contemporary Judaism. Indeed none of the films have a Reform Judaism setting, for example, though Medved tells us that the rabbi in *Crimes and*

Introduction

Misdemeanors is Reform rather than Orthodox [17]. We have to be clear: the films discussed here give rather random glimpses on a very small scale into a phenomenon which is in itself vast.

Judaism is one of the oldest religions in the world, which is why its history and contemporary variety is so extensive. Scholem's use of mysticism is only one way to structure its investigation, but has relevance for our films here. He shows us that Jewish mysticism is almost co-extensive with the Kabbalah, conceding only Merkabah or "throne" mysticism in a period of the first to the tenth centuries as preceding Kabbalism. Most of the chapters in his book then deal with the development of different forms of the Kabbalah, and mostly it is only the later period of this development that is relevant to the films in this book, but what his scholarship shows is important however: the real Kabbalah is very different to the populist New Age version promoted by media celebrities such as Madonna, Demi Moore and Britney Spears. It is also a rich and complex tradition, not all of which is to be admired. He says:

> If one turns to the writings of great Kabbalists one seldom fails to be torn between alternate admiration and disgust. There is a need for being quite clear about this in a time like ours, when the fashion of uncritical and superficial condemnation of even the most valuable elements of mysticism threatens to be replaced by an equally uncritical and obscurantist glorification of the Kabbalah. [18]

In more than one of our films the Kabbalah leads the protagonist astray. At the same time its interpenetration with the everyday Judaism of ordinary Jewish communities means that it repeatedly enters the stories in our films under discussion, or provides a context in which everyday Judaism emerges on screen.

While some modern forms of the Kabbalah have been modified sufficiently to attract women – as the celebrities just listed show – Scholem wants us to be clear about the masculine nature of the Kabbalah, "made for men by men" as he puts it.[19] Indeed Judaism itself will appear in many of our films to be an entirely masculine venture where women struggle with the apparently more limited religious and social roles allotted to them. We explore this in depth in the chapter on Gendered Judaism, but we should not hold these difficulties to be a uniquely Judaic problem. All the ancient faith traditions have dealt with or are beginning to deal with similar issues, and, it seems, filmmakers are particularly interested in dramatizing this aspect of faith.

Introduction

Returning to the idea of Judaism as a religion of struggle with G-d, we note that Scholem is not the only Jewish thinker to understand the Jewish religion in terms of history and drama – so does Steinberg:

> To Judaism history is the unfolding of a design of which the denouement is to be man's ultimate fulfillment and redemption. Behind this drama stands G-d: playwright, director, animator, spectator, critic, and – from within every character and setting – actor also. [20]

Martin Buber's vision of Hasidism

Scholem's friend, Martin Buber, wrote a remarkable set of essays on Hasidism, a mystical branch of Judaism that will feature in many of our films. The editor's introduction to Buber's book, *Hasidism and Modern Man*, states this: "Hasidism is the popular communal mysticism that went far toward transforming the face of East European Jewry in the eighteenth and nineteenth centuries. ... Hasidism, as Buber portrays it, is a mysticism which hallows community and everyday life rather than withdraws from it, 'for man cannot love G-d in truth without loving the world.'" [21] We will see this sentiment confirmed in a number of films, but we need to be clear as to what the "world" is that man is commended to love here as a prerequisite or accompaniment to loving G-d. It is the human world, not that of Nature. It is the world of the community of Jews, termed "Israel"; it is the world of the extended family; it is the world of Talmudic scholars in debate with each other. It is not the world of rocks, plant-life, and animals and the animist spirits within them. It is not the world of art, science and politics. As Buber says about the teachings of Hasidism:

> They can be summed up in a single sentence: G-d can be beheld in each thing and reached through each pure deed. But this insight is by no means to be equated with a pantheistic world view, as some have thought. In the Hasidic teaching the whole world is only a word out of the mouth of G-d. [22]

All this will be explored in the films of the Hasidim that we will consider. Buber's work adds subtly to that of Scholem, particularly when he points out that the mysticism of the Hasidim is a *communal* mysticism. The mystic who retreats from the world may have a dramatic inner life – and we know this from their autobiographies – but that does not easily transfer to film. The Jewish mystic, however, is deeply part of a community, and whenever there are people bound together in their livelihoods and faith there will be a drama if not trouble – all of which makes excellent material for the screenwriter.

Plotinus's vision of Beauty

We may concede to Gertel and Medved that many films touching on Judaism are inaccurate or disrespectful. I have to show that there are worthy exceptions to this. We may be nervous that the vision of Judaism embodied in the work of Scholem and Buber is not the best starting point for this analysis. I have to show that it is in at least some respects appropriate. But above all we may be puzzled about the "beauty" of Judaism. What is this beauty and why should Plotinus, a philosopher of the third century BCE, who may have been a native Egyptian of Roman, Greek, or Hellenized Egyptian descent, but anyway not a Jew and largely innocent of the discourse around the G-d of the Jews, be the one to describe it for us? His philosophy is Greek. As Scholem makes clear, Judaism has nothing to do with the Greek tradition, except for a small overlap in the Kabbalah where Greek Gnostic influences are felt.[23] Despite all this I have chosen Plotinus's work on beauty as my starting point because he uses the term to describe both aesthetic beauty and moral beauty, the latter surpassing the former in religious importance. His work on beauty is found in the sixth tractate of the first *Ennead*, and it begins like this:

> Beauty addresses itself chiefly to sight; but there is a beauty for the hearing too, as in certain combinations of words and in all kinds of music, for melodies and cadences are beautiful; and minds that lift themselves above the realm of sense to a higher order are aware of beauty in the conduct of life, in actions, in character, in the pursuits of the intellect; and there is the beauty of the virtues. What loftier beauty there may be, yet, our argument will bring to light.[24]

Plotinus is here reminding us that ordinarily we reserve the word "beauty" for visual experiences, although also for lyrics and music. Hence we can certainly use the word beauty to describe exceptional cinematic passages which can be a combination of all three. But he also insists that there is a higher order in the conduct of life – which we can call moral – and in the "pursuits of the intellect." For those who appreciate modern mathematics or science the term beauty can be applied to a theorem for example. It is less familiar however to describe justice or acts of moral integrity as beautiful; nevertheless Plotinus gives us a justification for it, in a work treasured for centuries since its re-discovery.

Plotinus asks us: "is there any such likeness between the loveliness of this world and the splendors in the Supreme?" [25] In a sense the entire Neoplatonist tradition, with its later emergence in the New Age, and its interpenetration with the Romantic, answers: yes. The artist, the poet, seeks nothing else but the beauty that has some resonance with the "splendors" of the ineffable, the eternal, the Supreme – call it "G-d" if you will. But Plotinus calls the beauty of the senses "fugitive" – that is it really belongs to the realm of the manifest changing world, not to that of eternity.[26] He continues: "But there are earlier and loftier beauties than these. In the sense-bound life we are no longer granted to know them, but the soul, taking no help from the organs, sees and proclaims them. To the vision of these we must mount, leaving sense to its own low place." Plotinus is insisting on a hierarchy of beauty: in the sense-realm there can be beautiful sights and sounds, but for the soul there are greater beauties, for example noble conduct. To act morally, that is with no selfish aims, is to live in beauty and truthfulness, or in "Truth" with a capital "T". To fall from such conduct is to shrink and become ugly – perhaps no religion would disagree with this.

Kierkegaard's vision of Faith

That we can draw on a thinker like Plotinus in applying the word "beauty" to a religion is a little unfamiliar, so I want to reinforce the notion by drawing on works by the Danish philosopher Søren Kierkegaard. It is not that Kierkegaard expounds on the term "beauty" but rather that he juxtaposes the literary tradition of the Romantics – certainly one obsessed with beauty, and one indebted to Plotinus – with the Christian religion. For him, the love that the Romantics possess falls short of the love of G-d, the essential basis of both Christianity and Judaism.

In his essay "Works of Love" Kierkegaard shows that the romantic love of the poets is the secret self-love which is merely the erotic, not the eternal. This is quite consistent with his attacks on the German Idealist tradition in philosophy, particularly on Hegel. For example, Werther's all-consuming love, in Goethe's highly influential *The Sorrows of Young Werther*, is usually painted as sublime for the elevation of its object – Charlotte – to the role of transcendent inspiration and muse, and her rejection of Werther leads to his dramatic suicide. Kierkegaard's point here is quite precise however: the erotic love, which appears to place its object so central as to lead the poet to a state of self-abnegation, is in fact purely selfish. This is

Introduction

simply because this love is based on preference, as it is in friendship for that matter. To love one's neighbor as oneself is to love all neighbors, with no preference: after all it is easy to love the beautiful, the articulate, and the athletic, but what about the poor, the halt and the lame?

"…it is Christianity's intention to wrest self-love away from us human beings," he says.[27] He adds: "If the commandment about loving the neighbor were expressed in any other way than with this little phrase, as yourself, which simultaneously is so easy to handle and yet has the elasticity of eternity, the commandment would be unable to handle self-love in this way." He keeps returning to the idea that eternity lives between self-love and the love of the neighbor as oneself, in other words that selfish love is narrow and claustrophobic, whereas the love of others is the straight road to eternity. Steinberg tells us that this is also central to Judaism:

> In the second century Rabbi Akiba son of Joseph found the "great principle" of Judaism in the commandment laid down in Leviticus: "Thou shalt love thy neighbor as thyself."[28]

We also find this in the New Testament of Mark 12:31 or Matthew 22:39 where Jesus places it as the second most important commandment, the first being to "love thy G-d with all thy heart and all thy soul and all thy might." As a Christian, Kierkegaard is naturally drawing on the Gospels, but Jesus says this in response to the question as to which are the most important commandments, or *mitzvot*, and as a Jew well-versed in the Torah, he is quoting Leviticus 19:18, where the full statement is: "Thou shalt not avenge, nor bear any grudge against the children of thy people, but thou shalt love thy neighbor as thyself: I am the LORD."

The love of G-d takes various forms, and in medieval Christian mysticism it became a solitary longing, spoken of using the metaphors of romantic love. This form of religious love is largely foreign to early Judaism, as Scholem points out: "Not only is there for the mystic no divine immanence, there is almost no love of G-d. What there is of love in a relationship between the Jewish mystic and his G-d belongs to a much later period …"[29] Instead, the love of G-d is shown in observances of His law.

Kierkegaard belongs to a far later, Christian, period, though with a fondness for the Hebrew Bible as shown in his extraordinary meditation on the story of Abraham and Isaac in *Fear and Trembling*, which we look at shortly.

In the films that we examine it will certainly help if the cinematography is of a high standard, but the beauty we are looking for is a religious one, not an aesthetic one. The Romantics go wrong, says Kierkegaard, when the poet has become the priest. [30] Kierkegaard does not simply juxtapose the aesthetic and the religious however. In *Stages on Life's Way* he writes: "There are three existence-spheres: the aesthetic, the ethical, the religious. ... The ethical sphere is only a transition sphere, and therefore its highest expression is repentance as a negative action. The aesthetic sphere is the sphere of immediacy, the ethical sphere of requirement (and this requirement is so infinite that the individual always goes bankrupt), the religious the sphere of fulfillment ..." [31] Of course, this entirely reverses the secular position where fulfillment is only of the senses.

Turning now to Kierkegaard's analysis of the story of Abraham and Isaac in his book *Fear and Trembling*, we find him absorbed in a foundational story of the Judaic faith, one that appears in a number of the films we will look at. Kierkegaard is amused at the popular saying: "Only one who works gets bread", because he saw that many live very well without working at all, indeed in the physical realm it rains on the just and the unjust alike. Instead the homily about work applies only in the spiritual realm, just where most people are rather lazy. Applying this idea to the story of Abraham and Isaac he says:

> Now the story of Abraham has the remarkable quality that it will always be glorious no matter how impoverished our understanding of it, but only – for it is true here too – if we are willing to "labor and be heavy laden". But labor they will not, and yet they still want to understand the story. One speaks in Abraham's honor, but how? By making it a commonplace: "his greatness was that he so loved G-d that he was willing to offer him the best he had". [32]

The idea that the Kierkegaard's "stage of religion", or the spiritual sphere, requires "labor" is important to this book. Kierkegaard explains that the story of Abraham and Isaac will not be glorious if one merely accepts the conventional response, that Abraham was willing to sacrifice to his G-d the very thing that meant most to him. One needs to *work* at this terrible story. More than that, it takes courage. We do not have to think that Kierkegaard's own response to the story is the best, or even an acceptable one. The point is that he has worked at it. In some of the films we will be examining we will find difficult narratives, but if we work at them instead of either accepting a simplistic response or dismissing them as not conventionally Judaic enough, then we have gone deeper into the spiritual life.

Introduction

What though might be a specifically Judaic way of "laboring" at such a difficult story as Abraham's? The films will show us again and again: religious debate. The Jewish faith, as Scholem says, is in the first instance a dialogue between G-d and man, a vocal one at that. But in the yeshiva – the religious school – the dialogue between man and man also forms a part of the "work" we do on earth, along with prayer, good works and observance of the 613 *mitzvot* or commandments.

Selecting Religious Films

Apparently Jeremy Kagan, director of the first film we look at in this book, *The Chosen*, is reported to have said that "you would hear the Hasidim say that they didn't go to the movies … but Rabbi Schneerson felt that, if it existed in this world, then Ha'Shem, the Lord, meant it to be used for holiness." [33] My book *Luminous* is one of many volumes that explore the idea that movies can be "used for holiness". It concluded however that in most cases a direct attempt to embody or convey spirituality or the beauty of a religion fails, and that some of the best films succeed quite accidentally in this through their primary pursuit of being works of art. [34]

Film has much to recommend it however in the pursuit of the understanding of faith, and even as an adjunct to the practice of faith. Even though Judaism is an intensely book religion, it is also intensely human, so to witness competent actors on screen articulating some of the central issues in Judaism, or as protagonists struggling with their conscience, or even performing for us a Judaic rite or ritual, can be illuminating. If something of the texture of the religion can be visually conveyed by sets, costumes and actions, then does this not add to any textual description? And above all film is a shared experience. A group of people can watch a film together, or agree to watch it separately in their own homes and then convene to discuss it. As Judaism is a religion of debate, we can anticipate a lively discussion on any film that is a serious attempt to convey the core issues in the religion.

I collated many film listings in order to discover what I think are the key films about Judaism. As pointed out earlier, this meant dismissing many films that in the end turned out to be about Jewishness, particularly a secularized Jewishness. The films I have chosen may not always paint Jews in a positive light, but so much the better: there would be no need for religion if people were perfect. What I was looking for was something hinted at in the manifesto of Powell and Pressburger: that engaging with the film should sustain as opposed to diminish us. The Powell and Pressburger oeuvre is not that challenging, it has to be said, but we could

Introduction

not properly explore Judaism if we did not look at some quite difficult films.

I have grouped the films together in order to explore specific themes, that is apart from the first chapter which aims to give a general introduction to Judaism on film. Many of the films could easily appear under more than one of the headings, and sometimes are revisited in different chapters. What has suggested this division into themes is not however anything in the structure of Judaism, or its scholarly study: instead the structure is entirely suggested by the available films.

In Appendix I provide a list of the ten best films on Judaism, with short descriptions of each, culled from the forty-odd films under discussion. They are a personal choice, but the merits of these particular films over the others – as I see them – will become clear in the following chapters.

Terminology

I have drawn on many sources in this book, some old and some new. This also includes the subtitles of many films all of which means that many specialist terms I encountered have considerable variety in their spelling. Hence I have taken the rather unusual step of not quoting verbatim as is the normal citational etiquette because that could be rather bewildering to the reader. Instead I have standardized spellings and terminology to be as sympathetic as possible to the Judaism that Jews practice. For example I refer to the "Hebrew Bible" instead of the "Old Testament". In deference to the important idea that the Ultimate should not be named in the conventional manner I use the spelling "G-d" instead of "God", even when quoting sources using the conventional spelling. I also use Ha'Shem, meaning The Name, instead of Hashem, simply because, by dividing it into two parts, it helps the English speaker to remember the meaning of it. For the holy day of the week I use Shabbat, rather than Sabbath, because the latter could refer to either the Christian or the Jewish holy day (in one film the variant "Shabbos" is used). I hope that I have not made too many errors in navigating the terms, Yiddish or Hebrew, that are used by Jews in their faith and culture. I have included a Glossary of these terms at the end of the book to help the reader.

1. Essential Judaism

Preamble

In this chapter we look at three key films: *The Chosen*, *Ushpizin* and *The Quarrel*, set respectively in New York in the 1940s, Jerusalem in the present time and Montreal in the 1940s. As we follow the story of each film many of the essentials of Judaism come into view. I have selected *The Chosen* as the first film, and if my exploration here fails to convince the reader that film can convey the beauty of a religion then all the following films will hardly change that. This film is widely recognized to be amongst the best or possibly even the film that tops all others in its depiction of Judaism. It is however set over half a century ago, in the period leading to the creation of modern Israel, and depicts only two forms of Jewish thinking in a highly diverse tradition. The glimpses that it affords into the otherwise closed box of the Jewish religion are augmented by those of the other two films in this section, which, taken together I believe are essential viewing. Films in the later chapters, while not always reaching the heights of these opening films, certainly help further fill out the picture.

The Chosen

The Chosen is based on the novel by Chaim Potok, and is set in Park Slope, Brooklyn, New York City. Two Jewish boys, one of whose fathers is modern Orthodox and the other traditionalist Hasidic, get to know each other, and through their eyes we acquaint ourselves with two rather different versions of the Jewish faith. This takes us straight to Scholem's point in his survey of Jewish mysticism, that Judaism is always changing, whether led by Jewish mystical rabbis or by the changing world that Jews find themselves in. *The Chosen* juxtaposes what appears to be an ancient, rigid and resolutely anti-modern form of Judaism – Hasidism – (which was in its day quite possibly heretical), and modern Orthodoxy bent on a new "heresy": Zionism. Michael Medved is critical of the film:

> …the entire arc of the story involves the need for the rabbi's son (Robby Benson) to escape his father's domination and to liberate himself from the restrictive

bonds of a nostalgically portrayed but utterly outmoded religious tradition.[35]

This critique is found in a section headed "Jabbing the Jews" in which Medved, as we saw earlier, complains about the treatment of Judaism in film. It is good to bear such criticisms in mind, and also those of Gertel, but their approach is perhaps of the "glass-half-empty" type. Film, it has to be said, is bound to question all assumptions, and so we should not regret with Medved that a rabbi's son is searching for truth in his own terms, and in terms consistent with a world unimaginable to the Polish-Ukrainian setting of 250 years previous. Indeed in the struggle between son and father much of what is beautiful in Judaism is uncovered, I would argue. Kathryn Bernheimer appears to agree with this when making it the first film covered in her book *The 50 Greatest Jewish Movies*. She says this:

> One of the most profoundly Jewish films ever made, *The Chosen* explores the still-pressing issue of tension between different branches of Judaism. *The Chosen* is virtually unique in dealing with divisions within the Jewish world rather than with the conflict between the Jews and the hostile host culture.[36]

In her book *Seeing and Believing* Margaret M. Miles tells us:

> *The Chosen*'s director, Jeremy Kagan, was committed to making the film as accurate as possible. He secured the advice and help of the Lubavitcher community, a Hasidic group led by Rabbi Menachem M. Schneerson, on costuming, set design, and the choice of neighborhood for filming. Brooklyn school yearbooks from the 1940s were canvassed to get the "looks" of the boys.[37]

The film opens with a baseball match, which theme inspired the directors of the later film *The Yankles*, about a baseball team made up of students from an Orthodox Yeshiva. In *The Chosen* the boys of the Modern Orthodox team stare at the Hasidic boys marching to the pitch as Reuven Malter muses that although they only live five blocks away it might just as well have been five thousand miles. They kept to themselves. When Danny Saunders comes to bat, Reuven attempts conversation to no avail – it seems only to offend the Hasidic boy. So, when Reuven pitches against Danny some animus escalates into a strike that smashes into Reuven's face, breaking his spectacles and nearly blinding the boy in one eye. It is operated on, and there is some doubt about recovery. Danny comes to apologize to Reuven at his hospital bed but is rebuffed to the sound of jazz music – a sound quite foreign to Danny. But he does not give up and visits his victim in his home, patch over his eye and still uncertain over his recovery. Danny wants to explain, and does so with very modern, almost Freudian, honesty, that in that moment of hitting the ball he had wanted to kill Reuven. He no longer does, to which Reuven comments that he is weird, that he looks like he has walked out of another century.

"You play baseball like Babe Ruth. You talk like you're from outer space," he adds.

"Thanks for the compliment," returns Danny evenly.

We discover that Danny is intellectually brilliant: he learns a "quota" of four pages of the Talmud every day but he has never been to a movie or knows who Benny Goodman is. This last is after Reuven rattles of some jazz lines on the piano, then a jazz improvisation on what sounds like Yiddish music: to Danny's ears a little Hasidic. One has to say that whatever one thinks of this film, the screenplay is highly attuned to the cultural context of the day.

Both boys are clearly very bright in a typical Jewish manner – that is demonstrating a hereditary intellectualism diligently coached within the family – and their friendship now grows. They will learn from each other about their respective worlds, at the same time five blocks and five thousand miles apart. We also learn in this first blossoming of their friendship a key fact about Danny: his father only speaks with him when studying Talmud. "My father wishes that everyone could speak … in silence," he adds. We next see them exploring a key Jewish idea that spans the religious and secular worlds – that dreams are full of meaning. Here we begin to understand that Danny is on a path to secularism – as mourned by Medved – and that Reuven is making the opposite journey. Hence Freud meets Jewish religious word-play in their discussion, and Danny is forced to confess that he reads beyond the Talmud in the local library, in direct contradiction to his father's orders. He is reading Adler, Jung, and Freud.

Reuven is to visit Danny's father, introduced to us as a "great man," and on the way Danny explains Hasidism to him, saying that its founder lived with poor people in Poland during the 1700s. He continues:

> They called him the Ba'al Shem Tov, the master of the good word. He had studied Kabbalah, the secret books of Jewish mysticism. He preached a popular idea that G-d is everywhere, that he should be worshipped in joy and singing and dancing, that to be a good Jew didn't depend on how much you know, but on how much you felt.

These Hasidic ideas might represent ancient tradition for Reuven, but we learn from Scholem that they were radical in their day, and that the movement of Ba'al Shem Tov represented the latest phase of a Hasidism that had its first major period in the twelfth to the thirteenth centuries. Scholem says:

> The whole development centers round the personality of the Hasidic saint; this is something entirely new. Personality takes the place of doctrine; what is lost in rationality by this change is gained in efficacy. The opinions particular to the exalted character are less important than his character, and mere learning, knowledge of the Torah, no longer occupies the most important place in the scale of religious values. [38]

A key religious idea is broached here in the film – and hinted at earlier in the juxtaposition that Danny enthusiastically shares with Reuven between head and heart – of feeling as more profoundly religious than learning. This is a Hasidic idea. In his book *Hasidism and Modern Man* Martin Buber declares: "In fact, nowhere in the last centuries has the soul-force of Judaism so manifested itself as in Hasidism." [39] Even if this is overstated, we are at least encouraged that this film is likely to be revealing of Judaism in general as we follow Hasidic ideas in their specifics.

We arrive at the yeshiva of Reb Saunders, up the steps under the watchful eyes of bearded elders, and into the synagogue, and for me this is now the first test: do we read this as a moment of religious beauty – the religious costume, the pews, the feeling of religious anticipation – or are we dead to it? Why should not a Christian, a Muslim, a Hindu, or a Buddhist also feel that religious anticipation in witnessing this gathering with others to pursue their faith in a space dedicated for that purpose? And is it not a beautiful feeling?

But I do not wish to preach to the converted. The scene for many, one has to concede, merely represents perhaps a burden placed by the past on the present. For Danny however, his passion for Freud and other secular works found in a modern library have not dulled his religious feelings. His eyes are lit up as he sits with his friend, still with a patch over one eye. His father approaches and quizzes Reuven on his eye, on his learning of the Torah and the Talmud. We then cut to the celebratory Shabbat meal where there is singing and clapping, the men sway, children are present. For those skeptical of religion, or even frightened by it, here is a difficult scene indeed. What is this singing? What is this swaying of the body, this clapping, this ritual intonation over the breaking of bread, the traditional braided *challah*? Danny stands in silhouette, clearly enjoying himself; the pace fastens, and we focus on Reuven. He appears to represent our modern discomfort with all this, but his face too breaks into smiles before long. He is captured by the beauty of it, though this all happens very fast.

The film has a story to get through, and so cannot dwell on this moment, the implications of which could bear a longer filmic presentation. Instead, just as Reuven is about to join in with the singing, there is silence. The old Rabbi speaks:

> This man was on a boat and fell into the sea and the captain of the boat, he saw this man was drowning, so he threw this man a rope and "Hold onto this rope!" he shouted. "Hold onto this rope. Hold tight. Hold tight, because if you let go you may lose your life." Are we, too, not drowning in a sea of ignorance, cruelty, debt?

The scene is lit as in a Rembrandt painting; we cut to a cherubic infant held in the arms of his bearded father staring in rapt attention across the table at the rabbi. Saunders continues:

> Who is our captain? G-d. And what is the rope that he throws us? It is our Torah! Now, it is not an easy task to study Torah. It is a task that takes all day. It is a task that takes all night. And there is a great danger. Did not the Reb Meir say, "He who is walking by the way and studying and he breaks off that study and he sees a field, and in that field, he sees a tree. Him does not the scriptures consider! As if he had forfeited his life! ... Only, only through the Torah, through the Torah, can you lead a full life. Only then will G-d, the master of the universe, only then will he hear your words!"

The assembly is stunned by the force of his speech. There is a pause. The old man permits a smile, and then says "Amen." "Amen!" shouts the group. Then, with great modesty the rabbi enquires of Reuven what he thought of his "little talk". Was it all right? Was it good?

"It was very good," replies Reuven nervously. But the rabbi presses him as to whether it was correct. Reuven is stumped but Danny offers this with conviction:

"It was written in the name of Rabbi Yakov, not Rabbi Meir." There is a chorus of agreement from the others, and the old man concurs. He has not finished with Reuven however.

"Is it true," he asks him, "that a man, he should spend his whole life only studying Torah?"

Reuven replies hesitantly: "Torah should be combined with work and good deeds."

There are mutters of agreement. "And whose words are these?" presses the rabbi.

"Simeon the Righteous, I think."

"You think?" Reuven has to commit himself, under pressure from this inquisition, but he is correct, there is laughter and the group breaks into song again. Danny is in his element; Reuven is deeply flustered. But how can a young Jewish man not enjoy this? It is in his DNA. We note too that Scholem's characterization of the Hasid "saint" in this tradition is of a man whose actions are more important than his learning. "Work and good deeds" are actions in the world, and Plotinus agrees that "noble conduct" in this respect has more beauty than anything in the sense domain.

Buddhism has an equivalent to this cut and thrust of religious dialogue called "dharma talk," an unimaginable adjunct to the religious life of the Church of England for example. It is not in the British temperament, and only a little more in the American. The whole experience was therefore new to Reuven, but it is a rewarding feature of religious life if amiable and informed dispute takes place regarding tradition and text without fear of being branded a "heretic." Reuven's education has only begun however, as he now meets the family, including the women, and learns how Reb Saunders rescued his group from "bandit gangs of Cossacks", which had attacked them in their small Russian town, and brought them to America. Reuven cannot understand that a whole group would uproot themselves like that just to follow a rabbi. But Danny tells him that his father is more than a rabbi, he is a *tzadik*, a righteous man, a bridge between G-d and his followers. "Zaddikism", as Scholem terms it – the elevation of the good teacher over the good text – characterizes the Hasidic legacy of Ba'al Shem Tov. [40]

This vision of the religious life is contrasted in the film with the worldly activist religion of Reuven's father, David Malter, who is involved in the campaign for the establishment of the State of Israel. Danny learns of Reuven's world and continues to study in the library, further exploring the works of that great Jew: Sigmund Freud. It turns out to be David Malter's guidance under which Danny is exploring secular thought, and at the moment of this revelation being imparted to Reuven David hands Danny *Totem and Taboo* by Freud. Perhaps only *The Future of an Illusion* and

Civilization and its Discontents amongst Freud's works – or perhaps amongst all fiercely atheist polemics – stand more for the destruction of all religion, I would venture. One could say that I would have no need to write books like this if Freud's legacy was not so strong amongst us still. Everything that Danny's father wished to conserve is under threat through the kindly tutelage of David Malter, a man we can characterize as an Enlightenment Jew. David concedes his own limitations in the face of Reb Saunders's great gifts as a leader but we will later see how Malter's secular vision for Israel became at one level a new turn for religious Judaism. In turn Reb Saunders knows just what threats face his son, or rather his own vision for his son – his most important "possession" – but nevertheless allows him to attend the same modern college as Reuven. This is towards the end of WW2, and the friends are studying both the Talmud and modern subjects. Alarmingly for Danny, Freud's ideas are dismissed as medieval magic and unscientific. He has to do "proper" psychology: running rats through mazes.

In an art gallery Danny brings up an issue central to the Judaic tradition: the proscription on idolatry or even any representation. They stand under a Greek nude in marble, and Danny declares with feeling:

"It's a deception. Have you ever noticed how we have no pictures or paintings on the walls of our house? It's because the images detract from what's real. From what's true." Danny's eyes are fixed on the nude, a female.

"I see you haven't stopped looking," points out Reuven.

"That's…'cause it's…it's beautiful," says Danny, practically in a trance. This is a clash of worlds.

Here is a good point at which to turn again to the question of beauty. Plotinus wants us to understand beauty in a new way. He says: "Almost everyone declares that the symmetry of parts towards each other and towards a whole, with, besides, a certain charm of color, constitutes the beauty recognized by the eye, that in visible things, as indeed in all else, universally, the beautiful thing is essentially symmetrical, patterned." [41] Certainly the marble statue that Danny is fixated upon fulfils this requirement for symmetry. But Plotinus wants us to consider different things such as "methods in life" or "expression of thought" or the virtues. The latter he calls "a beauty of the Soul", and in all these things there is no obvious role for symmetry. Hence he moves us away from aesthetic beauty to what we can call for – the sake of simplicity – moral beauty. And so far in this story we are faced with some moral questions: will an injured boy forgive his assailant? Will a Hasidic father permit his son to study secular subjects? Will he ask his son's forgiveness in the end?

The statue is however not a moral act. It has only physical beauty. It is profoundly Greek. It belongs to Kierkegaard's aesthetic stage of life, one that has not yet discovered the moral, or yet discovered the one higher still, the religious. For a traditional Jew it also represents idolatry, and the passion that this arouses in all three monotheisms must not be underestimated. There are countless realistic statues in the Greek style across the Mediterranean and Middle East which have been defaced – noses broken off, eyes gouged out – in the legacy of this animus towards representation. This hostility originated in Judaism. In Karen Armstrong's *A History of G-d* she describes how this came about as a reaction to earlier nature religions, and the attempt to absorb them into the early Jewish faith. In this rather alarming passage she tells us that it was the Deuteronomists who ushered in the strict rejection of images and idolatry, previously associated not just with nature religions but goddess faiths:

> Josiah instantly began a reform, acting with exemplary zeal. All the images, idols and fertility symbols were taken out of the Temple and burned. Josiah also pulled down the large effigy of Asherah and destroyed the apartments of the Temple prostitutes, who wove garments for her there. 42

This is part of the ancient history of Judaism, and, while such things as fertility symbols and Temple prostitutes have played no part in the religion for millennia, the original feelings which drove Josiah's revulsion linger on. Without this history the scene between Danny and Reuven in the museum would be incomprehensible.

A little later we are reminded of the moral drama between father and son in a scene where Reb Saunders is playing with his younger boy, which Danny witnesses with a sorrow in his heart. What is the moral justification for his father's silence to him, while he denies nothing to his other son? What cruelty is this? His father indulges the little one, plays chess with him, but only interacts with Danny as his Talmudic tutor.

But now another moral question looms, one with profound religious implications: as war ends the pressure grows internationally over the possible establishment of the new state of Israel. The news has begun to filter through of the Holocaust. In Danny's first movie outing with Reuven the newsreels that precede the feature are full of the concentration camps, and show mountains of corpses. All Jewish communities are devastated.

"All is reduced to … bones," is Reb Saunders' shocked commentary. There was nothing left of the Hasidic communities in the Old World – countless villages, towns and cities had been ethnically cleansed of Jews. How are they to respond to this?

Reuven's father is galvanized in his efforts to secure a Jewish homeland. His speaking engagements take him away from home for a while so Reuven stays at the Saunders' house and witnesses the full religious life of the rabbi's family. He meets Danny's sister Shaindela, who Reuven discovers with sorrow has already been spoken for in the traditional way. His immersion in the Hasidic world culminates in a wedding held with traditional music, singing and dancing. Reuven can't dance, he says, but is swept up in it all. To slow violins and handclaps the rabbi himself gets up to dance, using the ancient hand gestures and movements. Who knows where in the East these traditions originated, but the religious meaning and chasteness of them – the men and women celebrate and dance separately – are profoundly different to the sexualized dance of modern America.

"When the messiah comes he will lead our people to the land of Israel," says Reb Saunders over supper one day. Reuven tells him that some think that Palestine should become a Jewish homeland without waiting for the messiah. The rabbi is incensed. He shouts:

"It is written that the Messiah and the Messiah only will bring the Jews to the new land!" He is furious and declares that G-d alone will achieve this: "G-d, not Ben Gurion and his henchmen! No!" He shrieks: "Never!"

It is hard now to understand the vehemence of this Hasidic anti-Zionism, but perhaps there was more than one source to it. On the one hand there was the theological objection: Israel will only come about when the Messiah comes. On the other hand was the broader faith objection: the "founding fathers" of Israel, David Ben Gurion and his "henchmen" including perhaps Menachem Begin, Ariel Sharon and Moshe Dayan, represented to Saunders an atheist militarism utterly removed from his Hasidic pacifism, and one bent on establishing a modern secular state more Marxist than Mosaic.

Afterwards Reuven asks Danny: "How was I supposed to know that Zionism is a contaminated idea?" The stumbling block, Danny explains, is that this proposed Jewish state will not be a religious one, at least not Orthodox. On the streets of New York the Hasidim hand out leaflets and shout: "No Israel without the Messiah! Fight the Jewish goyim that want to make the false state of Israel!" We cut to David Malter declaring the exact opposite at his podium in front of a much larger Jewish constituency. The very meaning of his life, he declares, is the protection of those fighting in Palestine, the victims of Arab aggression – this must have been during the 1948-1949 Arab-Israeli war. And it is the Holocaust that gives him the moral justification. A Jewish state will give meaning to that horror, will mean that the Holocaust will never happen again. "Never again! Never again! Never again!"

There is equal passion on both sides.

The film has taken us to the heart of the modern contradiction within the Jewish faith, and it is played out for us again in the college canteen where a fight breaks out over it. Worse, Reb Saunders reads David Malter's speech and in his fury excommunicates Reuven from his house. This is a terrible blow to Reuven who, whatever his father's ideology, has been captivated by the profound religiosity of the rabbi's home. Even worse, striking now at the heart of their friendship, and deploying an old weapon again, Danny is forbidden to speak with Reuven. Their friendship is over. What moral beauty is there in this? As Reuven reflects: "The silence between us is ugly." It is indeed, and religion was the cause of it. But Reuven was committed to Zionism, to his father's cause, to the point where he becomes involved in arms running at the port. "Farm equipment" is destined for Haifa – in reality they are boxes of rifles. Both sons follow in the footsteps of their fathers, but Reuven is thinking to become a rabbi – a rabbi for the modern world, not like Reb Saunders.

A little earlier David Malter was taken ill, but in convalescence he listens with Reuven to the UN vote on the Palestinian partition plan. It is the most momentous event in modern Jewish history, and *The Chosen* is not the only film to dramatize Jews grouped around a radio, listening with pounding heart to the fate of their people in the hands of an international vote – we also see it in *Sunshine*, a film about generations of Hungarian Jews. The decision of each country is announced in turn, so, for example, the Soviets back it, but traitorous Britain abstains. The vote is carried however to immense joy. Shortly afterwards Danny speaks with Reuven, when the ban on Danny's friendship is lifted by Reb Saunders as the Jewish state has become a settled issue. Indeed the vigorous anti-Zionist campaigns such as mounted by most New York Hasidim were abandoned overnight, and it would now become a matter of faith for Jews everywhere to support Israel. (For example the New York Hasidic Rebbe, Menachem Mendel Schneerson, whose name was mentioned by the film's director, became a leading supporter of Israel consulted by generations of Israeli leaders.) Danny has to apologies again, for another injury to Reuven: he was not there for Reuven during the sickness of his father. But for Reuven the silence was sadistic, nothing less.

In the last scene Reb Saunders summons both young men. Reuven tells him that he is going to be a rabbi, which is received with a nod. The old man is in reflective mood and has something to tell them, or rather he has something to explain to Danny and clearly wants his best friend there as a witness. Quietly Reb Saunders says:

> When my Daniel was four years old, I saw him, he read a book. He didn't read the book, he swallowed it. He

swallowed it like one would swallow food. And then he came to me, and then he told me the story that was in the book. And this story was about a man whose life was filled with suffering and with pain, but that didn't … it didn't move Daniel. You know, Daniel was happy. He was happy because he realized, for the first time in his life, what a memory he had. "Master of the Universe," I cried, "what have you done to me? You give me a mind like this for a son? A heart … I need for a son. A soul … I need for a son. Compassion and mercy I need from a son. And above all, the strength to carry pain. That I need from my son."

The old man pauses and then continues to explain himself. How was he to teach all this to his son, the son that he loved, and not lose the love of his son? He reminisces how he used to hold him close, to laugh, to play. But the boy became indifferent to people less brilliant than he was. Saunders saw what he had to do. He had to teach his son through the wisdom and pain of silence … as his father had done to him. The rabbi is speaking as a sorrowful father, but more, as a spiritual teacher. It was a harsh discipline, but it worked. He had to teach Danny "through the wisdom and the pain of silence, that a mind without a heart is nothing."

Steinberg confirms many times that this is how we should understand Judaism. The intellect is important, so he quotes the ancient rabbis: "'An ignorant man cannot be truly devout.'" [43] He continues with a mention of Maimonides who held that perfection consists in the possession of the higher intellectual faculties. This might have been Aristotelian to some degree, but is also highly Jewish, and would appear later in Baruch Spinoza's idea of the intellectual love of G-d. But Steinberg adds:

> The main stream of the Tradition does not go so far. In its eyes moral excellence stands higher than intellectual, the merciful and just heart above the head no matter how informed and discerning.

Reb Saunders is, then, acting fully in accord with his religious tradition. But Danny is in tears. The old man asks Reuven if he thinks he has been cruel. Maybe, the rabbi reflects, but not really because Danny has learned. Let him become a psychologist. But he is not afraid because his Daniel is now a *tzadik*, righteous man. Tears stream down Danny's cheeks, his father says in a trembling voice "it is good." He says "I don't know, maybe you should forgive me for not being a wiser father?"

What worse suffering is there in the Jewish tradition than to be estranged from or rejected by one's father? And what greater blessing than a reconciliation? They hug each other in Reuven's presence.

The rejection in any shape by one's father causes psychological pain, yet it is much more than a psychological story that we encounter in *The Chosen*. It is much more than a drama of young friendship. And it is much more than a useful reminder that Zionism was not universally held by Jews prior to the founding of Israel. It is a deeply *religious* story. The rabbi was a religious teacher who could not stand by and watch his son develop in the wrong way, that is develop his mind at the expense of his heart. It was a horrible cruelty, and the old man was right to ask his son's forgiveness. But silence is traditionally a tool of religious practice and here we find a deeply Judaic issue. St Paul continued it into early Christianity when he said that without the heart we are as sounding brass; that "knowledge puffeth up a man"; and again when that early tradition turned its back on the Greek academy, on philosophy, on geometry, on "Athens".[44]

The Chosen demonstrates this about morality: it is not simply a question of keeping the Ten Commandments, nor even the 613 *mitzvot*. How can any system account for the infinite variety of human circumstances? How can even Jewish Law in its huge ramifications account for the decision of a father to impose silence on his son, a punishment added to when the son is later forced to repudiate his best friend through the same silence? One could say that moral beauty and moral ugliness are a hair's breadth apart here, and we, along with Reb Saunders, must doubt the wisdom of his decisions. But we cannot doubt the beauty of his doubting, the beauty of his asking for forgiveness and the beauty of forgiveness granted. We believe at least this at the end of the film: that Danny has become a *tzadik* – if only a probationary one. The rest of his life will tell.

The film, then, is a demonstration of Judaism's first postulate, as stated by Steinberg, "The simultaneous love of G-d and man." Saunders has to negotiate these two commitments as best he could, posing as they do for him a moral quandary. There is however no negotiation with Nature at all, confirming Scholem's observation on Judaism that "the scene of religion is no longer Nature, but the moral and religious action of man and the community of men." For Saunders the man who spares even a moment from Torah studies to contemplate a tree in a field has forfeited his very life.

Ushpizin

In the case of the film *Ushpizin* it is the Jewish holiday of Sukkot that prompts a moral dilemma in the protagonist. This holiday is also known as the Feast of the Tabernacles, or Booths, and lasts a week during which the observant move into tent-like structures built to resemble the fragile shelters the Jews constructed in their exodus from Egypt. This story is set in an orthodox neighborhood of Jerusalem, so we visit it again in the chapter on Israel Judaism. Given that this film is played to some extent as a comedy, we have some relief and contrast to the seriousness of *The Chosen*, but at the same time the issues themselves are far from trivial.

Ushpizin opens with a text explaining the nature of the *Sukkot*, and mentions that blessings are to be made on the "four species": date-palm branches, myrtle, willow and citron. The citron, or etrog in Hebrew, is a yellow fruit looking a little like a lemon, and a magnificent etrog will be at the heart of the story. Three Orthodox Jews examine this etrog as if they were diamond traders – indeed they later refer to it as "the diamond" – and into their shop walks Moshe, a devout and impoverished Haredi Jew, who is immediately love-struck with the fruit. However at a thousand shekels it is an expense far beyond his means.

Moshe has a dubious past, and has turned to religion as atonement. The devout lifestyle of Moshe Bellanga and his wife Malli means they often do not have enough to eat, let alone purchase a 1,000-shekel etrog to mark the upcoming festival; in fact they cannot even put a shelter together, and are terrified of their landlord. Moshe belongs to the local yeshiva, and we obtain a new picture of men at prayer, complementing the scenes in *The Chosen*. Here the synagogue scenes are less family-oriented, better-lit – under a Mediterranean sky – and of course, located in Jerusalem, not Brooklyn. But Moshe is not completely familiar with this world as he shows us when he attempts to light a cigarette in the synagogue, and is castigated for it.

On the eve of Sukkot there is ritual blowing of the ram's horn (*shofar*) and Moshe is miserable, broke. He and Malli pray in different ways for the means to celebrate the festival. He has given her no money, and he has also failed to give her a son. In his yeshiva there is no money for him and he has not demanded any, but at the end of the day an additional thousand dollars turn up; it is the habit of the wealthy and devout from outside the small community to make such donations. Rabbi Zwibel (possibly a play on "onion" in Yiddish) has no idea who to give the money to but tells his agent simply to pick a number. As the number is correlated against dwellings we cut to a scene of Moshe sitting on a bench and praying to G-d almighty that he needs a miracle. And so it is: the number chosen is that of their house.

Meanwhile, two ex-convicts are converging on their locale. In a Jerusalem café an Orthodox Jew is asking for donations. "Good evening," he says, holding up the contribution box. "Are you into spirituality?"

"Sorry, man, I'm broke," says one of the convicts, who we later learn is called Eliyahu. But he calls the man back in order to examine the collection box. It has the name "The Hidden Light" on it, the name of the yeshiva attended by Moshe.

"Breslau, right?"

"Yes, Breslau." This is the name of the Hasidic Orthodox yeshiva of Moshe and his wife Malli, and, though fictional, appears to be an intentional reference to the Breslov Hasidic group, founded by the great-grandson of the Baal Shem Tov who we encountered in *The Chosen*. Eliyahu has struck lucky and he knows it: he shakes his coins for good fortune and deposits them in the box. He can draw on the friendship of Moshe, it seems. And Moshe in the meantime has returned home to a miracle: a thousand dollars. The etrog – "the diamond" – is now within his grasp.

Moshe now has a superb "booth" or *sukkah*, and on his way to the ritual bath – the *mikveh* – he peers into it, only to find his old acquaintance Eliyahu and his friend Yossef there. He is taken aback for a while but then realizes that the Lord has sent them as guests. This is a central part of the *sukkah* festival: the hosting of guests or *ushpizin*. For Eliyahu and Yossef their luck is in: the police would hardly look for them in such a place. Moshe runs back into the house to find *yarmulkes* – skullcaps – for them. Comically the fugitives had earlier asked for Moshe at his yeshiva, holding hands on their heads in the place of the skullcap; now they will be properly equipped.

When Moshe changes into his traditional Hasidic dress and his fox-fur hat – a *shtreimel*, which has possible Tatar origins – it prompts enquiries and ribaldry from his new-found festival friends. On learning that such an item can fetch as much as $2,000 Yossef works out that a street-full of Orthodox Jews are worth $200,000 and many such hats could be rounded up by motorcycle.

"Could you fence them?" he enquires earnestly of Moshe, who sternly rebukes him for talking criminality.

The *Sukkot* celebratory meal starts as an ordeal for the convicts because Moshe sings the appropriate prayers, a blessing that clearly is too long-winded for the guests. But the singing is beautiful, and if it takes a comedy like this for us to experience it, well, why not? The sacred chant echoes around the streets, and after food Moshe tells the guests of the religious meaning of the holiday. It is about the impermanence of things, which Yossef can relate to, though perhaps not quite in the spiritual manner intended: Yossef may be thinking more of the impermanence of the ownership of things. Moshe indulges them; we guess that their world was his not long ago. Is he a real convert to the religious life? Eliyahu for one does not buy it. Moshe is a man with a violent past, and now he is Moses?

This is of course a little ironical, because Moses not only slew the Egyptian but legislated that "accidental" killers should have their own Jewish cities – Hebron is one of them – a part of Jewish religious history that has no counterpart in any other religion, as far as I can tell. In turn Malli's unease over the guests prompts Moshe to say that, sure, they are not the ideal *Sukkot* guests, or *ushpizin*.

"Are we any better?" he asks. Eliyahu has finished their wine, so he and Moshe turn to the hard stuff, after which Moshe says that going to the synagogue next day will be difficult.

"Every day?" queries Eliyahu.

This prompts an unexpected rant from Moshe: "Rabbi Nahman from Breslau says the light descending is beyond spirit and soul – endless light. It cannot be conceived by the mind," he roars, "except for one thing." Only through faith. Eliyahu is not fazed by the big man's roaring. He tells of a time when Moshe, enraged by the tauntings of Americans, breaks a bottle and lunges at them with it. He even demonstrates by breaking a bottle himself and holding the vicious weapon in a threatening manner, to Moshe's alarm who shouts at him to drop the thing. Devout neighbors gather at the disturbance, and Eliyahu stares at him.

"That's why I'm amazed to see him with this beard and the whole act," says Eliyahu. "The entire city of Eilat was afraid of him." But he suddenly hugs the spiritually-garbed convert to religion. Perhaps it takes the wildness of a criminal to recognize the wild heart of religion – we will return to such themes in the chapter on Crazed Judaism. In the meantime Moshe just mutters "I hope I'll manage to repent for all I've done in the world."

Moshe later confides in his rabbi concerning the unsavory nature of his *ushpizin* but the rabbi says that this is the whole point. "Don't forget where you were until not long ago," he tells Moshe. One could say that this is real religion: the insistence on the possibility of repentance, and so Moshe prays in the synagogue with the palm frond he has bought, offering it in the four directions. He is working hard at his atonement, and his *ushpizin* are a trial and a reminder of the temptations of his former life.

In the end the trial becomes too much for him however, so he concocts a lie, telling his guests that he and Malli are leaving to visit relatives. The fugitives take this in, believe it, and remove their *yarmulkes* on their way out. But his wife regrets the lie, saying their rough guests were a test and they have failed it. "We blew it," she says later over food in the Succoth. The two criminals are not fooled for long however and return to embarrass them. Now the couple wait on their guests, all aware of the lie, the penance now becoming a circus: they indulge every whim of their friends in the belief that the Lord has sent them back. If the Jews in the desert were good hosts, even to heretics, then this was the meaning of the religious festival now underway. So the guests from hell can abuse them in any imaginative way they choose, which includes break-dancing as they grill their breakfast. The devout look on dumfounded. The children are hastily removed as the scene gets ugly with shouts of "Profanity! Thieves! Psychopaths!" All this for playing pop music.

Moshe seeks advice from the rabbi, for his wife leaves him over the episode. When a man has passed a test, then an even harder test will arise, the rabbi tells him. "No rest, no rest in this world," he adds. A prayer shawl and the "four species" are brought, date-palm branch, myrtle, willow and etrog, and he again performs the ancient ritual with the rabbi. He returns to the Sukkah to a meal, including salad, prepared by the fugitives whose turn now it is to act penitently: they understand that they have driven Moshe's wife from him. Eliyahu now concedes the Moshe really has changed, and he has respect for that, the little lie now forgotten and forgiven. But then Moshe discovers that the etrog used for the salad is "the diamond" and he runs crazed to avoid taking his anger out on the hapless Eliyahu. It was his hope for his wife's fertility, based on an old religious belief. He struggles with himself to avoid anger – to avoid becoming again the man who would attack Americans with a broken bottle. The holiday ends with what seems only misery for Moshe, and he dismantles his Sukkah with the others.

But his wife returns with news of a new miracle for him: she will have a child after all.

The film ends with this blessing upon them. Moshe, as a properly religious man who has endured serial tests of his faith, dances in the synagogue for the circumcision ceremony of their baby son.

Underlying the outer story of the film and the humor of the great etrog is an inner story of atonement. Steinberg tells us this:

> The memory of old evils will and should remain with him; the sense of guilt will persist. But with time something else will emerge; a conviction of having won through to regeneration, to a recaptured oneness with moral values and the G-d behind them. This is the experience which the ancient rabbis knew and voiced when they portrayed G-d as saying to penitents: "Inasmuch as ye have come before Me in judgment and departed from Me in peace, I do reckon it unto you as if ye had been created anew." This is the "returning" implied by *teshuhah*, the classic Hebrew term for repentance. [45]

Atonement has a beauty in the Plotinian sense, and when thus perceived can also be seen within the Jewish festival of Yom Kippur, the Day of Atonement. I devote a chapter of *Luminous* to the subject of violence, compassion, forgiveness and atonement, and note that the film *Atonement* – based on the novel of the same name by British novelist Ian McEwan – was constructed to show that atonement is only a fantasy. [46] From the secular mind we can expect nothing more, but atonement for the religious mind is a reality, hard-won it is true, but one of the most important possibilities for a human life.

The Quarrel

As Omer Bartov says, *The Quarrel* is more of a filmed play than a film,[47] but for our purposes this does not matter at all. The story concerns two Jews, a writer called Chaim Kovler and a rabbi called Hersh Raseyner. What this film illustrates about the essentials of Judaism is found in religious debate between Jews, the beauty of a friendship held despite opposing world views, and a moment at the end of the film where they sing and dance together, their verbal disputation exhausted.

It is Montreal in 1948, much the same era as that in which *The Chosen* is set, but without reference to the creation of the new Jewish State declared to the world in May of that year. It is the Jewish New Year, *Rosh Hashanah*. Chaim has had a sleepless night in a hotel under Mount Royal; he sits in a café with bacon and eggs while other Jews go to the synagogue. A man stares at him through the window and he cannot eat the bacon, he cannot eat anything. As he leaves the man asks if he will be the tenth to make a quorum or *minyan* for a religious observance. It is a really big *mitzvah* – religious obligation or kindness – for a sick man in hospital, he is told. Chaim stopped believing in such prayers years ago, but grudgingly joins the observant Jews at the sickbed, and is further put out when the rabbi – who could have made up the obligatory ten males – comes and goes saying his synagogue needs him. The singing of the men is religiously beautiful, even if, as Chaim thinks to himself, the sick man is beyond help. It is also a challenge to the secular mind. What kind of comfort could ten men, some of them no doubt mere acquaintances or even strangers, afford you if you were dying in hospital? What kind of song would a secular group choose to sing, and how many would know the words, and how comforting would they be? What humanist substitute could we possibly imagine for this? We cannot. But if we know the meaning of religion, then regardless of our particular faith we can see the beauty in it.

Afterwards Chaim is in the park and sees more devout Jews praying by the water, throwing crumbs into the lake for absolution of their sins. One wears the fox fur *shtreimel*. Chaim talks to himself:

> On Rosh Hashana Jews stand by the water and empty their pockets of sins. My mind wandered and there was Białystok before me, men standing by the banks of a river, praying, throwing crumbs into the water. Only a few of the women, the truly devout, would come. Off to the side was the dignified Rabbi Yakuv and around them the yeshiva students. That was *me* there, and beside me my friend Hersh Raseyner. But, Białystok no longer exists, except in the memories of its survivors. Yet the images were so powerful.

As Chaim remembers his old life before the Nazis destroyed it, he says that the images of it were "powerful." Is this not another way of saying "beautiful"? It does not matter which term we use, the point is that the religion of Judaism holds a place in Chaim's memory that pulls at him hard. He is staring across the water. Who is the rabbi leading the yeshiva students here by this lake? It looks like Hersh Rasseyner, his dearest friend, his bitterest enemy. Impossible, did he not die in the camps? Chaim approaches tentatively, wonderingly. The rabbi stares at him.

"Chaim… you are still alive?" They cannot believe it, but it is true. Both sets of families died under the Nazis but against all odds these two have survived – one still true to his faith, the other now a hard-boiled secularist. They clasp hands. "Let's walk," says Chaim.

They begin to compare notes about the terrible chain of events that had separated them from each other and from all their loved ones. Chaim, it seems, had made the wrong choice, one that sent his wife and two children to their deaths without him.

"There was no right choice," observes Hersh. He in turn has been haunted by the terrible fight the two had when Chaim had left the yeshiva. "I thought that G-d had kept me alive so that I could see you one more time," he confides, "so I could ask you to forgive me." The forgiveness is assured and also reciprocated. Chaim is amused however: his friend the rabbi has a *yeshiva* in a city with a cross in the middle – the cross of Mount Royal.

Chaim is bitter. His bitterness is that of millions of post-Holocaust Jews who neither believe in G-d any more nor trust in life. He sleeps with a woman, a literary fan, but has no dreams of marriage to her or having more children – his sexual encounters are clearly random. Why should he think of having children? For what? To have them taken away again? For Hersh G-d exists in the miracle that the Jews survived at all; for Chaim what is left is only rage. Hersh says: "Auschwitz was not created by G-d. Man did it. The question isn't how I can believe in G-d. It is how you can believe in man."

One could say that the whole film becomes a debate about this point. The Holocaust has polarized them: the same event has driven their lives in diametrically opposing directions. "G-d abandoned us," says Chaim forcefully. "No," he corrects himself, "G-d humiliated us."

Their quarrel then turns to Shakespeare and novels, dismissed by Hersh as mere tales of lust. Hersh has no patience with merely contrived tragedy, when all that is left of their *yeshiva* is a burnt wall, a real tragedy. "Do you remember what we used to say? Once you study *Musar* you can never enjoy life again. You will always be wounded, a cripple, all your life. Because you traded your serenity of soul, for what? Lust that will never be satisfied."

The *Musar* movement was a nineteenth century form of Judaism practiced in Eastern Europe, particularly amongst Orthodox Lithuanians,[48] though as Białystok is mentioned it seems that the Musar yeshiva of Hersh and Chaim was located in Poland: unlike the traditions in the previous two films it is non-Hassidic. The *Musar* tradition is one of ethics and moral behavior, and Hersh has summed up in a few words what all such traditions teach. The characters in Shakespeare and in Chaim's novels – and even if Hersh hasn't read them he already knows them – will pursue desires that will remain for ever unfulfilled precisely because they are not religious feelings. In contrast true religion wounds one because it shows glimpses of a serenity that is beyond satisfaction or non-satisfaction. Chaim concedes that he did for many years believe this too. "I was sure that art was lustful, it was evil, it was the dark side." For a secular man to say such a thing shows that he had come from a different world indeed. But now for him writing was the holiest act – he was a creator on par with The Creator, and it felt like a blessing. In a sense Chaim has known all three of Kierkegaard's "stages" but has been confounded in the middle stage of the ethical. Rather than see, as Kierkegaard suggests, that atonement is so "infinite that the individual always goes bankrupt" and make his home instead in the sphere of religion, he has retreated from the ethical to the aesthetic.

Hersh pleads: cannot Chaim see that his life itself is a work of art, without a foolish audience or a name on the cover? It is a good argument. In effect Hersh is pointing to the author of Chaim, G-d. He is still utterly convinced that when Chaim left Judaism it was not the fault of the yeshiva. "You still have the spark of the yeshiva in you," says Hersh.

Towards the end of the film a yeshiva student catches up, he had been worried about Hersh. The student knows Chaim and accuses him of "spreading poison" and demands to know why he left the yeshiva back in Białystok. This angers Chaim who strides back down the hill deaf to the pleas of Hersh to forgive the young man. "All that he knows is that you once touched the beauty of the Torah and that you left."

It comes down to an argument over the "chosen people" and the role of the yeshiva in maintaining that identity: for Hersh the religious life is what will preserve them, for Chaim it is secular tolerance.

Of course, they cannot resolve these issues, nor can they overcome the guilt of surviving when others perished, including close family. They have shared the particular pain of all post-Holocaust Jews, and all that remains, given the secular-religious divide between them, is to dance. At the end of the film they are sitting on a park bench in the sun after the rain to the drone of cicadas and the laughter of children playing in the background. They are still exploring the guilt of past actions; Hersh in hurting his father only days before his execution by Nazis, Chaim that he left his family on the belief that the women and children would be safe; he then was persuaded that the only life he could save was his own when he could have returned to join them in their inevitable deportation and murder.

Nothing more can be said. Hersh finds the tune that they had been searching for earlier, his humming joined by Chaim.

They sing a little to start with, to find the mood and rhythm, and then sway in silence, their hands upraised. Anyone who has a feel for the sacred origins of such dance, as found in cultures as far apart as Judaism and Hinduism, will appreciate that the raised hands, moving in ascending spirals, and around each other, are both expressive of the relationship with G-d and between each other, two seekers of truth. This is heartbreakingly beautiful; something shared with us through film. All religious feeling is found in it.

Oblivious for a short while, they are broken from their trance by the applause of a small group that has gathered around them in the park. Does one not mourn that such a moment has become infinitely rare in the arid secularized playground of the modern world? Two men whose Jewish faith has shaped them to the core, unable to agree on their response to the modern world and the Holocaust, unable to absolve each other's guilt, but able to express the depth of their friendship in the lost religious song of a Musar rabbi, and express it in universal terms so that complete strangers in a park honor them for it. If two men danced in a park to applause anywhere in the world now it is far more likely to be a break-dance or equivalent, a celebration, not of faith but of art or sexuality.

The two men go their separate ways at the end of the film, but not before Hersh shares a little story with Chaim. Hersh had been on a train when a woman – a modern Jewess – tells him that she gets angry whenever she sees a Jew dressed like him in the old style of another century. "You make the rest of us look ridiculous," she says. "Madam," he replies, "you are making a mistake. I am not Jewish. I am Amish." The woman is confounded and apologizes profusely: she has such respect for the Amish and the way they keep their traditions. Chaim laughs at it and so they hug and part company from each other, happy to have met again.

Summary

These first three films have given us many entry points into the otherwise closed box marked Judaism, closed to an outsider that is. I would never underestimate the many points at which the secular mind balks in these films, but surely it is clear that the films have integrity of purpose. At the least one can see that the characters in them belong to a coherent world of faith, even when they reject some of its older certainties – as Danny Saunders does in studying the modern "science" of psychology – or even when they reject Judaism in its entirety, as does Chaim Kovler. We have glimpsed many essential beauties of Judaism in these films, including religious debate and instruction in a yeshiva, traditional religious life in the family of Reb Saunders, the celebration of a wedding, the celebration of the festival of Sukkot, the dance of an old rabbi at a wedding, and the more surprising dance of the hands of reunited friends. We have witnessed a deeply controversial act undertaken in the name of religion: the imposing of silence on Danny by his father, yet we must find beautiful his confession of it to his son and the request for forgiveness. Atonement was the underlying theme of *Ushpizin*, and despite, or perhaps because of, the comedy of the etrog, we feel that Moshe has made genuine strides along this deeply human and uneven path that the religious life sets out for him.

2. Musical Judaism

Preamble

In *The Chosen* Danny tells Reuven that the Hasid Ba'al Shem Tov preached that Jews should worship G-d in "joy and singing and dancing." In the film *The Dybbuk*, discussed later in the chapter on Mystical Judaism, a rabbi dressed in white and wearing the fox-fur *shtreimel* is surrounded by his congregation. They sing: "With joy and song shalt thou serve the Lord." The films in the previous chapter dealt with serious issues, not withstanding the humor about an etrog in *Ushpizin*, so it is appropriate to look now at films which are about joy and song: two musicals, and two versions of a film about a Jewish singer.

The contradiction between traditional Judaism and modernizing forces, as in *The Chosen*, is represented again in the four films we now look at: *Yentl*, *Fiddler on the Roof* and two versions of *The Jazz Singer*. In each case forces both internal and external to Jewish tradition create difficulties for the protagonists, while the vehicle of song helps to give poignancy to the drama. Dance is not forgotten here, either.

Yentl

Bernheimer says: "*Yentl* stands as the most prestigious Hollywood production to favorably centre on a female Jewish character. It is for these reasons *Yentl* is ranged among the greatest Jewish films."[49] There is no reason to doubt this assessment, but does *Yentl* range amongst the greatest films on Judaism, as opposed to Jewishness? Medved objects to the film on this basis:

> The premise of this movie is that traditional Judaism is so irredeemably sexist that it forces the intellectually ambitious heroine (Ms. Streisand, of course) to disguise her gender in order to satisfy her desire for Jewish learning. Ultimately, she abandons the masquerade and flees to America, leaving behind both the social restrictions and the superstitious religiosity that have stood in her way. [50]

Both these views, one positive and one negative, are true about the film, but we are seeking something different: anything that hints at the beauty of Judaism. The film *Yentl* is based on Isaac Bashevis Singer's short story "Yentl the Yeshiva Boy," and became a project for Barbara Streisand when she wrote the screenplay, directed it, and played the lead role. Yentl is a young Jewish woman who "shall be married," but instead wants to learn the Talmud, which is forbidden to women in her 1904 Ashkenazi community in Poland. So she dresses herself like a young man and goes to the *yeshiva*.

The film opens with a bookseller and his cart, working its way through a town square. A young man enthuses over a new book which puts forward twenty-five interpretations of Genesis, while the women discuss the price of cabbage. "Storybooks for women, sacred books for men!" shouts the bookseller. The young man reading the book tells another of a key idea expressed by its author: "He relates the mysticism of creation to the mysticism of language." You may recall that we met this idea in the Introduction as a key feature of the Jewish religion.

Yentl wants to buy the sacred book, but the seller says it is against the law. "Do yourself a favor, buy a nice picture book," he tells her.

At home her kindly rabbi father, Reb Mendel, is teaching a boy, asking him questions, but she knows all the answers. They can hear her somewhat impatient replies to these questions from the kitchen where she is doing woman's work – clearly she would love to be in the boy's place. "Yentl knows Talmud?" asks the boy. "My father says that a woman who studies Talmud is a demon." Her father excuses her however as we understand that her mother and brother have died, leaving her perhaps to take inspiration from the rabbi and model her aspirations on his.

Later she sits down to study with her father, so we now understand that she does receive such instruction from him.

"Where were we?" he asks.

"Hillel's argument …" she says. "Hillel's argument that knowledge…" However she breaks off because she can see that her father is very tired: he is not long for this world. Note that Hillel was a famous rabbi of roughly the first century BCE; his mention along with the earlier reference to language mysticism suggests that the film will be well-informed on Judaism.

Mendel retires and later Yentl hesitantly takes a *tallit* from its red covering and wraps it around her. It is her first transgressional act: this is something reserved for the men. In song she asks G-d as to "The reason why a bird was given wings if not to fly?" It is a moment of real piety. It seems that she is expressing a longing – unfathomable to secular feminism – for the infinite, apparently denied to women in so many patriarchal traditions. She wants to know where she belongs in the scheme of things. "If not to hunger for the meaning of it all, then tell me what a soul is for," she sings. It is a good sentiment. "What a waste to have a taste of things that can't be mine," she concludes.

Later, in the synagogue, she looks down from the balcony where she is confined and watches the men participate in their relationship with G-d in the manner denied to her. She clings to the wooden spindles of the balcony as if to the bars of a cage, but already there is gossip amongst the women that she is studying the sacred books.

"Children are more important than the Talmud," her father tells her, but his health is failing and before long he dies. At the funeral Yentl is guided in the traditional rending of the lapel of her jacket: "You must tear it over your heart," a female mourner tells her.

At one point somebody asks: "Who is to read *Kaddish*?"

"I will," says Yentl, reaching for the prayer book and starting to recite in Hebrew, the *Kaddish* being the traditional prayer for the dead.

"It must be a male relative," objects one.

There is muttering as she reads, but she persists and they rejoin as appropriate.

Seven days later, she takes the black shroud off the mirror in their house – this is a traditional Jewish sign of mourning – and cuts her hair. Now she is left alone she has made up her mind to disguise herself as a boy, with the name of Anshel, and seek admittance to a *yeshiva*, a Talmudic school. As a plot device we have to buy it, though Streisand makes a rather unconvincing male.

An intriguing scene now plays out in an inn where Jews are discussing the Talmud, or are discussing the relevant merits of yeshivas, or are playing chess. Yentl appears to have convinced the men that she is one of them, to the point that one challenges her at arm wrestling, which she naturally loses. She is rescued from further humiliation by a young man called Avigdor who also has a ripped lapel: he has just lost his brother. She gets into a discussion of a certain Rabbi Akiva in which she proves her erudition. Whatever the origins of this scene in the original story and its reworking for the screen, we are left with something unique: an inn, a public house, where, whatever other manly pursuits take place, the emphasis is on religion, its whole milieu is religious. Yentl is in the element she craves.

She tells them that she is looking for a quiet yeshiva.

"A *quiet* yeshiva?" queries one. This is not a quip for the sake of it: the whole point of a religious school is debate, something Yentl has not yet known, nor that it can become close to raucous. Rabbi Zalman is recommended as a genius at the Bechev yeshiva, a fictional location in Poland, actually filmed in Žatec in what is now the Czech Republic. This is poignant because its synagogue was the second largest in Bohemia, torched by the Nazis on Kristallnacht, but still surviving. We catch glimpses of it in the film.

At Yentl's interview the rabbi explains to her after she questions him. "No, Anshel, the point of study is to teach us how to live, not only to study." She quotes Hillel: "'He that increases wisdom increases life,'" she says, and adds: "Wisdom is the most important thing." But the rabbi counters: "Wisdom is the means, living is the ends." Despite her argumentative stance, or perhaps because of it, she is admitted to the yeshiva and celebrates with her new-found friend Avigdor.

She soon finds her voice in Talmudic debate in the courtyard of the synagogue – she revels in it. There is a dispute over sources, which is argued this way and that until she finally says: "Forgive me. It's *Bava Kamma*, but it's 31b." The *Bava Kamma* or "The First Gate" is one of a series of three Talmudic texts that deal with civil matters such as damages and torts. Yentl certainly knows her scripture, but it has to be said that her manner is a little submissive if she is to pass as a man in that context, as her "forgive me" indicates.

Yentl and Avigdor lodge with the family of Avigdor's fiancée Hadass, but his marriage hopes are dashed when they learn that his brother had committed suicide, an act deeply stigmatized in Jewish tradition. Avigdor has by now formed a strong bond with Yentl, and, on the rebound from his despair, hits on the plan that Yentl should marry Hadass in his place. He quotes the law that says if a man dies a brother should marry the widow: it is a sign to Anshel of how much he values the friendship with this young man, though Anshel / Yentl of course reads all this differently.

For obvious reasons she initially refuses, but in the end agrees – despite enormous trepidation – to prevent Avigdor leaving town and therefore losing his friendship. The preparations for the wedding and the wedding itself are traditional, and afterwards Avigdor gives the couple a wedding present, a book allegedly by Nachmonides, the *Holy Letter*. In an interesting essay on the subject of this text, Evyatar Marienberg calls it "a Hebrew Kabbalistic text on marital sexuality" and draws our attention to the dispute over its authorship by Scholem and other scholars.[51] We return to it when considering the film *A Stranger Amongst Us* and also in the chapter on Family Judaism.

"Never force her," says Avigdor, the irony of it of course hidden from him. "Be patient until her passions are aroused." It seems that he has studied this text.

It is here that the initial religious impulse of the film is lost in what becomes gender politics, touching as they are. We are treated to scenes of the Jewish wedding, and then the ploy that Yentl hits upon to avoid sexual contact with Hadass, which backfires because Hadass understands this as tenderness from her "husband" and subsequently forms an emotional bond with Yentl. "Everything you do shows me you love me," she says. In turn Yentl tries to teach Hadass the Talmud, explaining to her that it is series of commentaries interpreting the Torah, the first of which is the *Mishna*, the code of law. "What is so incredible Hadass," she tells her, "is that it's a masterpiece of literature, folklore and philosophy. It deals with astronomy, architecture, medicine…"

This is rather telling. The Talmud for Yentl – and perhaps for all of secularism – is a masterpiece of literature, folklore, philosophy, astronomy, architecture and medicine. She omits that is a masterpiece of religion, and that in the secular America where she will finally migrate to, there are potentially many equally convincing masterpieces of astronomy, architecture and medicine, and possibly even of literature, folklore and philosophy.

Obviously in the end Yentl / Anshel will have to reveal her identity to Avigdor. He is naturally first disbelieving, then bewildered, and then in a rage. Anshel has broken every commandment, every second of the day! "What are you, a demon?" he bellows.

As his anger abates he comes to recognize that his friendship for "Anshel" was unusual all along, and finally, as this new constellation coalesces in his mind, he proposes that they start a new life in a different town, marry and have children. But Yentl, thrilled at this outcome, wants more. Avigdor remonstrates with her over her determination to continue her studies: "You know everything without opening a single book. What more do you want?"

This might be a stock male response in the Jewish tradition, but is interesting none the less. We saw in *The Chosen* that book-learning was downplayed by the Hassidic Master, the Ba'al Shem Tov, who "preached a popular idea that G-d is everywhere, that he should be worshipped in joy and singing and dancing, that to be a good Jew didn't depend on how much you know, but on how much you felt." For these reasons Reb Saunders didn't want a son with a brilliant mind, but with a soul. So, is Yentl's longing to study taking her to G-d or to mere cleverness? Is it just "astronomy, architecture, medicine" that Yentl is drawn to? The film cannot ask this question however, because what is at issue is her freedom as a woman to pursue the same course as a man. Her biology has condemned her to a path for which she has no instinctive desire: she does not wish to provide the Jewish community with children, and be bound to that role in its traditional form.

Whatever her feelings for Avigdor, his refusal to budge from tradition means only one thing: she will travel to a place where she might be free to pursue her true desires without subterfuge, America. She leaves Avigdor to marry and find his happiness in the traditional manner with Hadass, after all.

An Ethical Assessment

Yentl is a film that can be criticized in many ways, including its romanticized presentation of Eastern European *shtettl* life and the rather slushy nature of the film's populist songs. Yet it is precisely the joy that drives the singing, as in *Fiddler on the Roof*, that is an important reminder of Judaism's love of singing and dancing in the service of the Lord. *Yentl* also conveys a yearning for religion, or to go deeper into religion, despite the secular elements of scientific learning and gender politics that enter the story. From a modern perspective the film *Yentl* has a moral to it: that patriarchal tradition has long suppressed women, and that a modern woman of courage, whether Barbra Streisand in making the film against all the odds in a man's world, or Yentl succeeding in her ambition to become a Talmudic scholar, is to be admired. We should not dismiss this point at all, but I would like to suggest that there is a moral weak point in the story of Yentl.

At every turn we see her as resourceful and determined in the pursuit of her goal. We see her as a strong woman, even if her submissiveness here and there undermines this a little. But she yields to Avigdor's pleas to marry Hadass. Why? Because, as Kierkegaard might see it, she has forgotten the command laid down in Leviticus 19:18: "Thou shalt love thy neighbor as thyself." She has inflicted a horrible deceit upon Hadass in marrying her. True, this is a plot device, and true, it all works out because Hadass will divorce "Anshel" and marry Avigdor in the end. But when Yentl yields to Avigdor's rather crazy plan to marry Hadass she has yielded to her own *preference*: she wants to keep Avigdor near her. She belongs to the world of the romantic, in fact, to the aesthetic world where the "poet has become the priest" – and we can see her singing in this light also. But she has not attained to the moral world, because she has not undertaken the hard path of turning away from her own preference in order to avoid an injustice to another – and we have to point out that this is to another *woman*. At the least we might expect an act of contrition, or a moment of doubt: if Reb Saunders doubted the treatment of his son, undertaken as a method of spiritual instruction, then should not Yentl doubt her treatment of Hadass, undertaken as deceit for personal gain?

Fiddler on the Roof

Fiddler on the Roof is perhaps the most famous Jewish film ever made, and there is no doubt that its star actor, Topol, made his character Tevye into a universally-loved figure. Kathryn Bernheimer says of him:

> Tevye is much more than a Jew: He is the Jewish people. Like the Jews, Tevye has a direct, personal relationship with the Creator. He *kibitzes* and *kvetches*. He offers suggestions and sometimes even curses his Maker, but it is clear the relationship is founded on mutual trust. G-d will not let Tevye down, and Tevye will not let G-d down, no matter how much *tsuris* is heaped upon him. Like the Jews, Tevye is severely tested by forces that threaten to destroy him – forces from without and forces from within his own family. Like the Jews, he suffers. And like the Jews, he survives.[52]

Bernheimer is surely right in what she says, but we are not so much interested in what makes for a Jew as to what makes for Judaism. In that sense *Fiddler on the Roof* does not match a film like *The Chosen* or even some of the more anguished representations of Judaism in the more obscure films we shall look at. But its energy, the vitality of Topol, of rousing music and memorable songwriting, of vivid images of forced exile, all help us see Judaism in an incrementally illuminating fashion. Above all, song is seen as central to Jewish religious life, and if the song *kibitzes* at times – gossips – or *kvetches* at times – complains – all the more true to the Jewish temperament in which Judaism is forged.

The portrayal of religion in any serious sense is not the strength of this film, but we are aware of its centrality from the start as we are introduced to the life of a Jewish community in the Russian village of Anatevka, one that coexists with the larger Russian Orthodox Christian section. "Tradition is everything", we are told, in that heads are covered and the Jewish population wear the *tallit* or little prayer shawl for their prayers.

"This shows our constant devotion to G-d," Tevye tells us. He elaborates: "Because of our traditions every one of us knows who he is, and what G-d expects him to do."

Tevye was three when he started Hebrew school, we learn, but he must spend the bulk of his day as farmer and milkman in order to feed his family. Of course if Tevye "was a rich man" he, just like Yentl, would devote all his time to studying the Talmud. As to the Christian part of the village: "The Orthodox, we don't bother them and so far they don't bother us."

Musical Judaism

The film is based on the Broadway musical, which in turn was based on "Tevye and his Daughters", a story by Sholem Aleichem set in 1905 Tsarist Russia, now Ukraine. The film won Oscars, including for cinematography, while the image of the fiddler on the roof comes directly from a painting by the great Russian-Jewish artist Marc Chagall. The Judaism encountered in the film is that of rich tradition, with little deeper concern about the relationship with G-d. Nevertheless, if one can accept that the pure depths of the religious impulse are somehow still present in the outer forms of the religious life, then *Fiddler on the Roof* usefully portrays some of the outer religiosity specific to Judaism.

Tevye always talks with G-d. "Am I bothering you too much?" he asks at one point. At first glance his relationship with G-d is one of supplication, a series of requests to make his life less hard, and then specific complaints that he is being visited with sufferings that perhaps could have been held at bay. If G-d wasn't too busy dealing with other, greater, disasters that is. The tone of his supplication is however not whining or greedy, it is more a continuous conversation with his deity.

It is in the little details that Jewish religious life is always present, for example when Tevye touches the *mezuzah* in traditional fashion on his visit to the butcher regarding marriage to one of his daughters. The *mezuzah* is a little ornamental box affixed to the doorpost containing a small parchment inscribed in indelible ink with specified Hebrew verses from the Torah. The box is usually touched with the tips of the fingers on entering a property and the fingers then kissed: we will see this in a number of films.

The exuberance and energy of *Fiddler on the Roof*, when not conveyed in rousing song, is shown in other events such as the dance match between a Cossack and Tevye. The athleticism of this should not be underestimated. Tevye's life is hard enough as a milkman with five daughters to feed, and it is the marriage of three of them that occupy much of the film. In the normal fashion Tevye arranges a good match for the eldest, Tzeitel, but she thwarts him as she loves an impoverished tailor. He accepts this with all the grace he can muster. At the same time the possibility of a pogrom always hangs over them, as in his wife's bizarre dream of a graveyard wedding (a little like in Tim Burton's film *Corpse Bride*, also based on a Yiddish folk tale). The dream is silly nonsense perhaps but a portent of a changing world, one of revolution, communism and women's emancipation.

The next daughter, Hodel, decides that she will marry the socialist revolutionary lodger, Perchik. He is a Jew but represents the face of modernism, willing at every turn to overthrow tradition. At one point, after announcing that he must return to Kiev to work for the revolution, he tells Hodel, "Everything's political. The relationship between a man and a woman has a socioeconomic base." Within his stream of explanatory socialism Hodel perceives an offer to marry her, which he clumsily agrees he is making. Tevye has to swallow this one too.

But when the third daughter, Chava, marries a Russian Cossack boy without parental consent, this is too much. The tailor and the revolutionary were Jews, but to marry outside the faith is a step too far, an unforgivable step. Tevye's generous nature has his limits and the shutters come down. "Chava is dead to us," he declares bitterly. There is no joking here.

Prior to this, at the wedding of Tzeitel and the tailor, we are witness again to the Jewish talent for celebration, to the way in which all the solemn occasions of life are accompanied by singing and dancing of a religious nature. Also, towards the end of these celebrations, the forces opposing their community become apparent as Russian Cossacks deliver their warning in the form of targeted vandalism and intimidation. (We may recall that the fictional Reb Saunders and his people were driven from Russia by the Cossacks.)

As Tevye contemplates the marriage of Chava and the Russian boy he repeats one of his catch-phrases, "on the other hand." His thought processes are thus illustrated, with effective camerawork that places him in and out of the landscape. And to complete the poetic nature of the imagery there is a scene of men and women dancing in orange-red semi-silhouette, representing Jewish tradition. "How can I accept them?" asks Tevye. "Can I deny everything I believe in? On the other hand, can I deny my own daughter? On the other hand how can I turn my back on my own faith, my people?"

The last "on the other hand" wins out as we saw, and he disowns his daughter as dead to him and their family.

In the end the inevitable news comes via the local Russian constable: the Jews have three days to leave their village. Perhaps it is part of the general anxieties about revolutionary activity, which have resulted in the arrest of Hodel's husband and his exile to Siberia. Or perhaps it is part of the general anti-Semitism made clear when there is talk of "Christ-killers" amongst the Russian Orthodox Christians. Or perhaps it is down to the long enmity between Jews and Cossacks – partly due to the historic role of Jews as tax-collectors – that created the conditions in which Hassidism itself arose. But the villagers, though initially defiant, know that all protest is useless, and pack up their belongings, resigned to their fate. One old man says: "Our forefathers have been forced out of many, many places at a moment's notice." The rabbi takes down the scrolls from the shrine in their beautiful little synagogue: since 70 CE or so Judaism had become a "portable" religion. Some will go to America – New York or Chicago – others to relatives in Europe. They leave the village in the middle of winter: no doubt many will die on the uncertain journey ahead. These make for deep cultural memories. To see the village column walk over the wooden bridge at the end of their village, the icy water flowing underneath, is to see a horrible fate. To survive a Russian winter with home and hearth and a huge log pile is hard enough, but that same winter spent in a tent is a near-certain killer.

The somberness of this last scene is mitigated with the music of the fiddler of course: we know that Jewish humor comes in part from just this squaring up to tragedy with defiance. In the director's comments we learn that the montage of leaving scenes was based on photographic research, "the same as Spielberg used in Schindler's list." The scenes are of course a symbol of the Diaspora, the near-two thousand year history of forced expulsions and migrations, and of the hostility facing a group with a strongly religious identity that refused to disappear through assimilation. It is a history almost unique in the world's religions – perhaps the Tibetan Buddhists are the closest modern analogue, forming a more recent diaspora.

The film, as pointed out earlier, is about the breakdown of tradition, but perhaps also about the strengthening of it through hardship. In another director's comment the question came up of why the film was such a success in Japan with no common cultural history with the film's setting. The Japanese response apparently was to explain that they too – in the late twentieth century – were absorbed with the question of the breakdown of tradition. But, the Japanese asked in turn, why was it successful in America? They assumed that tradition there had long since disappeared. In reality its success is probably in the first instance simply because it is an excellent film. Each element, the acting, singing, songwriting, set design, cinematography and so on are beautifully crafted, and overall it tells a universal story.

The Jazz Singer

We will now look at two versions of *The Jazz Singer*, the first released in 1927 and featuring Al Jolson in the lead role, and the second released in 1980 and featuring the popular singer Neil Diamond. Both films portray a Jewish cantor's son seeking fulfillment outside the synagogue through the popular music of the day, and both are a little overshadowed by the separate fame of the singers playing the character of Jakie Rabinowitz in the early film and Yussel Rabinovitch in the later one. Both lead actors are Jewish by birth, and neither sings jazz as the term is more usually understand, but that is not significant to their stories as iconic American entertainers. In the United States Al Jolson was once called the "concentration of our national health and gaiety," while Neil Diamond's rock anthem "America" is a patriotic song often played in national contexts, for example he sang it at the centennial rededication of the Statue of Liberty in 1986.

The Jazz Singer (1927)

Apparently Harry Warner, whose studio was contemplating making *The Jazz Singer* as their first "talkie", was a devout Jew but not sure of the gamble with this particular film project. His decision to go ahead was proved right however: the movie was an instant success.[53]

The film is set in the Jewish quarter of the Lower East Side of New York, where today there is still an Orthodox Jewish community with yeshiva day schools and a ritual bath, a *mikveh*. Jakie Rabinowitz runs away from home after he is discovered singing in a jazz club, and becomes Jack Robin, writing home to his mama, but refused contact by his father, the cantor. The boy has all the talent of his father, but directs it to the popular crooning of the day rather than to religious ends. His career does well and he returns to star in a show on Broadway. Of course he visits his parents and is then faced with a terrible choice: should he appear on the opening night of the new show in which he stars, or should he sing the *Kol Nidre* on the festival of Yom Kippur to please his dying father?

Glimpses of religious Jewish family life are shot through with humor, for example when his father's birthday is honored by friends and family with a thoughtful present – including from Jack. With equal lack of imagination each has bought him a new *tallit*. Otherwise the film rather declares Broadway the future and Judaism the past. Its high point for us is when Jack capitulates in the end and appears in the synagogue; the whole film is worth watching just for this.

Jack is singing in the distance as we watch his father sit up in bed at the sound. The window is opened to the synagogue over the street and we cut to Jack in *tallit* and ceremonial hat, flanked by men holding the Torah scrolls; the choir answers at each point in the singing. His father passes away, glad that his son has returned to the fold. The candle-flames of the seven-branched candlestick dance in front of the impassioned Jack, and we briefly see the ghostly spirit form of his father, dressed as cantor, who touches his son on the shoulder in a blessing. "As a jazz singer – singing to his G-d," comments his Broadway girlfriend. She and the producer who had pleaded with him not to let the show down look on in admiration, moved by … by what? Is it the religiosity of it? Is it the musical gift? Is it the admiration for a son who does the right thing by his father and mother? The *Kol Nidre* is sung before the evening service on Yom Kippur, the Day of Atonement. The characteristic gestures and body movements that Al

Jolson have used so far in the film to sing rather maudlin popular songs are at first strange when coupled with the religious intensity of the *Kol Nidre*, but we soon get used to it. It is passion that we feel, a religious longing for forgiveness, for atonement, and the whole cinematic presentation – though far too brief – is one of unforgettable beauty. Has not the son, after all, taken a profound step towards his father, a step to make up for the gulf that grew between them, a step in recognition of the generations of cantors before him, including his father, and in recognition of a divine gift? This sequence of images, permanently etched into the vintage emulsion of a film roll, is the kind of gift that only cinema can bestow, and which it has done for nearly a century.

The Jazz Singer (1980)

The 1980 version of *The Jazz Singer* opens with Neil Diamond as Jess Robin, real name Yussel Rabinovitch, singing in the synagogue or *schul*. Shots of the building exterior confirm it to be of the Eldridge Street Synagogue in Essex Street, Brooklyn, New York. Jess is assistant cantor to his father but plays in a popular music band on the side and is in a rush to join his black friend sitting in the congregation, who is given a yarmulke in order to attend. It keeps falling off his head as he taps his watch in a reminder to Jess.

Later on Jess is blacked up to sing in his band in a nightclub, just as Jack puts on blackface in the earlier film. However some members of the audience are furious at the applause for his singing: "He ain't no brother, he's a white boy!" A fight breaks out on stage, the police are called, and Jess's father has to collect him from jail the next day. He has only one comment on the whole pop music and blackface issue: "It's not tough enough being a Jew?" Jess has to explain the whole thing to his father, including his professional name.

"Five generations of Cantor Rabinovitch," his dad lectures.

"I sing in the synagogue, Pop, for what?" says Jess.

"For G-d."

"G-d doesn't pay so good, Pop."

His father – played by Sir Laurence Olivier – is outraged. "You think it an accident that you can sing? G-d gave you your voice for *his* use. Not yours." He tells his son that their people were killed for singing their prayers in a certain way, and that they owe it to them to keep singing it that way, not in English. "You can't change what has always been."

Jess's wife Rivka is also a singer: she teaches it to youngsters in a lovely scene and agrees with his father: "You've got too much talent to waste it on music that doesn't mean anything."

"It means something to me," her husband replies.

Jess devotes himself more to his role in the synagogue for a while, including the coaching of a young boy learning a song in Hebrew for his bar mitzvah. However Jess's talent as a popular singer – and the efforts of his band members – results in securing a recording contract, which means spending two weeks in Los Angeles. Naturally his wife objects.

"Aren't you curious about what's out there?" he asks.

"Why should I be?" she says. "I have what I want. It's all here."

"Oh really," he says. He has been pleasing his father with traditional versions of songs. "Think of him, if not of me," she says, but he is determined to go. He tries to tell his father about the importance to him of the recording to which the old man just says "No!" But, faced with his son's determination, he then cries and gives in.

The two weeks away is soon extended however as opportunities open up. When Jess performs at his first major venue Rivka comes to see him, but his career is not what she wants: it is incompatible with the traditional Jewish way of life which means everything for her. The crowds of young fans and the parties have not the slightest attraction for her, nor the money he is earning. So, before long they divorce, and he stays in California, and the very thing that his father feared has come to pass. Jess now lives with a non-Jewish woman called Molly Bell, musical assistant to the record producer.

Eventually his father visits, looks for the *mezuzah* on doorpost, but finds none.

"Pop, the world can do without another cantor," is Jess's defense.

"You're wrong," says the father and uses the religious argument that when so many died this family of cantors was spared. He should sing in *shul*. Jess can't do it any more, saying that he needs to express his life, his feelings, maybe they come from G-d too, and then confesses to the divorce. Just then Molly bursts in and the situation becomes clear to the old man. He is devastated.

"I have no son," he weeps and tears the lapel of his jacket: he is saying that Jess is dead. It is in utter anguish that he performs the *keriah*, the tearing of a piece of clothing over the heart, an act associated with bereavement – as we saw in *Yentl* – and leaves them. When Jess explains the tradition, Molly asks: "who's dead?"

"I am," he replies. The old cantor has disowned his son just as Tevye disowned Chava, both offspring "lost" to their tradition and as good as dead.

Jess, in despair, heads off on the open road, bumming his way around bars with his guitar, a man attempting to deal with a past, one that has placed an impossible choice upon him, torn between his love for his Jewish family and heritage and the feeling that he serves G-d better as a popular singer. Eventually he is tracked down by a band member with the news that he has a son by Molly, so Jess returns and picks up his life with the new family and pursues his career again. He lands a prestige appearance, during which a family friend turns up to say that his father has become too ill to sing the *Kol Nidre* on Yom Kippur. He asks if Jess could come to the service to be cantor and hopes that it will bridge the distance between father and son. Jess initially says no, but is convinced by Molly that he should go. Unlike in the earlier version of the *Jazz Singer* Jess does not have to choose between a top performance and the *Kol Nidre*.

In this film the *Kol Nidre*, for those with a religious bent, is also hauntingly beautiful, and speaks of a sacred world utterly at odds with Jess's heavily orchestrated rock anthems of modern secular America. But here is the frustrating part: it is too short again. We have lengthy Diamond ballads, but just this short glimpse of sacred singing. After the service and eventual reconciliation between father and son it is Neil Diamond's "America" that concludes the film, a patriotic song symbolic perhaps of his new allegiance: not to his Jewish faith but to the American dream – a country of the First Amendment, where liberty is the new god and which act prohibits Congress from making laws "respecting an establishment of religion."

Unlike in *Yentl* it is the Jewish woman here who wants to retain tradition, specifically the tradition of cantor within the Jewish community. The term "cantor" is used to cover the lead singer in any religious service, while the specifically Jewish term is *chazan*. For those with an ear to sacred song, a good cantor is a prize indeed, because a congregation led by one of poor musical talent will often grind its way untunefully through sacred song, well-meaning perhaps, but a much lesser offering. A traditional religious song, led with power and artistry by a gifted cantor, is a beautiful experience, whether in Judaism, Christianity, Buddhism or any other faith. But Jess wants to take a talent that was traditionally cultivated in the service of G-d for another, secular, purpose. Of course, having said this, we should also be open to his claim that perhaps G-d wants him to express his being in this new way.

The same impulse fuelled the trajectory of the Romanian sculptor Constantin Brancusi, one of the founders of modernism in the arts. He once wrote an essay on the subject of "an art of our own" meaning an art independent of religion, and this phrase later became the title of a book devoted to the spiritual in the art of the twentieth century. Although Brancusi sought to be free from subservience to the Church, he retained a deep spirituality in his life and work. [54] Jess on the other hand follows a trajectory from subservience to the Jewish religion to an art that lives in the cathedral of secular populism. In seeking freedom to be who he is – and maybe this is what G-d wishes for him – he appears to have chosen the "aesthetic" of Kierkegaard's three "stages."

Summary

The four films in this chapter provide some valuable material for rounding out our picture of Judaism, even if some of their characters are on the arc to secularism. *Yentl* certainly starts out with images of Judaism that suggest a profound piety, but the film loses its way a little in its gender politics and the suggestion that learning for its protagonist may land up as a rather secular activity. We are also not so sure of the deception she participates in regarding marriage. *Fiddler on the Roof* at no point suggests a deep engagement with Judaism, so at least it does not disappoint in that respect, while the two films about the jazz singer are clearly about a young man cutting his ties with tradition. Despite all this there is much of the beauty of Judaism to be found in the singing and dancing in these films: a deep celebratory impulse at the heart of the religion. We also glimpse details of the daily round of the religious Jew in an Eastern European setting. What stands out in my mind are the two renditions of the *Kol Nidre* – the very soul of Judaism pleading for forgiveness and atonement in haunting and gifted solo voice, filmed in a sacred synagogue setting complete with seven-branched candlestick, the ceremonial Torah scrolls and the sung responses of the choir. It is nothing less than magic on film.

3. Mystical Judaism

Preamble

Scholem's remark that there is as much that is not admirable as there is admirable in Jewish mysticism is relevant to us here: it could be said about all mysticism. At its best mysticism seems to be the wellspring of the profounder truths of religion, while at its worst it seems to be the self-interested pursuit of magical powers. In the Judaic tradition it is mostly the Kabbalah that becomes this knife edge on which its practitioners walk between that which takes one closer – perhaps very close – to G-d, and that which takes one away even while apparently drawing near. The three films in the Kabbalah section of this chapter – *PI*, *Bee Season* and *A Stranger Among Us* – show us this tension in different degrees, while among the three films in the *dybbuk* or ghost section we find in *The Dybbuk* the pure soul of a Kabbalah student overbalanced by romantic love.

Mysticism has a considerable scholarly literature but ultimately not much consensus on its nature. For example there seems to be a naturalistic mysticism of oneness that involves no supernatural element, which is more a shift of identity from the personal to the universal. On the other hand for many there is no mysticism without the spirit world, occult gifts such as clairvoyance and reincarnation. But, following Plotinus, it is clear that what is beautiful in mysticism is that which is also moral. Hasidism, as Buber portrays it, is a communal mysticism, meaning that the greater depth of mystical insight or experience is measured by the greater the mystic's service to the community. If Reb Saunders dances in mystical ecstasy, the value of that exalted frame of being for him is the value of his being for the community.

Kabbalah Films

Preamble

As argued above mysticism can be divided into two strands: a naturalistic mysticism in which nothing directly contradicts the laws of science, and a magical mysticism in which events take place with no possible material explanation. For example the idea of *Ein Sof* – a characterization of G-d as infinite, or *the* infinite – may be a subtle idea, but in the first instance we are dealing with a concept, infinity, that is familiar to philosophy and the natural sciences. On the other hand when a ghostly Messenger materializes and dematerializes in front of our eyes – as in *The Dybbuk* – we are most definitely dealing with the supernatural.

The Kabbalah seems to span these extremes. We saw earlier that Scholem outlines the entire history of Jewish mysticism of which the Kabbalah is a development that seems to dominate all mystical thought of the Jews after the tenth century CE. Scholem is quite clear about the basic character of the Kabbalah:

> Language in its purest form, that is, Hebrew, according to the Kabbalists, reflects the fundamental spiritual nature of the world, in other words, it has a mystical value. Speech reaches G-d because it comes from G-d. ... All creation – and this is an important principle of most Kabbalists – is, from the point of view of G-d, nothing but an expression of His hidden self that begins and ends by giving itself a name, the holy name of G-d, the perpetual act of creation. [55]

This statement on the Kabbalah makes a good background to the movies we now examine.

The following films – *Bee Season*, *Pi* and *A Stranger Among Us* – reference the Kabbalah in a variety of ways, the first two being explicitly about the language mysticism and numerology of the Kabbalah, but neither showing us mystical pursuits with direct relevance to the community. In *A Stranger Among Us* community looms large again, but we cannot quite see the relevance of the Kabbalah for it. The Kabbalah is present in *The Dybbuk*, *A Serious Man* and *The Possession*, which I examine as a group because they are premised not just on the Kabbalah, but also on the supernatural possibilities of communication with the dead. The latter two films are not that interesting for Judaism, but as *dybbuk* stories – Jewish ghost stories – they form an introduction to what is perhaps one of the most remarkable of our Jewish mystical films, *The Dybbuk*.

Bee Season

Bee Season opens with a little girl Eliza – known to her family as Elly – at a spelling bee being given her last spelling challenge of the competition. She thinks to herself as she stands on the stage: "My father told me once that words and letters hold all the secrets of the universe. That in their shapes and sounds, I could find everything and see beyond myself to something special, perfect. My father told me once that I could reach the ear of G-d."

It is no surprise then that Eliza's father, Saul Naumann, turns out to be a professor of Judaic Mysticism at a San Francisco university. The novel, which the film follows fairly well, has at its heart the Judaic and Kabbalistic concept of *Tikkun Olam* which means repairing or healing the world. Scholem tells us that this concept arose in Lurianic mysticism after the exodus from Spain, the shock of this expulsion driving the Kabbalah through one of its periodic shifts in emphasis, leading not only to a more messianic Judaism, but also to the wide adoption of the concept of the transmigration of souls. [56] Even if that idea does not surface in this film it leads, suggests Scholem, to a more individualistic kind of salvation. He says: "The doctrine of *Tikkun* raised every Jew to the rank of protagonist in the great process of restitution, in a manner never heard of before."

In a family scene Elly is taught Hebrew by her older brother Aaron who in turn is taught by his father. "How do we reach the ear of G-d, Aaron?" Saul asks of him, who replies in Hebrew. "Exactly," says Saul. "We speak with him." Here is perhaps the most direct confirmation yet in our films of Scholem's point cited in the Introduction, that the gulf between man and G-d in Judaism is crossed "by nothing but the voice."

This is promising: here is a modern family absorbed in the Jewish religion and Jewish mysticism. Perhaps typically the Jewish father takes a greater interest in his son's religious and educational development than his daughter's. As well as the Torah, the cello forms part of Aaron's instruction, which Elly is left out of: the preference for the boy is symbolized by his ready access to his father's study, a place Eliza has no right to enter. Hence she is convinced that her father has no interest in her achievements.

Saul teaches Kabbalah to students at his University and we follow one of his lectures. He tells the class:

> G-d is everything. A perfect luminous essence. But even G-d wants more. To experience more, to give. So G-d creates a vessel, a container that can receive this gift of G-d's pure light. This divine light pours into the vessel. The vessel, of course, can't contain the magnitude of this light, and it shatters, destroying the vessel and scattering its broken shards in a big bang of creation. Now, man's job is to locate and gather these shards to make a vessel, our world, whole again. Now the Kabbalists call this fixing, this mending *Tikkun Olam*, the fixing of the world.

Saul tells his students that it is their responsibility through acts of goodness and kindness to try and restore what is shattered. We note too that Saul has updated the language of the Kabbalah to include a reference to a concept familiar in science, the big bang.

Elly meanwhile is winning spelling competitions. She seems to see the letters of the words forming in a swarming cloud of indistinct particles, perhaps dandelion seeds blowing in the wind, beautifully animated. Her mother gives her a kaleidoscope in which images are fragmented and also have this animated quality. Somehow when Elly closes her eyes a voice says the word; it changes into something else, and then she can "see" it, the word.

Her brother accompanies her to her spelling successes, and before long her father wakes up to her talent. He becomes excited about it because her gift resonates with his own Kabbalistic interests in the letter-formation of words, and also, as a typical American father, success, "winning," is important to him. This means that Elly begins to displace Aaron as the favorite. Saul invites her into the previously forbidden study, and he is going to cram her.

Elly's mother Miriam works in a science lab but appears left out of Saul's passions. She steals something from a stranger's house – a beautiful thing, not valuable, just shiny – and at first we have no idea what this is about. In the meantime Elly's tuition begins under Saul, starting with Hebrew letters, animated letters in charcoal; she is in a trance. He instructs her: "Close your eyes. I want you to open your mind to all the words in the universe that begin with the letter 'e'." Before long Saul introduces her to the Kabbalah in the university library, to the work of Abraham Abulafia, a thirteenth century student of the Jewish philosopher Maimonides. Scholem tells us that Abulafia was "the least popular of all the great Kabbalists," [57] in contrast perhaps to the populism of the Lurianic movement of the later period.

"What's a mystic?" asks Eliza.

"A mystic is a person who believes that you can talk, really connect, with G-d," says Saul. "This is all about talking with G-d and a response, something more than mere words of praise, something that almost no one can do. Something beyond words." He pauses. "Let G-d flow through you."

She closes her eyes.

"Abulafia believed that by concentrating on letters the mind could be opened up and reach what he called *shefa*," Saul tells her. "It is the most special way of being together with G-d."

Mystical Judaism

Shefa, or *ohr*, in the Kabbalistic lexicon means "light" or "Divine influence." Abulafia's mysticism was of an ecstatic kind, triggered by personal revelation and one which would be largely familiar to students of mysticism in any tradition, though it is uniquely Judaic because of its emphasis on the name of G-d and the "science of the combination of letters." [58]

Aaron, feeling increasingly left out and alienated from his parents, goes to a Catholic service in search of his own personal religiosity, but finds that it does not suit him. Later he meets a Hare Krishna girl in a park and tells her that his mother was Catholic and had converted to Judaism. This is California, after all, and so we should not be surprised at this melting pot of religions.

Saul shows Elly his translation of Abulafia's words, his guide for reaching *shefa*, in his notebook. "Cleanse your heart and soul," he instructs his daughter. "Permute the letters back and forth. This will arouse in you many words, one after the other. You will feel then as if an additional spirit is within you. You will experience ecstasy and trembling. In this manner you will reach beyond yourself. Go slowly, as the path is dangerous and must be traveled with caution."

Saul himself is not able to do it but he thinks Elly has the gift that he lacks. At the same time as she "permutates" the word "library" in an animated visualization Aaron is performing a Hindu ritual with the Hare Krishnas. Their mother steals again, but we still have no idea why she does this. What we can see, from the perspective of the Jewish faith, is that this family, while religious in its various ways, is modern in this respect: it is entirely "nuclear." There is no extended family, no near relations that could assist in the development and guidance of the children, no synagogue, no rabbi, no community. The mother in particular is confined, apart from her job, to a traditional role, but without the network of support from other traditional Jewish women or the broader community. She is going downhill.

We now witness intercut scenes of Aaron dancing and singing with the Hare Krishnas and Elly in Saul's study attempting a deeper stage of the Kabbalah. Her single intoned vowel hits the same pitch as the Hare Krishna singing – is it the Hindu "Om" – is it the Jewish "Amen" – or is it just the letter "o" or "a"? Aaron thinks Elly moves the way Abulafia described it.

Miriam's story unfolds a little: in a flashback we see glass shards everywhere, a broken windscreen, broken glasses, a cut-glass fanlight in a front door, the broken splintered images in the kaleidoscope. Perhaps she witnessed the death of her parents in a car crash and has never received therapy. Finally her obsessive behavior deteriorates to the point where she is arrested for stealing an item of no particular value in a stranger's home.

Saul is asked to accompany a policeman to a garage where she has been storing all her stolen items; he is grim in the car. When he looks round he is astonished: it is an art "installation" – if you like – of glass and reflective objects strung from the ceiling, heaped in piles. It is mesmerizing, most of it stolen, shards of other people's lives. It is beautiful. In the police car on the way back Saul starts to cry, as he sees that all his scholarship had availed him nothing in his marriage, in his obligations as a husband, in the simple human capacity to help his wife in her desperate unraveling. She had been seeking through other means the *Tikkun* he read and wrote and lectured about. They had been on the same journey and he had been a useless companion.

In the mental hospital his wife just says: "It is beautiful isn't it?"

"I've never seen anything like it."

"It's beginning to hold the light," she says. He does not understand.

"The shards," she explains, "putting them together. *Tikkun Olam,* to make things whole. Hold the light."

He shakes his head. "You showed me," she says. He tries to explain that it was a metaphor, a poem.

"Yes," she says, "I made a poem." But they cannot reach each other and she says that all he does is talk and talk and talk.

"Are they empty words?" she asks. "Do you want to understand? Understand me?" Had his powers of understanding been directed at her, his wife, instead of abstract theories, perhaps there would have been a true healing.

On his return Saul tells Aaron that she is in a mental hospital, but the son just says that it is him, Saul, who is sick. Later he says that Saul craves all the attention of success, of control. Elly just says: "He needs Mom."

Elly is however still working towards the national spelling finals despite all this havoc. As she focuses her unique ability we see a collared dove on the window sill of her hotel room, and as she works on the spelling of the word "origami" the creature turns into a paper bird; they are preparing in a hotel, the night before the finals. In her mind she hears a repeat of Saul saying "You will feel then as if an additional spirit is within you," the words of Abraham Abulafia. She opens the Kabbalah that she has secretly brought with her.

"Light, light, light," she repeats. "Let G-d flow through you." She "permutates"; spots of light float around her, she picks one on the end of her finger, it is an "n," she has an ecstatic climax, and then falls and we see trance-like kaleidoscopic images, but it looks as if she is having a fit. What indeed is the boundary between the ecstasy of the mystic and the fit of the epileptic? Between the G-d-intoxicated one and the schizophrenic? The secular world does not know how to answer this question, or even how to ask it.

She recovers however with no ill effects.

So, we reach the national finals. She is on stage, Saul and Aaron are in the audience bound by their anguish over Miriam who is sitting on her sofa in the mental ward watching Elly on TV. The final reaches its last round in which she has a single competitor left, and she has been given the word "origami" as she had practiced earlier. In her imagination the paper bird, the collared dove, flies across the auditorium. One by one she spells out the letters. She pauses. The nation looks on. Her father looks on; her brother and her mother look on. Looking ahead, any doubt gone, it is time for the very last letter. The whole film, starting with the flash forward to this scene, has led to this point, we know that her success is assured. But she says in a firm voice: "y." She is dinged out: the word is spelled wrong. Her competitor spells the last word correctly and wins the final.

She was teaching her father a lesson.

Elly whispers to herself: "And like the ancient mystics, G-d would flow through me, and we would be together." Through her tears her mother says "She's my daughter." She is indeed, and in this act of sanity we hope for her mother and for the whole family. But what exactly is this deliberate failure a rejection of? In the first instance it is a rejection of the American ideal of winning, the counterpart of which is to come second, third, last it does not matter: then you are a "loser." She had to show her father that it did not matter. But is she also rejecting Abulafia, the Kabbalah, her religion? We cannot be sure. However we can suggest that the knife-edge on which the Kabbalistic mystic must stand is made very clear in this film, and this young girl, gifted in religion, is also gifted in the sanity needed to traverse it.

Pi

The term *gematria* has been known to European culture since the sixteenth century when the Renaissance scholar Giovanni Pico della Mirandola made translations of lost works by Greek, Egyptian and Kabbalist authors. *Gematria* is associated with Jewish tradition and is a form of numerology in which letters of the Hebrew alphabet take numbers. Abulafia's "permutations" are part of this tradition.

In the film *Pi* it is *gematria* that obsesses a group of Jews who provide the incidental sub-theme to the protagonist's computer-driven mania with numbers. The film – also known as *Pi – Faith in Chaos* – is about the attempt by Max Cohen, a reclusive mathematical genius, to understand the whole of nature through numbers. The film is a compelling portrayal of obsession.

Mystical Judaism

Although *Pi* is located in the modern world of math and computers – as in the film *A Beautiful Mind* (also about a mathematical genius on the borders of madness) – its portrayal of Judaic observational essentials and preoccupations is instructive. For example the film explains the use of the *tefillin* or phylacteries, strapped to the forearm and head. Cohen is instructed in their use and also told that wearing them is a *mitzvah*, a duty or observance that all Jewish men should perform as a purification. Rather like the *mezuzah*, the *tefillin* contain small parchment scrolls with text from the Torah.

At the start of the film Max is walking past Tai Chi practitioners in the park and tells us: "Restate my assumptions. One: mathematics is the language of nature. Two: everything around us can be represented and understood through numbers. Three: if you graph the numbers of any system, patterns emerge. Therefore, there are patterns everywhere in nature."

This is not so much Kabbalistic or Jewish, as Pythagorean. Max believes that the Stock Exchange is an organism which also has a pattern, hiding behind the numbers. He calls his bizarre stack of mainframe computers "Euclid," which again suggests a Greek origin to his metaphysical obsessions. However when an Orthodox Jew introduces himself to Max in a café the story effectively veers from the Hellenic to the Hebraic. On learning that he is a Jew the stranger asks:

"Do you practice?"

"No, I am not interested in religion."

"Did you ever hear of Kabbalah?"

"No."

"Jewish mysticism," explains the stranger. "It is a critical moment in time. You ever put on *tefillin*?"

Max shakes his head, not really interested in any of this.

"*Mitzvahs*, good deeds. They purify us," concludes his interlocutor. (Note: the proper plural is *mitzvot*.) Max is fed up with all this; he is more worried about having an "attack" – a period of acute anxiety of panic that is the outcome of his obsessive life. A little later he plays Go with math professor Sol; the game too has mathematical regularities, but Sol is worried about him, concerned that Max is Icarus, the renegade pupil (another Greek reference). He warns Max that his obsession is costing him his health: "The world can't be summed up by math, there is no simple pattern." Sol tells Max that once he is obsessed with the number 216 he will find it everywhere, that he will effectively read it into nature, and that by discarding scientific rigor Max is no longer a mathematician, but a mere numerologist. Here we shift back to the Hellenic, especially a little later when in a rather beautiful sequence we see the patterns in sea shells, sunflowers, pine cones, and learn how Archimedes had begun much of this mathematical work; the film also references the golden rectangle and the work of Leonardo da Vinci. It is no surprise then that later in the film Max should say:

"Remember Pythagoras. Mathematician, cult leader, Athens, c. 500 BC. Major belief: the Universe is made of numbers."

Pythagoras can be understood as the first teacher in the Neoplatonist tradition, despite the fact that the tradition draws its name from Plato. In fact Croton rather than Athens was Pythagoras's city for the major period of his life, where he established his religious community. *Pi* references Neoplatonism, not just in the emphasis on numbers and the reference to Pythagoras, but also in respect of the Kabbalah. Ordinarily, one would assume that the Hebraic and Hellenic traditions remain religiously antithetical to each other, but in fact the Kabbalah shows a kind of synthesis, as Scholem points out. What the Kabbalah has in common with Pythagoras – and may have drawn on him historically – is the emphasis on numbers.

Just as the esoteric discipline of astrology gave way to the scientific discipline of astronomy; just as the esoteric discipline of alchemy gave way to the scientific discipline of chemistry; so the esoteric discipline of numbers – called numerology in its broad sense and *gematria* in the Hebrew context – gave way to mathematics. In this sense Max is making a backward journey in time.

Max first learns of *gematria* from the Hasidic scholar Lenny Myer in the café, who tells him: "Hebrew is all math. Aleph, a, is one, Bet, b, is two …" Lenny explains that when the word "child" is written down in Hebrew and the letters added together they come to 44, which is the sum of "father," value 3 and "mother," value 41.

"The Torah is a long string of numbers, a code, sent to us from G-d," Lenny asserts, and goes on to give the numerical equivalents of the Tree of Life, *Etz haChayim*, 144 and 233. Max interrupts him to say that the numbers are part of the Fibonacci sequence.

"If you divide 144 by 233 you get theta."

"Theta?"

"Theta," repeats Max, drawing a spiral. "The Greek symbol for the golden ratio, the golden spiral."

"Wow," says Lenny. "I never saw that before. It's like that series you see in Nature? Like the face of a sunflower?"

"Wherever there are spirals," says Max, tipping some cream into his coffee.

"See, there's math everywhere," says Lenny. Spirals emerge in close-ups of swirls in his coffee and swirls of cigarette smoke as Lenny exhales.

Mystical Judaism

Myer and his group of Kabbalistic scholars are seeking a numerical pattern in the Torah while Max is seeking a numerical pattern in the numbers of pi. The stories converge as it appears that both are seeking a number with 216 digits: to the Rabbis it represents the name of G-d and to Max it is the key to stock-market fluctuations.

When Max is hounded by the corporate lady who wants the secret of his algorithms it is Myer who provides him with a distraction: he offers to show him *tefillin*. He has a car, he will take him to the *shul*. Myer tells Max that they now realize who he is and that his work in mathematics has inspired them. Wearing the *tefillin*, they will now say a prayer:

> Shma Yisroel
> Adenoi Eloihenu
> Adenoi Echod

Max repeats these lines hesitantly in the strange synagogue he finds himself in, a Star of David behind him, but he does not connect to the religious element in all of this. This short prayer, known as the "Shema Yisrael" (spellings vary) is said to contain the monotheistic essence of Judaism. In English it is "Hear, O Israel: the Lord our G-d, the Lord is one." One could also say that it is mystical, a reminder of the oneness of all things.

Later when Lenny Myer and his group of Jews rescue him again they appear no less ruthless than the corporate types in their quest to obtain what is in Max's head: the 216-digit number that is the lost name of G-d and the intonation of which will usher in the Messianic age. Max is knocked out in the struggle but wakes up in the *shul* of Rabbi Cohen, now with a *yarmulke* on his head. The rabbi is flanked by bearded men who insist that Max has to give them the number. The rabbi lectures him:

> The Talmud tells us it began 2,000 years ago, when the Romans destroyed the second temple. The Romans also destroyed our priesthood, the Cohanim. And with their deaths they destroyed our greatest secret. In the centre of the Temple was the heart of Jewish life, the holy of holies. It was the earthly residence of our G-d. The one G-d. It housed the Ark of the Tabernacle which stored the original Ten Commandments which G-d gave to Moses. Only one man was allowed to enter this holy of holies, on one day, the holiest day of the year, Yom Kippur. On the Day of Atonement all of Israel would descend on Jerusalem to watch the High Priest, the Cohen Godul,

make his trip into the holy of holies. If the High Priest was pure, he would emerge moments later and we would secure a prosperous year. It meant that we were one year closer to the Messianic age. But, if he was impure, he would die instantly and it meant that we were doomed. The High Priest had one ritual to perform in the holy of holies. He had to intone a single word. That word was the true name of G-d. The true name which only the Cohanim knew, was 216 letters long.

"So that's what happened," muses Max. He reflects. "I saw G-d," he tells them, thinking back to ecstatic moments he had in the pursuit of his obsession. The rabbi tells him that he is not pure enough. But Max insists that the sacred number was given to him, that it is changing him. He saw everything. But the rabbi tells him that it is killing him. He is not ready to receive it. Max shouts at him: "Rabbi, I was chosen!" He rushes onto the streets again.

Apart from the Neoplatonist-Kabbalist elements in the film, and the visual representations of many related themes, *Pi* also usefully portrays in Max a certain kind of autism, or rather a mild Asperger's syndrome, and a radical solution to it. As Eric Wilson, writing on Gnosticism in film, says, *Pi* "portrays the insanity that might issue from the Kabbalistic attempt to grasp G-d's secret code."[59] The solution that Max is driven to – auto-trepanning – is a suitably bizarre solution to his predicament of looming insanity. It leaves Max on a park bench, smiling benignly and in the warmth of human relations with a little girl. At the start of the film she would come up to Max and give him long multiplication or division to do in his head, checking his genius against her calculator. He barely had time for her earlier, but now, "cured" of his autism, he is happy to listen to her prattlings. He can no longer do the math though.

A Stranger Among Us

A Stranger Among Us is the first of two films by Jewish director Sidney Lumet to be considered in this book. This film is often compared to Peter Weir's *Witness* because both have tough secular-minded cops enter a closed religious community. In *Witness* it is a policeman amongst the Amish, while in *A Stranger Among Us* it is a policewoman Emily Eden (played by Melanie Griffiths) amongst the Hasidim. Where Elliot B. Gertel is mostly critical of the portrayal of the Jewish faith in American media, he is largely enthusiastic for *A Stranger Among Us*, saying for example that:

> What Avrech [the screenwriter] and Lumet attempt here is admirable. In both the humorous scenes and in the sad scenes they depict the sense of the sacredness of human life and deeds, which are so central to Hasidic teaching and to Judaism in general.[60]

Emily Eden is a policewoman based in the 83rd Precinct, Bushwick, Brooklyn and is called in to investigate a murder amongst the Hasidic Jews of the diamond-trading district of West 47th Street in Manhattan. In the film the Jews travel to work in special buses from what is probably the Williamsburg section of Brooklyn, historically known to be the home to Hassidim of the Satmar dynasty (who incidentally are noted for having been extremely anti-Zionist). In order to penetrate the closed diamond-trading community – for Emily believes that it is an inside job – she has to fake an identity as a Jewish woman and live with the family of the rabbi at the centre of the community. His son was a close friend of the murdered man and is destined to inherit his father's role, which will exclude any marriage outside his faith. Hence we are set up for an inevitably doomed romantic attraction, and, more interestingly for us, a glimpse of the Hasidic world through the eyes of an outsider. By bringing in the whole freight of modern assumptions and mores with Emily we both see many of them debunked and at the same time understand some of the challenges faced by a traditional faith community located in one of the most modern cities in the world.

Gertel concludes:

> *A Stranger Among Us* does get across the flavor of Hasidic life, the Shabbat, the rituals for every aspect of life, the emphasis on Torah study and community. (These are, of course, important to any expression of Judaism.) The Hasidic outlook, however, is not sufficiently explained, nor its place in Jewish history.[61]

This criticism, that the Hasidic outlook and its place in Jewish history are not sufficiently explained, is perfectly valid, but our strategy is to take the entirety of the films under consideration here to provide something of a composite understanding. Even if that fails, the strengths of each film lie in the deeply visual texture of cinema, and in *A Stranger Among Us* it provides a memorable journey into Judaism. I will focus mainly on one element in this chapter: the presentation of the Kabbalah in this film, leaving other elements, particularly the emphasis on family life, to later chapters.

Mystical Judaism

From the opening shots of the film – a fly-past east over Manhattan Bridge – we are submerged in the Jewish religious life of the yeshiva and Hebrew school where children are chanting, taught by a man in side curls and yarmulke; behind them, in the stained glass, is the Star of David. We later learn that the man's name is Ariel. The contrasting daily round of the policewoman Emily Eden is equally introduced to us but it does not concern us much until she takes on the Jewish murder case.

In the synagogue, dimly lit with candle bulbs, an old rabbi adjusts the *tefillin*, the phylacteries, on his head; another is tied on his left arm. He walks to the podium, the *bima*, and begins to sing his prayer. In a number of films we see such a moment, where the rabbi moves through his congregation to begin the service. Martin Buber, who was rather disaffected by the splendor of a Hasidic synagogue in his youth, tells us this however:

> The prayer house of the Hasidim with its enraptured worshippers seemed strange to me. But when I saw the rebbe striding through the rows of the waiting, I felt, "leader," and when I saw the Hasidim dance with the Torah, I felt, "community." At that time there rose in me a presentiment of the fact that common reverence and common joy of soul are the foundations of genuine human community. [62]

Later on in the yeshiva a student called Jaakov tells Ariel:
"You shouldn't learn Kabbalah. Mysticism can shorten your life."
"On the other hand it can lengthen your life," responds Ariel, absorbed in his book.
"The rabbi says we shouldn't study Kabbalah until the age of forty. Besides, only the most brilliant students can understand it. Only the brightest can hope to understand its mysteries."

This is a common sentiment: the Kabbalah is only for brilliant students and is dangerous. However I know of no study of the world's great mystics that suggests a shortened lifespan on account of their pursuits, unless of course you count execution for heresy, something hardly facing New York Jews. The room in which the men are studying is to my mind rather beautiful: I have never visited it in real life and yet the movie camera gives me this glimpse of it, an image that I could never gain solely from perusing the texts of the Jewish religion.

Jaakov and Ariel converse on other matters, then Ariel returns to his text as a counterpoint: "G-d counts the tears of women." He is not sure what it means but has just come across it in the Kabbalah.

Mystical Judaism

We now come to the moment when Emily walks through the Orthodox district, passing street signs for Forest and Putnam Avenues, and shop signs such as "Boruch's Kosher Pizza" and "Yechel's Newstand," eventually arriving in a home just like that of Reb Saunders. She waits in a room full of Orthodox men who all avert their eyes from her above-the-knee skirt; she then meets with the rabbi.

"Jaakov Klausman is reported as a missing person?" Emily wants this confirmed but a young woman distracts her by discretely covering Emily's knees with a drape, and then further distracts her by covering her shoulders with another.

She is told that diamonds are missing to the value of $720,000.

"Perhaps your son ripped you off," suggests Emily to the parents of the missing man. "I've seen it a hundred times."

"In your world, not ours," says the rabbi tersely.

Later on Emily accompanies the Jews to their gem house. The rabbi, his son Ariel, and others touch the *mezuzah* and then kiss their fingers as they enter the heavily fortified diamond room.

"What do you call those?" asks Emily, pointing to Ariel's sidecurls.

"*Payots*" he replies. He explains that idol-worshippers used to cut their hair in that area as part of their cult, and Jews are forbidden from imitating them. She casts a professional eye over the scene of the crime, saying she knows human nature, as a cop. The rabbi says:

"With all due respect, you do not know our nature."

"With all due respect sir," she answers him, "inside every honest man there is a thief trying to get out."

"You're positive?"

"When you've seen what I've seen in this life, okay?"

He walks up to her and just looks at her, as if he wants to investigate her soul. She turns away and looks around again. Sending Yaakov's parent's out, she investigates further and discovers the body of the missing man in the false ceiling. It was Jaakov's life that was shortened, it seems, not Ariel's.

At the funeral Emily witnesses the rituals we saw in *Yentl*: the bereaved cut or tear their suits, and they say *Kaddish*, the Prayer for the Dead. Ariel insists: "Yaakov only knew Hasidim. We don't kill each other, we don't kill anybody."

Later at the precinct police station Ariel has to give evidence. He is then challenged by Emily:

"You don't trust a female cop, do you?"

"Actually the Kabbalah says that women are on a higher…"

"The what?" she interrupts him, her eyes curious about this man.

"The Kabbalah. Jewish mysticism. It's very intricate, very esoteric. It concerns itself with creation, transmigration, meditation..."

"I bet it's from California, right?"

This is a stock response that we could expect from a secular woman such as Emily, but it is not altogether unreasonable as we saw in the film *Bee Season* which was set in California, and in which many individuals seek spiritual paths verging on the New Age. At the same time Ariel has alerted us to the fact that transmigration of souls – reincarnation – has a significant place in the lexicon of the Kabbalah, where it is known as the doctrine of *Gilgul*.[63]

"Ah no, it's wisdom from before the beginning of time," explains Ariel. "Most of us don't study it because it presents great difficulties in certain areas."

"The point?" asks Emily, impatient with his long explanation. He apologizes.

"The Kabbalah says that women are on a higher spiritual plane than men," he concludes. "Therefore it would be foolish of me not to trust you."

It would be no exaggeration to say that at this stage of their acquaintanceship they are talking at cross-purposes. He turns away and then tells her how Yaakov was his friend, a special friend. She realizes the extent of his loss and offers him a chocolate éclair, but he cannot eat it as it is not Kosher. Emily wonders whether he ever break the rules. Of course not, he says. Ever, ever? No. Wow.

"You guys got a lot of rules?" she asks.

"Actually there are 613 rules or commandments," Ariel tells her, smiling. "248 positive commandments and 365 negative ones." He is referring to the *mitzvot*.

"No shit," she says.

Emily will give him a ride home in her police car, something that rather goes against the gender etiquette he is used to, but they reach a compromise. As they leave the 83rd Precinct police station we see a modern art piece above the entrance, which is still there today. Location filming like this, even in a film shot in the early 1990s, helps locate the characters in their proper setting and also brings home the point that religion lives on in the present, amidst concrete, glass and steel, and in an era of forensic policing and modern art.

Emily, now kitted out in the rather frumpish unfashionable style she needs to adopt to plausibly be a visiting Jewish woman amongst the community, goes to the Klausman home with Ariel. We see the Hasidim touch the *mezuzah* on the way in; the mirrors are covered, as in *Yentl*. The mourners have discarded their shoes because "leather shoes in ancient

Mystical Judaism

times were a sign of wealth, and when somebody dies we are no longer wealthy," explains Leah, daughter of the rabbi and the person assigned to guide Emily in her new world.

"Wow," responds Emily, a bit shaken. She murmurs uncertainly: "I don't know."

"What?"

"You people you really *care* about each other."

"Of course."

In the room they share, a little later on, Emily asks about the word "rebbe" as opposed to "rabbi".

"It's more than a rabbi," responds Leah. "A Hassidic rebbe is a great presence."

It also turns out that she and Ariel were adopted by the rebbe after their parents were killed in a car accident.

Emily is a good pupil of Ariel's. Back in the modern world of policing she tells a colleague about the *tzitzit*, the tassels on the *tallit*. "Pay attention," she tells him, "it's from the Kabbalah, it's very mystical. It's numerology, Ariel told me all this stuff." She explains to him that every letter in the Hebrew alphabet has a numerical equivalent, so *tzitzit* comes out to 600. With all the knots in them it comes out to 613. "It's very cool shit, I mean stuff," she adds. She doesn't tell him that 613 is the number of *mitzvot*, which if properly adhered to would most likely rule out the use of bad language.

Leah has told Emily at one point that the rebbe is a survivor of Auschwitz. On learning this she feels mortified at having lectured him on human nature earlier on, and now gets a chance to apologies. He responds:

"We are both on intimate terms with evil. It does things to your soul, doesn't it?"

"I don't know about that," she replies hesitantly.

"You have a soul, Emily," he says. "I've seen it."

They look at each other. He smiles.

"Have a good Shabbos," he says.

"Shabbos?" she murmurs.

There now follows a Shabbat scene which I describe in more detail in the last chapter, Family Judaism. At one level it is not dissimilar to the rather "exoticized" presentation of the Amish celebration on house-raising that police officer John Book participates in at a similar point in the film *Witness*. But if we can get past the obvious clumsiness in the too-eager attempt to make the unfamiliar accessible, then there is much to contemplate in it concerning the intersection of the Jewish religion and Jewish extended family life.

Later on at night Emily finds Ariel in the courtyard studying. He asks her about her gun; has she killed anyone? She has, in the course of duty. He understands that she has to, but points out that his religion holds that "When you kill one person you annihilate an entire universe."

Emily wants him to teach her from the book he is reading from. Had I not read Evyatar Marienberg's article on the *Holy Letter*, cited above in connection with *Yentl*, I would not have known that Ariel is reading from this text. Marienberg tells us that the screenwriter, Robert J. Avrech, claims not have seen *Yentl* at the time of writing.[64] Apparently, Ariel's version condenses passages from the *Holy Letter*, but cannot be mistaken as coming from anything else. It seems that Avrech regards this scene as one of his best, but really it is rather unremarkable. Ariel's knowledge of sex comes from a book – as did Avigdor's in *Yentl* – while Emily's comes from real life. How can she be anything other than a little sarcastic with him? We know already that his tradition regards marriage as a holy union, and that Emily's sex life is more modern. No wonder she just says: "Okey dokey."

They then discuss his forthcoming marriage to the daughter of a rebbe in Paris, a woman he has not met. This is met with more doubt, but he tells her that he believes she is his *basherte*, destiny. Earnestly he explains to Emily the ancient theory found in the *Kabbalah* that G-d created every soul to have a match (outside of Jewish tradition this is an idea more commonly associated with Plato). A man seeks his *basherte*, the woman who is his soulmate or destiny, while the woman seeks her *bashert*, the male equivalent, though "seek" is not quite right because of the role of the "matchmaker" or *shadchan* in this, as found in *The Fiddler on the Roof* and a number of other films we will look at.

But the conversation becomes a little heated as his ideas of sex as part of marriage and children rather grate on her. He tells her it is a *mitzvah*, a duty, but she is getting angry. We understand that where he continuously chooses the Kabbalah she would like him to have chosen her – it always was to be a romance that would go nowhere for her.

Emily returns to the room she shares with Leah, who then compares Emily to one of the women in the Torah, Deborah, and other great female warriors of the Hebrew Bible.

"Emily," then confides Leah, "Ariel is special."

"What?"

"Talmudic genius at six years old. He is to Jewish learning what Mozart was to music," she says. "Ariel has a great soul. Ariel can look down at the sky."

None of this is any comfort to Emily, but we are reminded perhaps of Danny Saunders, though Ariel seems to have had an easier time of his growing up than Danny, as stepson in the house of a rebbe.

Mystical Judaism

The "thriller" aspect of the film reaches its violent conclusion. Marienberg tells us that Avrech "describes himself on his web site as 'an observant Jew, a religious Zionist, a conservative Republican, and a member of the NRA.'" No member of the National Rifle Association would be disappointed with the finale, where the reluctant Ariel is given a gun by Emily and is forced in the end to shoot the murderer – a woman called Mara who has come under the Rebbe's wing and has betrayed them all. Ariel collapses weeping afterwards.

The film finishes with the wedding of Ariel and his French bride. In all, this is a film that stands well alongside *The Chosen*, *The Quarrel* or *Ushpizin*, for glimpses into the Jewish faith, as long as one can forgive the implausible ending – "silly" as Gertel calls it.

Gertel's enthusiasm for the film extends to its portrayal of women:

> Also, mirabile dictu, the Jewish woman is depicted here not as shrill or spoiled or a shrew, but as knowledgeable and knowing, attractive and spiritual, devoted yet indomitable, especially in Mia Sara's low-key portrayal of Ariel's sister, Leah, with whom Emily rooms. Mia Sara is able to communicate the classical quality of Yiddishe *chen* (pronounced, "khayne"), graciousness and understanding, traditionally extolled in Jewish women (see Proverbs 31) but cherished in men and women alike. [65]

Emily herself is clearly touched by this encounter with the Jewish faith but her life will no doubt largely revert to its previous secular track. In *Luminous* I explored the case of Martha Livingston, another secular chain-smoking woman officer of the judicial system, in a film called *Agnes of G-d*.[66] Her encounter with Miriam Ruth, Mother Superior at a monastery where there has been a suspected infanticide, has something of the chemistry between Emily and Ariel. The antagonism is much sharper, but a similar friendship develops across the divide. Such films can be persuasive of the legitimacy of religion because they do not take sides.

Dybbuk Films

Preamble

Bee Season, *Pi* and *A Stranger Among Us* provide a glimpse into the Jewish mysticism of the Kabbalah. These are nothing more than glimpses, probably distorted by the nature of film making, and presenting only fragments of a huge historical system, yet they add to our total picture of Judaism. Nothing in these films requires us to step beyond the boundary of the natural however. We now turn to a very different film with Kabbalistic elements: *The Dybbuk*, in which the supernatural, in the form of ghosts, takes centre stage ("dybbuk" is Yiddish for ghost). This film is an early black and white feature, released in 1937, and can be compared to *Der Golem* (1920) and *The Cabinet of Dr Caligari* (1920). *The Jazz Singer* of 1927, which we looked at earlier, is of this period, and only hints at the supernatural at the end when the deceased cantor appears as a ghost to bless his son. The 1980 version of the film is far more accessible, even when we make allowances for the ground-breaking nature of the first talkies, because of the more naturalistic acting. In contrast *The Dybbuk* is easily the most difficult of our films so far as the acting is not just melodramatic and stilted as is typical of the era, but its context is foreign and its plot hinges on the supernatural. However it is potentially one of the most rewarding of all the films we deal with in this book for revealing the beauty of Judaism.

Before looking at *The Dybbuk* itself we look at two films in which *dybbuks* in different forms appear, and from which we can learn about the absence of religious beauty, or even religion.

A Serious Man

A Serious Man is the story of Larry Gopnik, a modern Jewish man whose life unravels and which prompts him to take advice from a succession of rabbis. His son – a product of what becomes a dysfunctional family not so different to that in *Bee Season* – is the beneficiary of guidance from the most venerable of these rabbis, one his father fails to secure an audience with. The film opens with a Yiddish folk-tale of a *dybbuk* which appears to have no relevance to the main film at all, unless we imagine that Larry's brother Arthur, who has imposed himself on the family, is a malevolent kind of ghost.

Carol Linnitt, writing in the *Journal of Religion and Film* says: "At a glance Larry's plight differs little from Job's: both stories are characterized by overwrought devastation, although Larry's devastation is more attuned to the uncomfortable hues of tragicomedy." She goes on to say:

> In *Dialectic of Enlightenment*, Horkheimer and Adorno write, "only thought which does violence to itself is hard enough to shatter myths." This notion invites what, throughout *A Serious Man*, Larry resists: the failure of religion. There are undoubtedly areas where religion fails in *A Serious Man*.

Mystical Judaism

> The task that Larry faces is to allow his own existential experience to refine his spiritual experience, to shatter the myths of religion. Larry must make the same decision Job did: to turn towards or away from G-d. But regardless of his decision, Larry must allow a certain violence to be done to religious thought, in order to allow his understanding of religion to deepen. [67]

In fact we do not need to say that much about this film because its attempt to deal with the failure of religion is hardly serious, and Larry Gopnik is not a serious man at all – perhaps merely solemn in a comic kind of way. It is not at all a serious film from our point of view. Gopnik's understanding of religion is virtually nil and fails to deepen at all through the film – clearly we are applying different criteria here than Carol Linnitt, and indeed it is hard to see why one would want to bring in the work of the Frankfurt School in an analysis of this film. We see mainly the absence of what we are looking for, though the reference to the *dybbuk* shows perhaps how the idea lingers in modern Jewish thinking.

The *dybbuk* story at the beginning appears as a flashback to a nineteenth century folk tale. A peasant tells his wife that a certain Traitle Groshkover, a friend of hers, who studied under the Zohar rebbe in Krakov, helped him when the wheel of his cart came off. She stares as he enthuses:

"He's quite a scholar. He can recite any passage from the *Mishna*!" (We may recall that Yentl explains to Hadass that the *Mishna* is the Jewish code of law.)

"G-d has cursed us," she says staring into the distance. He husband doesn't understand. "Traitle Groshkover is dead!" she spits out.

He roars with laughter, saying that he saw the man, talked with him.

"Talked with a *dybbuk*!" she retorts.

He is absorbing this, when the same fellow knocks at the door. What can he do?

"Reb Groshkover! You are welcome here," he says.

The wife is not fooled however and stabs the apparition, who is not killed exactly, but does bleed a little and wanders off muttering that he knows when he is not wanted. The husband thinks they are doomed because his body will be found in the snow; the wife praises the Lord for deliverance. Who was right?

The film then cuts to the 1960s and we are introduced to the family of Larry Gopnik, physics lecturer and tract-home dweller with wife and two children whose life is unraveling in a more twentieth-century kind of way. In the modern telling, Larry has accepted his brother Arthur – an incapable obsessive – into his house. But the loss of Jewish family life is indicated by this: instead of a deeper religious life through the extended family, quite the reverse is the common experience of secular living: to add family members beyond the nuclear core is to court disaster; it is effectively to invite the *dybbuk* into the home. When Arthur is ejected things go right again.

An attempt to bring seriousness into the film is made through Larry's presentation of Schroedinger's paradox, but quantum physics seems no more relevant to Larry's life than the equally mysterious concept of the *dybbuk*. There is a lovely moment however when Larry's son listens to the great Ukrainian-born *chazan* Josef "Yossele" Rosenblatt (1882-1933) on record. The boy is learning to sing, copying the cantor needle-scrape by needle-scrape. He is preparing for his *bar mitzvah* as was the boy in the later version of *The Jazz Singer* but without the benefit of a living cantor at his side. The recording is beautiful in contrast to the petty bickering of family life, much of which revolves over Larry's wife wanting a divorce. She taunts him that she wants to get ritual Judaic divorce, a *get*, without which she is an *agunah*, the meaning of which words are lost on him. This is secular Jewish filmmaking in which the meaning of religion is completely lost. That people see it otherwise reminds me of Hegel's saying: "by the little that now satisfies Spirit we can measure the extent of its loss."

The Possession

The film *The Possession* is a modern horror film centering on a "dybbuk box," though this is an invention: there seems to be no precedent in Jewish history for the idea that a *dybbuk* could be confined. A girl happens to buy the box in a yard sale and before long its curse is visited upon her and her family. Her father, Clyde Brenek, takes it to a Hebrew professor who tells him that the box originates in a Jewish village in Poland and that "dybbuk" is the Hebrew word for "dislocated spirit."

"So, was it used for something religious?" asks the father.

"The more traditional branches of Judaism, especially in the Hasidic sects, believe in various spirits, both benevolent and, um, …"

"Benevolent and …?"

"Evil. Like demons. The *dybbuk* box was made in the belief that somehow the evil could be contained."

As a result Clyde researches books and the internet for material on Jewish exorcism. He reads from one such book to help his daughter, by now possessed in various horrible ways. He intones:

"Whoever sits in the refuge of the most high, he shall dwell in the shade of the Almighty. I will say of Ha'Shem, He is my refuge, my fortress, my G-d. I will trust in Him for he will deliver you from the ensnaring trap, from devastating pestilence …"

The girl stares at him and the pages of the book rustle as if a wind were blowing. He continues hesitantly; then suddenly the book is blasted from his hands across the room. It is standard horror fare.

What is a little unusual is his next step: he visits a Hasidic yeshiva in Brooklyn in the quest for a real Jewish exorcist, where he is invited into a rather beautiful synagogue and is given a yarmulke to wear. The rabbi listens to his problem during which some Jews walk out in alarm. The rabbi tells him:

> The *dybbuk* looks for innocence, a pure soul. It will move back and forth from the box, searching for a proper host. The host begins to hear voices, experience visions. All of this is the deception of the spirit, to protect the host and drive others away. The final stage is when the *dybbuk* attaches to the host, the two becoming one. It will feed and take until there is nothing left. It wants only one thing, that which it does not have. Life.

The rabbi says that the *dybbuk* has to be forced back into its box by commanding it by its name, but then lets the father down by saying it is too great a risk to perform this ceremony of exorcism. The *dybbuk* could come upon anyone attempting to perform the ceremony. "It must be left to will of G-d."

This is not good enough for Clyde, who discards the yarmulke in frustration. However the rabbi's son, Tzadok Shapir, agrees to perform the exorcism. (Interestingly this character is played by Matthew Paul Miller, stage name Matisyahu – "Gift of G-d" – and also known as the "Hasidic Reggae Superstar".) The film follows the inevitable horror course in which the *dybbuk* at no time appears to be anything other than malevolent.

The Dybbuk

The treatment of the *dybbuk* theme in the last two films cannot possibly prepare us for the classic film *The Dybbuk*. Here we find not only the tenderest portrayal of Judaism in any of our films but also the tenderest portrayal of the ghost, the wandering spirit, the disembodied person, the *dybbuk*. Only one film is perhaps comparable in its treatment of the ghost: *The Sixth Sense*. I say this of it in *Luminous*:

> Its popularity is won by the over-simplification of its thesis and the shortcuts it takes, yet its moral strength and the value of its key insight is undeniable. In the world's

esoteric literature we find the idea that the spirit of the departed may linger out of fear, confusion, or the simple human desire to see something finished. "Listening" to the ghost – acting as therapist – is an act of compassion that recognizes this fact, and which defuses the rage and hostility otherwise accompanying the desperate state of the ghost. This may well be the real basis of exorcism. [68]

The Dybbuk is based on the play of the same name which was one of the most widely-produced in the history of Jewish theatre. Its "ghosts" are entirely benign, and the exorcism carried out at the end of the film – somewhat in the spirit of that in *The Sixth Sense* – is as far removed from that in *The Possession* as is possible. The film opens with a Prologue, which we read from pages of a book turning over in a breeze:

> Wherefore, from the highest height
> To deepest depth below
> Has the soul fallen?
> Within itself, the Fall
> Contains the Resurrection.
>
> All creatures are drawn to
> the source of the Divine Being.
> In these migrations it may
> happen that a wandering soul
> – a DYBBUK – enters
> a human being which once it loved.
> Thereupon these two souls
> fuse into the mighty
> "Shir Hashirim," the "Song of Songs"
> of Love Eternal, burning
> like an everlasting light
> never to be extinguished.
>
> "It is writ –
> When a man dies before his
> time, his soul returns to earth
> so that it may complete the
> deeds it had left undone and
> experience the joys and griefs
> that it had not lived through.

Mystical Judaism

This text hints again at the transmigration of souls, the doctrine of *Gilgul*. Scholem tells us this about *Gilgul*:

> Now it is very interesting and significant that this Kabbalistic doctrine of transmigration, the influence of which was originally confined to very small circles, extended its influence with startling rapidity after 1550. The first voluminous book which is based on the most elaborate system of *Gilgul* is the *Galli Razaya*, "The Revealed Mysteries," written in 1552 by an anonymous author. In a short time this doctrine became an integral part of Jewish belief and Jewish folklore. [69]

It would be an exaggeration surely to suggest that transmigration – more commonly known as reincarnation – is an integral part of Jewish belief, certainly not in the modern era, though its presence in Jewish folklore might suggest why the idea surfaces in this film. The real point is this however: the minute we accept the idea of ghosts, disembodied persons, or *dybbuks*, we also have to consider the idea of reincarnation, the moving of the spirit from one body to another. In this film we find a peculiar version of it: the spirit of a young man called Channon ben Nisan does not seek out a new body at conception or birth, as in standard doctrines of reincarnation, but inhabits the body of the woman he loved. The only parallel I know of in the world's religious literature is perhaps in the story of Chaitanya Mahaprabhu, the Hindu Vaishnava saint whose body is meant to have been inhabited simultaneously by the spirits of Krishna and his mistress, Radha.[70]

We will now work through the strange story of Channon ben Nisan, bearing in mind that more important than any particular Jewish views on ghosts we are also witnessing many general scenes of everyday Judaism. It is not an easy journey and many things can potentially alienate us: the subtitles, the melodramatic acting in some cases, wooden acting in others, the obscurity of many events, the fact that only a seemingly random portion of the Yiddish dialogue is subtitled, and that this is anyway a ghost story, including the presence of the mysterious Messenger who materializes and dematerializes at will and makes his pronouncements as if an automaton.

After the Prologue a rabbi in white with *shtreimel*, surrounded by his congregation, is singing: "With joy and song shalt thou serve the Lord." The subtitles tell us: "In religious ecstasy, immersed in the Holy Scriptures, the Chassidim – disciples of the Wonder Rabbi – absorb his mystic teachings." This sets the tone for the immensely reverential feeling of the whole film – a gestalt that to many will perhaps appear naïve and unrealistic. The story itself is fairly simple: two good friends, Sender Brynicer ben Henie and Nisan ben Rifke, have pregnant wives and agree that if their offspring are boy and girl they should be married. Nisan dies in a storm before his wife gives birth to the boy Channon, while Sender's wife dies in childbirth with the girl Leah. The pledge is forgotten; Channon and Leah grow up unaware of each other; only later does Channon arrive at the house of Sender. The two fall in love, but Leah is promised elsewhere; Channon invokes the satanic power of the Kabbalah to aid him; he dies in the process. His ghost, the *dybbuk* of the story, in the mutual desire for Leah and Channon to be united, enters her body, and an exorcism is called for. This succeeds but Leah dies in the process.

All of this drama unfolds within an intensely spiritual setting, as suggested above, much of which is conveyed through singing. The initial vow made by Sender and Nisan is consecrated in a rather beautiful and substantial synagogue during the festival of *Sukkot*, the Feast of the Tabernacles as we saw celebrated in the film *Ushpizin*. It is the day of *Hoshana Rabah*; the congregation hold the "four species"; the cantor sings the praises of the Lord, answered by the choir. Sender and Nisan, like the other congregants, hold the *lulav*, the closed palm fronds, myrtle and willow in one hand, and the etrog in the other. The whole scene conveys the solemnity of this festival, a little lost in *Ushpizin* partly through the comedy surrounding the etrog. Of course it is a bit hard not to laugh at the supernatural Messenger who appears at this moment to solemnly warn the friends: "Lives of the unborn should not be pledged."

This is just the preamble. Many years later Channon, the son of the deceased Nisan, wanders into the town where Sender is now a rich man and blessed with a beautiful daughter Leah. Channon is a devout Talmudic scholar, and joins both the local yeshiva and Sender's household. At the evening meal Sender comments:

"So you have discarded *Gemara* and have turned to Kabbalah."

Note that the *Gemara* is the component of the Talmud comprising rabbinical analysis of and commentary on the Mishnah, the first major textual edition of Jewish oral tradition.

"*Gemara* is cold and dry," answers the youth as Leah stands with ritual water for washing hands, "and so are the Laws." He turns to her, as Leah has brought Channon water and cup for *netilat yadayim*, the ritual washing of hands; they look into each other's eyes.

"Kabbalah," continues Channon, "turns your soul away from the earth and lifts you to the highest heights!"

"Flights in the mysticism of the Kabbalah are perilous," says Sender sternly.

Mystical Judaism

"I will not fall," declares Channon with conviction. "I go my own way," he adds. "It will lead me to my goal."

Leah and Channon then converse as her father sleeps at the table, and agree that they seem to have already known each other for a long time.

In the yeshiva in the following scene we are reminded of the exchanges between Ariel and Yaakov in *A Stranger Among Us*. Film titles tell us this:

> While the others study *Gemara*, Channon attempts to penetrate the mysteries of the Kabbalah. By means of symbols and by using numbers for letters he seeks to become a co-factor in the mystic powers that rule the world.

Channon takes a book of Kabbalah from the library and hides it in his coat.

"Are you going to the *mikveh*, ritual baths again?" another student asks him.

"Yes."

"You still fast on Shabbats?"

"It is harder for me to eat on the Shabbat," Channon declares, "than to fast all week."

"What do you wish to attain?" the other presses.

"I want to attain a clear and sparkling diamond – melt it in tears and absorb it in my soul." He then adds: "I want to secure two barrels of gold coins – for him who can count gold coins only." By this we assume he means for Sender as a dowry.

"Take care, Channon," admonishes the other. "You are on a slippery road. Holy powers will not aid you."

Channon is angry and grabs the other. "And if the holy powers will not – what then?" he demands, on which the other retreats in fear.

Inevitably, therefore, Channon misuses Kabbalistic powers for his own ends, performing "gemmatria" on Leah's name and his own, and finally pronouncing "Satan!" to conjure up the dark power. This backfires in the only possible way in a film of such moral integrity: he dies as a result. Leah is heartbroken but has to marry a wealthy suitor chosen by her father. In preparation for this ordeal she goes to visit the grave of her mother, but instead visits that of Channon, where the Messenger appears and tells her that a bride should not be alone in a graveyard as evil spirits will come and carry her off.

"There are no evil spirits," she declares. "There are only the souls of human beings dead before their time – unto eternity." Her voice is beautifully delicate, spiritual; we take her seriously.

"Not eternity," intones the Messenger. "The souls of the dead return to this world to wander until they achieve purity. Souls of the sinful return as beasts, fish and plants. Sometimes it happens that a vagrant soul enters the body of a human being whom once it had loved. That is a *dybbuk*."

"*Dybbuk*," she repeats wonderingly, and then stoops over the grave of Channon. "Come, my bridegroom, I shall bear both our souls – like unborn children."

When the Messenger speaks of souls of the dead returning as animals or plants he is talking of the doctrine of metempsychosis, more usually understood as a Greek idea than a Jewish one. In the text of the original play this passage is rendered slightly differently:

> The souls of the wicked return in the forms of beasts, or birds, or fish – of plants even, and are powerless to purify themselves by their own efforts. They have to wait for the coming of some righteous sage to purge them of their sins and set them free. Others enter the bodies of the newly born, and cleanse themselves by well-doing. [71]

As Scholem comments, the Kabbalistic doctrine of transmigration, or *Gilgul*, "is no longer mere retribution, it is also at the same time a chance of fulfilling the commandments which it was not given to the soul to fulfill before, and of thereby continuing the work of self-emancipation."[72] This makes it a little different from the emancipation or restitution embodied in the idea of *Tikkun Olam*; it makes it a more personal endeavor. This fits well with the film because it has a deeply romantic vision of the love between two human beings, and could therefore, in Kierkegaard's scheme of things, slip down the scale from the religious to the moral to the merely aesthetic realm of the lover's "preference." That selfish element in the film is greatly moderated however by the fact that these two lovers are laboring under an improper vow of their fathers' making, and by the deep moral structure of the universe portrayed at every turn in the film. Indeed it is hard to think of a story that so profoundly unites the romantic, the moral and the religious.

When it comes to it Leah cannot go through with her arranged marriage. At the very moment of placing the wedding ring on her finger she shouts "No! You are not my bridegroom". In that moment Channon's spirit enters her, and she speaks with his voice. "Into the bride has entered a *dybbuk*," intones the Messenger. There is thunder and lightning, rain; the celebrants flee.

This development leads to the finale of the film: the exorcism. *The Possession* was a film rightly compared by critics to *The Exorcist*, but *The Dybbuk* is utterly different to such mainstream fare in the treatment of this subject. At every step the proper dues of each protagonist – human and ghostly – are carefully weighed. There is hardly a mention here of the word "evil."

Leah is taken by Sender, her father, to see Azrael, the son of the great sage, Rabbi Itzele of Miropol, a distinguished rabbi in a distant town. Sender is treated to a sermon on the false path he has taken, the path of wealth, in the form of a parable from the Messenger:

> Once a rich man came to the Rabbi. He was a great miser. The Rabbi took him by the hand, led him to the window and said: "Look!" So he looked through the window. Then the Rabbi asked: "What do you see?" "I see people." "Look out again and tell me what you see *now*." He turns, and is shocked. "*Now* I see myself."

The Messenger explains this to Sender: "In the window there is glass, in the mirror there is glass. But the glass of the mirror is silvered. And no sooner is the glass silvered than one ceases to see others and one can see *only oneself*."

"Do you mean me?" asks Sender, but the Messenger turns and glides off. Of course the Messenger means Sender: this wealthy merchant would not countenance the marriage of his daughter to a poor man, even after the discovery that it was the son of his friend Nisan. Sender is now interviewed by Azrael, and on learning that Channon had eaten at his table Azrael says:

"Perhaps you wronged the young man or mistreated him." He waggles accusing fingers at Sender. "Try to remember," he admonishes.

"I don't know," mourns Sender with head bowed, "I am only human." But after a while he confesses that even when he finally learned of Channon's identity he still did nothing. Azrael is stern with him: he will have to answer to the long-departed Nisan before the Rabbinical Court.

"With a dead person?" asks Sender.

"You must accept this trial."

His dead friend is summoned by Azrael's envoy, bearing his staff. The dead in the first grave is petitioned: "Sacred dead, I am sent by Azrael the son of the great sage, Rabbi Itzele of Miropol to beg your pardon for disturbing you, and to deliver his command that you inform the pure dead, Nisan ben Rifke, by means known to you as follows: That the just and righteous Rabbinical Court of Miropol summons him to be present immediately at a trial at which he shall appear in the same garb as that in which he was buried."

We note that neither the *dybbuk* nor the dead in general are so much feared as respected. They are termed "sacred" or "pure" and are petitioned in the politest possible terms. Nisan duly appears in the Rabbinical Court – though not without some trepidation on the part of those in attendance – but will not accept the apology of his old friend. He is told that the verdict of the court was that Sender was obligated to keep the pact, and now pleads with Nisan to grant him complete forgiveness for not doing so. They cannot persuade the dead man to comply, so there is nothing for it but an exorcism.

In this final religious ceremony Azrael commands the spirit to leave Leah's body, but Channon, speaking through her, tells him that however powerful the rabbi is, he can do nothing against him. All roads are blocked to him, he has nowhere to go.

"Do not drive me away," he pleads.

"Wandering soul," says the rabbi, "great compassion for you fills my heart and I will endeavor to redeem you from evil spirits." But he insists that Channon must depart from the maiden. The rabbi seeks authority from his council to exorcise the spirit, which they bestow upon him. They lend their power for him to help the "Yiddishe Tochter." He turns.

"*Dybbuk*! Soul of one who has left our world! In the name and with the power of this holy congregation, I, Azrael ben Hodos, command you to leave the body of Leah. If you do not, I shall excommunicate you!" Channon tells him he is not afraid, so they go ahead. The congregation dons white sheets and holds the *shofar*. The rabbi tells Channon that through the power invested in him he rends the last thread that binds him to the living world.

"I do pronounce you excommunicated from Israel!" he proclaims. The *shofar* is blown, and Channon says that he can struggle no more. He pleads for *Kaddish* instead, the prayer for the dead. The rabbi asks Sender to say the first *Kaddish*, and they are satisfied that Channon has departed. Immediately Azrael, acting again with supreme compassion, revokes the order of excommunication:

"*Dybbuk*, by the same power and sanction with which I banned you I now lift that ban." He appeals to G-d: "Look Thou upon the suffering of this tortured soul. Regard not its transgressions. Prepare it for eternal rest within Thy holy palaces. Amen." All repeat "Amen."

The marriage, postponed over the possession of Leah by Channon, can now go ahead, but in their haste to welcome the bridegroom they all walk off and leave Leah alone – again. Leah gets up and sings. Channon's voice tells her he cannot exist without her.

"Take my soul, my bridegroom," she asks sweetly, and falls. She is dead. The Messenger blows out the light in his lamp. "Blessed be a righteous judge," are his last words.

The Dybbuk is a romantic tragedy that could match anything by the Romantic writers of the age, but is additionally imbued everywhere with religious piety and rigorous moral consideration. Channon transgressed – it is true – and met a sad fate quite over and above his failure to be with Leah. But at each stage the great Rabbi Azrael holds compassion for him; only resorted to the ultimate weapon – excommunication – when all else failed; and when that succeeds he is quick to reverse this terrible judgment on the soul of the young man. This tenderness is shown by all parties in the film and is palpable in the religious singing at different junctures.

Also moving here is something not transcribed from the Yiddish in the film: the use of the diminutive "Leahleh" instead of "Leah" by the girl's step-mother (just as Tevye and his wife call their daughter Chava "Chaveleh"). She holds her moral obligation to Leah's dead mother very dear and dreads that she has not done enough for her charge. The use of the diminutive expresses such love, as Yiddish- and German-speaking people will know.

Summary

Discarding *A Serious Man* and *The Possession* as of only tangential interest, we have four films – *Bee Season*, *Pi*, *A Stranger Among Us*, and *The Dybbuk* – which have afforded us glimpses into the Judaic mysticism of the Kabbalah. If we take some of the world's major religions, for example Christianity, Islam and Hinduism, then we will find that the mystics of those traditions are not always well received by the mainstream. If Sufism is one of the main mystical strands in Islam, then the martyrdom for example of Mansur in Baghdad, demonstrates this tension. But Scholem, as we saw, was clear that Jewish mystics, even if not popular in their day, like Abraham Abulafia, were not persecuted as in other religions. "Heresy" is not a common accusation in Judaism, it seems, and has not led to anything much worse than excommunication, as in the case of Baruch Spinoza. Of course excommunication from "Israel" is a terrible punishment to the faithful, as was hinted at in *The Dybbuk*.

Having said this, it is clear that the pursuit of the Kabbalah is not fully accepted by mainstream Judaism either. All these films either carry warnings, or insist that only the most brilliant scholars are suitable, or show dire consequences of Kabbalistic practice. Everything hinges, it seems, on what ends its study are pursued for. Saul's Kabbalistic hopes for his daughter were, ultimately, mere worldly ambition. Max's Kabbalistic friends were prepared to kidnap him for their Messianic ends, their means betraying their lack of moral integrity. Max's analogous secular pursuits were show to be not much more than madness. Channon ben Nisan wanted two barrels of gold as a dowry to persuade the father of his beloved Leah to let him marry her – when it had been an outcome solemnly vowed by their parents. Only Ariel in *A Stranger Among Us* seems to have had sufficient balance and integrity to pursue the Kabbalah pure-heartedly, but beyond some antique advice on sexuality we do not really know what this pursuit will further entail.

Along the way we have however had many glimpses into mainstream Judaism that reinforce and expand the picture built up in the previous chapters. In addition we cannot doubt that in principle the mysticism of *Bee Season* is deeply attractive, and that the well-balanced integrity of the daughter suggests perhaps a lifetime devoted to the Kabbalah would bear fruit in her. It is in *The Dybbuk* however that we find something utterly unique. While the use of the Kabbalah appears to be little more than magical hocus-pocus – and with fatal outcomes – the whole film seems imbued with mystical character. This is quite beyond the disembodied entities that populate it; rather it is in the *piety* by which all entities relate to each other. Although we have to "labor" at this film – as it were – the rewards seem to be glimpses of the beauty of Judaism quite beyond what we have so far encountered.

4. Crazed Judaism

Preamble

One of the chapters in Gershom Scholem's book on Jewish mysticism has the heading "Sabbatianism and Mystical Heresy." He tells us that messianic fervor was growing amongst Jews after the time of the Spanish Exodus, the catastrophe for Jews on the Iberian Peninsula that was preceded in scale only by the expulsion in the Roman period and only later exceeded in horror by the Holocaust. Each of these three major events has shaped Judaism. After the Spanish event a seventeenth century rabbi called Sabbatai Zevi became the receptacle of new hope, his claims to be the long-awaited Jewish Messiah falling on receptive ears. The key point that Scholem makes about him is this:

> Sabbatai Zevi, the Kabbalist ascetic and devotee, feels impelled, under the influence of his maniac enthusiasm, to commit acts which run counter to religious law. A latent antinomianism is discernable in these acts – harmless enough at first – to which the Sabbatians gave the restrained but significant name *maasim zari*, "strange or paradoxical actions." [73]

I believe that it is characteristic of Judaism, as a religion where orthopraxy is of more significance than orthodoxy, to downplay the idea of "heresy" in favor of the idea of "antinomianism," the latter meaning to be against the law, or willingness to transgress the law. We can understand how Jesus, thought by some Jews to be the Messiah, is seen by the later Jewish world as merely antinomian – for example healing on the Shabbat. Even though he says that he comes to fulfill the law he clearly at least has a unique interpretation of it, one not accepted by all the Jewish people of his time.

But how is one to know the Messiah? He is bound to be a person of unusual energy and charisma if nothing else, and this idea is picked up on in the film *Song of Songs*, examined below. Its protagonist David Cohen appears a little crazed in his rejection of conventional Judaism in a North London community, and at one point he challenges a teacher of the Talmud, saying that "...a messiah is a transgressor. That's how it works. He brings devastation. He is the end of the law." No doubt Sabbatai Zevi was such a transgressor. He had millions of followers and even after the unexpected and shocking end of his career as a Jewish Messiah – when he was forced to convert to Islam – his movement survived. Can a young Jew from Hendon start a similar movement in the twentieth century?

The quiet observation of all religious requirements, a meek but pure-hearted carrying out of all 613 *mitzvot*, makes for a certain kind of religious beauty. But it may be not much more than mechanical, in a life that is fortunate enough not to be tested by difficult circumstances. In contrast the intensity of a young person's struggle against received wisdom – with the possibility of a more profound insight gained in this furnace of antinomian rebellion – has potential religious beauty, and is dramatically more interesting for filmic treatment. It may also be a life bordering on the crazy.

So, what happens in Judaism when the "struggle with G-d" goes to extremes? Or if the personality is anyway unstable? In *Song of Songs* and *The Believer* we will look into Judaism through the extreme behavior of troubled young men: in the former it is an English Jew tempted by incest, and in the latter an American Jew who becomes a neo-Nazi. In both cases the young men are brought up in traditional Jewish families but their rebelliousness has a strong secular context. They both have high levels of personal energy and intensity, and so it is worthwhile looking back on two law-breakers portrayed rather vividly in *Ushpizin* – the young convicts on the run. Of these it is Eliyahu whose antinomian nature includes performing headstands on a bed, smashing a bottle to use its broken neck as a weapon – though only to remind his host of his own shameful past – and who then hugs Moshe skeptical of his conversion to the path of faith and peace, *shalom*. Towards the end Eliyahu acknowledges that Moshe is, after all, genuine. I suggested that it was perhaps Eliyahu's antinomianism that led him to recognize when a similar spirit, in offering his being to the Law, had found peace. Eliyahu may remain a secular law-breaker, but his acknowledgement of Moshe's – admittedly uneven – transformation has a certain wild beauty about it.

In the films *The Dybbuk*, *Pi* and *Bee Season* we have seen men act crazily from more esoteric causes. The male protagonists in each are pursuing the Kabbalah, or something akin to it. In each case we glimpse the beauties of the Kabbalah, the beauties of an understanding of the world based on numbers, or the numerical meaning of letters. These are visions of spiritual insights or ecstasies triggered by such means, but the warnings abound: without the deeper religious instinct of a girl like Eliza – a grounding in the moral world of human relations and responsibilities – insanity is just round the corner.

In this chapter we will divide the subject of crazed Judaism into two sections, as this preamble suggests: the secular and the religious. In the first section we look at individuals pursuing antinomian behavior in the modern secular context. In *The Believer* the context is contemporary far-right America, while in *Song of Songs* it is contemporary middle-of-the-road London. The third film in this section, *Time of Favor*, is partly set in a Jewish settlement in the occupied West Bank, and explores a different kind of craziness: that of a young Jewish man, crossed in love, who decides to blow up the Al-Aqsa Mosque, the great Muslim shrine on the site of the Second Temple, the Temple Mount. Although his motivation has a religious basis I suggest that it crosses the border into the political, and is hence at least partially secular.

In the second section we look at crazed Judaism in more mythological or supernatural contexts. *Der Golem* is a film about a homunculus, an artificial human, constructed through Kabbalistic magic. Just as the craziness of poor Channon ben Nisan leads to disaster, so does the craziness of the rabbi who unleashes the golem. Finally, in *Simon Magus*, we have a young Jewish man whose pursuit of magic also leads to his undoing.

Secular Craziness

The Believer

The Believer is perhaps the most difficult film we deal with in this book, not because of its style and period like *The Dybbuk*, but because of its political content. It is about a young American Jewish man raised in the religious manner who becomes a neo-Nazi. Distantly based on a true story it dramatizes a man's struggle with G-d in the most extreme form possible.

With anti-Semitism as a historic experience for countless generations of Jews, it is no surprise that the hatred directed at them might become internalized in various ways. The film is loosely based on events in the 1960s when it was discovered that within the Ku Klux Klan – an organization at times as anti-Semitic as it was anti-Black – there operated a high-ranking member called Daniel Burros who was a Jew and a former member of the American Nazi Party. In *The Believer* the protagonist Danny becomes a skinhead and flirts with neo-Nazi groups, becoming the boyfriend of one their female supporters. In the American context of the cultural elevation of violence, Danny's anti-Semitism becomes focused as a hatred for the perceived weakness of Jews: they are feminine; they are intellectuals; they didn't fight the Nazis. He dismisses the cosmopolitan cultural contribution made by the Jews based on books, numbers and ideas. "Marx, Freud and Einstein: what have they given us?" he says. "Communism, infantile sexuality, and the atom bomb."

Crazed Judaism

Abrams says of *The Believer* that: "it contains fairly accurate critiques of Judaism's belief systems. Danny Balint rejects his upbringing and background and, in externalizing his internal self-hatred, transforms himself into a mimic neo-Nazi. Yet, he still retains a reverence for Jewish learning and texts." [74] Abrams's key point here is that Danny retains his reverence for his faith, or to put it another way, he is mesmerized by the beauty of Judaism even while his revolt against tradition in his confused antinomian state forces him to not just reject Jewishness, but also to co-opt the apparatus of its persecution.

At various points in the film we glimpse his young self in Hebrew school challenging his teacher. The theme is of Abraham and Isaac, perhaps rightly chosen by the screenwriter as the most problematic of Judaic religious conundrums. The film opens with a scene where Danny is working out with weights; his skinhead appearance, three-armed swastika tattoo, and the grimace on his face a world apart from the educated American voice of his religious teacher echoing as a superimposed sound track saying:

> And it came to pass after these things that G-d tested Abraham, and said to him "Abraham," and Abraham said "Here I am." And G-d said "Now take your son, your only son whom you love, Isaac, and go unto the land of Moriah and offer him as a sacrifice on a mountain that I will show you."

The audio of the teacher fades out with these last words, clearly addressed to a class we cannot see: "So, everyone, what's really going on here?" As we saw in the Introduction, Kierkegaard was one amongst many who took the question of Abraham seriously, wanting to know what was "really going on here." In a later flashback, triggered in Danny's mind by discovering his old notebooks, we now see the class where young Danny sits, bespectacled, earnest, wearing the *kippah*. The scene is shot in a bright desaturated light, a cinematographic technique that well conveys the strange brilliance of formative memories. We hear the teacher again asking: "Everyone, what's really going on here? Shlomo?"

> SHLOMO: It was a test of Abraham's faith, of his devotion to G-d.
> TEACHER: Very good.
> YOUNG DANNY: (murmurs) Isaac wasn't his only son. Ishmael was his son, too.
> SHLOMO: (murmurs) The only son he loved.

YOUNG DANNY: (murmurs) Oh, they only kill them if they love them!

TEACHER: Danny, as usual, you have something to add?

YOUNG DANNY: It's not about Abraham's faith. It's about G-d's power. G-d says "You know how powerful I am? I can make you do anything I want, no matter how stupid. Even kill your own son. Because I'm everything and you're nothing."

TEACHER: Okay Danny, but if Ha'shem is everything and we are nothing, how are we then to judge His actions?

YOUNG DANNY: We have free will and intelligence, which G-d allegedly gave us.

SHLOMO: What are you talking about? G-d never lets Abraham kill Isaac. He gives him the ram so he doesn't have to.

YOUNG DANNY: Personally, I think that's a lie.

TEACHER: *You think*? Based on what?

YOUNG DANNY: There's Midrash supporting it. My father read a book by Shalom Spiegel that said Isaac died and was reborn.

TEACHER: *No-one* follows that Midrash.

YOUNG DANNY: I do! I follow it. But okay, say G-d provided the ram. So what? Once Abraham raised the knife, it was as if he'd killed him in his heart. He could never forget that and neither could Isaac. Look at him, he's traumatized. He's a *putz* the rest of his life.

TEACHER: Danny, watch your language.

The flashback fades out at this point, and returns to the dramatic narrative. The scene raises an interesting question however: if Kierkegaard found the story an increasing challenge to him as he grew older, and wrote an entire pseudonymous book to "labor" on it, how does the average kid in religious class deal with it? The Jewish writer Danny Rich says this:

> Hearing this story, the binding of Isaac, at a young age, say, in Hebrew school, is traumatic: first, there is what you're supposed to learn, which is the unquestioning nature of faith; then there is what you actually learn, which is the true nature of our grandfathers, just what those monstrous, psychotic, voice-hearing killers were capable of. [75]

Clearly, the fictional Danny is in good company with real living Jews who have also found the story challenging.

Crazed Judaism

Later in the film Danny shoots a fellow neo-Nazi skinhead after failing to kill a celebrity Jew they are stalking. His colleague has berated him for deliberately missing the target, and then discovers the *tallit* that Danny has bound around his waist. He accuses Danny of being a "kike" and there is something of a scuffle in which Danny fires his rifle at point-blank range. As Danny climbs into their truck leaving the wounded man behind, the sound-track of the old classroom fades up and we hear his young self declare: "I think the whole Jewish people were permanently scarred by what happened at Mount Moriah. And we still live in terror." We cut to the classroom again and another pupil responds.

> SHLOMO: Fear of the Lord is the beginning of wisdom.
> YOUNG DANNY: Fear of G-d makes you afraid of everything. All the Jews are good at is being afraid, at being sacrificed.
> (Teacher bangs gavel in outrage.)
> PUPIL: Do you even believe in G-d?
> YOUNG DANNY: I'm the only one who *does* believe. I see him for the power-drugged madman that he is. And we're supposed to worship this deity? I say never!

This is too much for the teacher who has Danny removed from his class. His parting words to Danny are: "And you. If you had come out of Egypt, you would've been destroyed in the desert with all those who worship the golden calf."

"Then let Him destroy me now," says Danny calmly. "Let him crush me like the conceited bully that He is." He looks up. "Go ahead," he invites. Of course, nothing happens.

One could say that Job was tested, Abraham was tested, and that the entire Jewish people now remain tested by the Holocaust. Indeed perhaps the way to understand Danny is to see his towering self-destructive instincts as entirely the product of this event, a monstrosity heaped on the Jewish people that remains spiritually undigested; remains spiritually indigestible. The accusation of "weakness" or "femininity" against the Jews since their allegedly meek capitulation to mass murder is an impossible taunt for a street-wise New York American Jew who has absorbed the macho shoot-first gun culture of his host nation. It is inevitable that somewhere, someone should be driven crazy by such a contradiction.

A great religious mind like that of Kierkegaard, or that of many learned Jews, such as Shalom Spiegel, "labors" at the Abraham story in a way that Danny Balint could not (note that Shalom Spiegel was William Prager Professor Emeritus of Medieval Hebrew Literature at The Jewish Theological Seminary of America). Danny had the right setting for this work – the Hebrew school – but his pent-up anger and leaning to violence saw him expelled from that context and so his studies ended there. Anyway, the kind of "work" that Kierkegaard insists on is simply too slow, too hard, and perhaps simply too unappealing to a young man of the modern world. Or more to the point, Danny just lacked a basic moral stand.

Danny's true colors – as if we had not read them in the opening shots – are shown early in the film when he follows a geeky young Jewish man on the Metro, pursues him under a bridge and knocks him to the ground.

"Hey, yeshiva bocher!" sneers Danny and gives him a kicking. It is a vicious attack and Danny just walks off, leaving the boy writhing in pain on the ground. Danny is drawn to a far-right group committed to general violence and which is happy enough to target Jews. A studious couple who run the group are impressed by him, and he quickly forms a relationship with their daughter, not a Jew, but who becomes fascinated with Judaism on a "know-thy-enemy" basis to start with.

Danny's intensely conflicted journey leads him to the attempted bombing of a synagogue, where other gang members force open the ark and loot the crowns. One of them holds the Torah scrolls by the wooden handles and is intent on destroying it. They say that the text is weird, read right to left; we see the Hebrew letters – "like squashed bugs," says one. Danny tells them that it is called the flame alphabet. "They think it's the word of G-d written in fire," he tells them. They challenge him as to why he knows so much about the Jews, to which he tells them that Eichmann had studied the Torah, the Talmud, the *Mishnah*, so as to know his enemy, the Jews. He is furious when they touch the Torah, but cannot explain himself further. When they desecrate it by spitting on it, kicking it, and tearing it, he looks on, conflicted. Secretly he takes it home with him.

They have left a bomb under the *bima* and later watch the news on TV. It fails to go off, the timer stuck at thirteen minutes. Danny becomes morose; he returns to study; he looks at the Torah scroll he has rescued, covered with his *tallit*. Earlier, when he had railed against communism, infantile sexuality, and the atom bomb as products of the Jewish mind he had added this: "it's the deepest impulse of a Jewish soul to pull at the very fabric of life … they want nothing but nothingness."

This is clearly how he sees the highest attribute of G-d – *ein sof* – as an infinity of nothingness. The religious soul is moved to song, is tipped into ecstasy, if it understands this *ein sof*, this infinity in the right way, but, as no words can describe it – any more than words can, or are allowed to, describe Ha'shem – the secular soul seizes on the word "nothingness" (or "emptiness", *shunyata*, in the Buddhist context) and understands it only as nihilism. So, perhaps we can understand Danny's path as a deeply religious one, but one traversed backwards, one denied the fundamental insight of religion, but so mesmerized by its beauty that only destruction remains.

He now begins to visualize a terrible scene in his mind – we see it as a monochrome flashback – of a Nazi atrocity in the Holocaust, a scene that was described to him earlier when he had to attend a court-ordered sensitivity training class, an alternative to imprisonment for violence against Jews. Danny is attempting to grapple with the meaning of this violence, his own violence. It is an important part of the film, but we look at it later in the chapter on Holocaust Judaism, focusing here on the Abraham and Isaac theme instead that also runs through the film.

Danny's girlfriend Rina suspects that he is a Jew as her fascination with the religion grows: "Is that why you became a Nazi, to talk about Jews incessantly?" This is perhaps a key to the film. What Jews fear most, according to some commentators, is assimilation, not hatred, because in the former they disappear while in the latter their culture lives on. "They don't want to kill us, they want to marry us," is a remark sometimes made almost regretfully in this context that would be bizarre if we did not understand this.

Rina becomes as obsessed with the Torah as he is, and at one point he berates her for being naked in front of it. He agrees with her that it is stupid, but insists: "Put something on." He cannot free himself from his religion, not in the smallest observance, while she wants him to teach it to her, as he knows Hebrew. He challenges her as to why she wants to study it. "Know your enemy," she says. She adds: "Because it's a basic text of Western culture and I want to read it in the original."

As they study it together Rina is baffled by this dictum: "Make no graven image of the Lord or the form of any figure, of man or woman, or anything that looks like anything, because He is not like anything." She asks: "Not only can you not see Him or hear Him, but you can't even think about Him? I mean what's the difference between that and Him not existing at all?"

"There's no difference," comes Danny's response.

"In Judaism there is nothing," she complains.

"Nothing but nothingness," he readily agrees.

He points out to her that Judaism is not about believing in things but doing things, "orthopraxy rather than orthodoxy" as Karen Armstrong says. In Danny's words: "Judaism is not really about belief," he says. "It's about doing things. Keeping the Shabbat, lighting candles, visiting the sick."

"And belief follows?"

"Nothing follows. Because you don't do it because it's smart or stupid, or because you get saved, because nobody gets saved. You just do it because the Torah tells you to and you submit to the Torah."

She swears, to which he objects: "Don't swear in front of it, okay?"

"Why should I submit?" she persists.

"You shouldn't," he tells her.

She turns to him earnestly. "You think I should because there's no reason?"

"I think you shouldn't," he repeats.

She bemoans that Judaism doesn't even need a G-d because it has the Torah. But she wants to celebrate the Shabbat. "Let's light candles on Friday and say the Kaddish," she says. "The Kaddish is a prayer for the dead," he corrects her. "Kiddush," she says, "Say the Kiddush. Light candles."

Later in the film Danny returns home to find that Rina has laid the table for the Shabbat: silver candlestick, wine, wine glasses and the challah bread properly covered. There is a box of matches made ready and a copy of the Torah.

"It's *erev* Yom Kippur. We'll have dinner, then go to shul. Atone for our sins."

He is sullen, other events have challenged his assumptions.

"Come on," she urges. "We can be like Eichmann. He studied Torah. He hated Jews."

"Is it like Eichmann?" Danny is skeptical. "Or are you just goofing?"

"I don't know," she says, shaking her head. "I just wanted to try it."

"Why?"

"Because G-d commands it?" she ventures.

She is beautiful in a white dress, vulnerable.

"I thought G-d didn't exist," he returns.

She looks down. "Well, He commands it, whether He exists or not. Look. We can fight Him and be crushed, or we can submit."

"And be crushed," he adds quietly.

"But, what if … what if submitting, being crushed, …" she sighs. "Being nothing, not mattering, what if that's the best feeling we can have?"

She pleads with him to light the candles and eat, but he just corrects her: that is the wrong way round because once you light the candles it is Yom Kippur and you are fasting. He leaves.

In the film's finale he leads the service at another synagogue targeted by his gang in a second attempt to blow one up. Inspection of the street signs visible as he walks to it confirms that it is the Ansche Chesed Conservative Synagogue in West 100th Street where location shooting, at least of the exterior, takes place for this part of the film. Danny has insisted on "davening" – praying – for his friend that evening, which means that he stands, properly robed in the tallit, at the very *bima* within which the bomb is placed. His inner conflict is visible on his face as he knows there is five minutes left before the bomb will explode. He interrupts the chanting, and hurries the evacuation of the building, but cannot move from his post: his girlfriend and the others have to abandon him. The minutes have gone by, now the seconds. We hear his teacher's voice again: "And you. If you had come out of Egypt, you would've been destroyed in the desert with all those who worship the golden calf."

"Then let Him destroy me now," says the young Danny in flashback. "Go ahead. Kill me, Here I am. Do it."

And so it comes about. But the explosion is only treated allegorically: the scene just whites out. The synagogue fades to the over-lit stairs which he had run down after expulsion from the religious classroom, but now he symbolically ascends the stairs – as a very material-looking ghost – encountering his old religious teacher on the landing:

"Glad you came back. I wanted to take up that discussion we were having..." starts the teacher

"I can't right now," says Danny as he passes him on the way up the stairs.

"About Abraham and Isaac. You remember what you said? That Isaac actually died on Mount Moriah?"

Danny continues to climb.

"I was thinking, maybe you were right about that." The teacher's voice follows him as he climbs to the next landing.

Surreally, the teacher is there again, and repeats himself. Danny passes him again.

The teacher adds: "Died and then reborn in the world to come."

The scene is repeated for a third time.

"Died and then reborn."

On the fourth ascent the teacher says: "Don't you know? There's nothing up there."

Danny simply keeps climbing, and in the end all we hear are his footsteps as he leaves our view.

"Nothing" is at the core of this film's understanding of the G-d of Judaism, and, despite its parading of the violent hatred of the Jews, it gives a glimpse into the religion via precisely what film is good at: drama. Perhaps Rina has understood it when she says: "What if submitting, being crushed, being nothing, not mattering, what if that's the best feeling we could have?" Has she a gift for religion? It is hard to predict; perhaps she just longs for the family life that Jews seem to have in abundance; perhaps she just longs for a family with Danny.

There are many interleaved themes running through this film behind the controversial and darkly unattractive scenario of Jew-as-Nazi. One commentator on the Internet Movie Database (IMDb) says: "Make no mistake about it, though: the film is uncompromisingly pro-Jewish, and the director, himself a Jew, has said that he became more religious because of his work on the film." [76] I don't find this surprising: the level of engagement with difficult aspects of Judaism goes as deep or deeper than in many of the films we have seen so far. Although Danny does not really work at the Abraham and Isaac story, we can say that the filmmaker, Henry Bean, did. In that sense I don't think that Abrams is right to say that the film contains "accurate" critiques of the beliefs of Judaism, after all, who is to say what is "accurate"? I would rather suggest that the film poses questions that are entirely within the spirit of Judaism to pose. At the same time the film is an agonized response to the Holocaust, as we explore later.

If these are its strengths, it has one weakness however, which is a certain Jewish narcissism. "All you talk about is Jewish, Jewish, Jewish," Rina complains to Danny at one point. In the novel *The Finkler Question* by the British Jewish writer Howard Jacobson a non-Jew becomes so obsessed by the amazing virtues of his Jewish friend Sam Finkler, that he yearns to become a Jew himself. [77] In the novel these virtues have nothing to do with religion, but involve sexual prowess, intelligence and so on. Had this been written by a non-Jew it might have been an interesting scenario, but otherwise it seems a deeply embarrassing exercise in ethnic self-glorification. Similarly when Danny defends his interest in the Jews to his fellow gang-member by citing Eichmann, it is not that convincing. We could say that Danny has gone wrong partly because he is obsessed with "Jew" over and above his interest in "Judaism", a religion with millions of converts from many ethnic backgrounds.

Song of Songs

The Believer has a bizarre enough plot, even if it did have some basis in a real-world case. Four years after its release *The Song of Songs* appeared with a similarly bizarre sub-plot and an emphasis on nihilism, transposed from violent New York to sleepy Hendon, a Jewish suburb of London, England. In this case the young man's transgression takes him into incest rather than neo-Nazism; his violence is imaginary rather than real. Very English you might say. *Song of Songs* opens with this quote from Ecclesiastes I:

> I have seen all the works that are done under the sun, and, behold, all is vanity, and a striving after wind. And I applied my heart to know wisdom and to know madness and folly. I perceived that this also was a striving after wind. For in much wisdom is much vexation. He that

increaseth knowledge increaseth sorrow. So I hated life because the work that is wrought under the sun was grievous unto me. For all is vanity and a striving after wind.

This is read by the protagonist of the story, David Cohen, and is accompanied by views of London, the Thames, and commuters going to work, including himself. In the meantime his sister Ruth is returning from a study trip to Israel. She attends her mother's sickbed, being pressed about marriageable young men; they alternate in reading from the Torah: the passage is a proscription on nakedness between family members. "You are reading well," approves her mother, but strangely Ruth vomits afterwards. Friends come round, then the Rabbi, who observes that Israel is having quite an effect on her.

"I am trying to keep more *mitvot*," she says.

David is teaching his class and has written an epigram from Blake on the board: "Sooner murder an infant in its cradle than nurse unacted desires." Brother and sister are portrayed as moving in opposite directions, confirmed when David asserts "I turned away from all that a long time ago. Community, religion. I won't go back to that." In contrast Rachel is looking for a suitable wig to wear as a sign of her deeper commitment to her faith. A little later we are given a clue as to the forces at work on the family: the father is gone, and when Ruth raises the issue of her father her mother's response is that these are worthless things. "All you have to do," she exhorts, "is to keep Ha'Shem in your mind." Despite all her observances and study Ruth does not seem convinced.

Ruth and David independently attend a seminar by Rachel Silverbaum, the leaflet for which has the word "Heresy" on it, but we cannot make out the exact title of the talk. Ruth is wearing the wig, prompting an old friend to assume that she is now married, but Ruth just snaps rudely at her kind words. The lecture begins:

> So now then we have the great sage known as Elisha ben Abuyah who becomes known as "Acher", meaning "Other." He hears a voice from heaven: "Return, O ye wayward ones, except for Acher." Everyone can return, everyone can repent, except Acher. So Acher goes on to break just about every law there is. According to some sources he even kills. What, then, is the heresy of Acher? Well, it is to believe that he is different from the rest. That he's been singled out. His act of transgression ... his acts of transgression are merely acts of narcissism. By breaking

Crazed Judaism

all the laws he wants to prove that he is different. That he cannot change, he cannot get back to Heaven. He wants to be special, and not to be guided by the same laws as everyone else. And that is why Acher loses heaven, because he cannot conceive the sharing of it.

David slips into the back of the lecture room and intervenes: "If Acher was so worthless, why would Rabbi Meir have followed him? Even after Acher has turned his back on the law, the great Rabbi Meir goes and follows him."

"True, but …" begins Silverbaum, but David cuts across her. His speaking presence is every bit as commanding as hers:

"Why would Rabbi Meir even imagine that he could learn anything from Acher?" David paces the room as if he were the professor. "Hm? Nobody?" He looks round, but no one dares an opinion. "Because a messiah is a transgressor," he tells them. "That's how it works. He brings devastation. He is the *end* of the Law."

"True," concedes Silverbaum, "but Rabbi Meir followed Acher only so far. Acher told him not to break the laws he himself had broken. Why?" She looks round for rhetorical effect; this is a competition of scholars. "Because," she continues, "he couldn't bear the thought of anyone else being special."

"No!" David contradicts her and pauses for the audience to absorb his challenge. Only Ruth does not turn her head to look at him. David explains: "Because you have to *deserve* to cross the line."

A man in the audience rises. "Excuse me, but…"

"No, I will not excuse you. It is inexcusable," says David imperiously. Ruth steals a glance at her brother. "None of you," he declares, "listen to anything but each other!"

The seminar now descends into chaos as David harangues them on the theme that there is a world beyond them, beyond the yeshiva, a world about to explode. "Boom!" he says. Silverbaum retorts that this is exactly where Asher went wrong: in violence. "Which one of you would die to make this world better?" David is asking as he is shoved out of the door. "Get *off* me Jew-boy!" he shouts as he evades them and starts dancing in the room. "Nagila Hava …" he starts singing and then takes a woman to dance with. He tails off. In the ensuing silence he looks at them and then walks out.

Ruth is as dumbfounded as the others, but she is aroused by his words, and when she leaves she tears off her wig. She has an idea, and returns to the seminar room. She locks its doors from the outside as Professor Silverbaum continues her lecture, and runs off. The seeds of law-breaking are sown it seems.

Crazed Judaism

Let us consider: what does the story of Acher mean? That when a man whose behavior we cannot fathom appears, a man who seems "G-d-intoxicated" – as was said of the excommunicated Jew Baruch Spinoza – when a man breaks the Law, we should follow him as did Rabbi Meir? Ruth is yearning to go deep into her religion as Yentl was; has she found her messiah, her teacher in her brother David? Or is David just another confused young man, like Danny in *The Believer*?

David passes under a bridge, not a New York overpass this time, but a bridge over a canal towpath in North London, and violently attacks a stranger, just like Danny. But, not really: it is just in his imagination. A little later he meets up with Ruth and they share the grin of recognition that appears on the faces of siblings after a shared transgression. Rather like Danny Balint with Rina, David will become Ruth's Torah teacher, though under strict conditions: it will be *his* Torah.

The unfolding of this messianic experiment goes nowhere however as the two become obsessed with the laws of sexual transgression – the purity laws – and the siren call of incest draws them closer. At one point Ruth performs the *netilat yadayim* for her dying mother on the Shabbat; she shares the plaited bread and holds the candlestick for her. As she leaves the sickroom with these items David is there; he lands up desecrating the *challah* bread by standing on it, and on her hand. It is sacrilege and masochism – that is all she will reap from his tutelage. She begins to withdraw her submission to the *mitzvah* most pressing on her, the care of her mother, and refuses to join in the recitation of some Tehillim, verses of the Psalms, to which she is invited by the Rabbi at the sickbed.

In the end David is shown to have no inner dynamic of gifted messiah-hood but merely one identified by Freud: a father complex. The rabbi reveals that David's mother has lied to him: his father is not dead but had simply left the faith. David's rage is stoked when Ruth admits that she had always known. This time he is really violent, but in hurting his sister, in violating the Law, he has made no breakthrough in religion at all.

The film ends incomprehensibly with a fire-lit scene with this offscreen recitation:

DAVID: Who is your father?
RUTH: a man who is infinitely kind.
DAVID: Who is your father?
RUTH: a man who is infinitely wise.
DAVID: Who is your father?
RUTH: a man of infinite compassion.
DAVID: Who is your father?

We have then to compare *Song of Songs* rather unfavorably with *The Believer*. What Plotinian beauty is there in it? Perhaps just a faint hint of what transgression can bring in a true messiah, but is nothing more than hinted at here, just a sweeping away of what is dead tradition with nothing to replace it. If we make a "commonplace," as Kierkegaard says, of any insight, then it slowly ossifies. The transgressor cracks open what has become rigid, releasing religious energy, which in the right hands flows in productive new directions. But David is merely a cesspit of contradiction, a boy rejected by his father. He did not deserve that – no child does – but we also see that he does not deserve to transgress either (as he puts it): he is no messiah. The Hebrew lecturer in this film, Rachel Silverbaum, has what Yentl dreamed of: the right to study Torah. Ruth also has what Yentl dreamed of, but what is she making of it? While Rina in *The Believer* was not even Jewish the possibilities for her Torah studies somehow seemed more promising.

Time Of Favor

Time of Favor is set in modern-day Israel and deals with a topic that has become more rather than less fraught since the making of the film: the issue of Haredi service in the Israel Defense Force (IDF). The ultra-Orthodox Jews of Jerusalem – who were against the founding of the secular State of Israel just as the Hasidim were in New York – have been excused military service from the onset of Partition. This was formally ended by legislation in March 2014, amidst much protest from the Haredi, a law then reversed by the Knesset in November 2015. Traditionally the Orthodox Jewish of Jerusalem had been supported by international donations to live the life of Talmudic scholars, largely freed from the obligations of material employment or military service. We saw in *Ushpizin* that Moshe was the lucky beneficiary of the largesse of a businessman, a donation of $1,000 to his yeshiva, and doled out at random. Such donations are perhaps still acceptable to secular Israeli Jews, but not the evasion of military service it seems, as pressure for a change in the law continues.

This is the background to the film *Time of Favor*, in which a controversial rabbi encourages his religious students to volunteer for a unit within the IDF, but the purpose of this unit is unclear and attracts suspicion from the outset. Because the setting of the film is Israel I will deal with some parts of the story in the chapter on Israel Judaism, while here I just want to focus on the character of Rabbi Meltzer in the story, the one who encourages his students to join the military unit. Is he a man like Sabbatai Zevi? Is he a potential messiah whose transgressions we must understand as the expression of religious energy and intensity, and who can see beyond the rest? Is his vision located on the razor edge between religious innovation and chaotic antinomianism?

Rabbi Meltzer teaches in a yeshiva that is part of a settlement community with beautiful views over rolling landscape. His daughter sees no beauty in it however because she wants to escape this context. The filming location for the settlement is in Kfar Adumim, located halfway between Jericho and Jerusalem, and therefore in the middle of the Palestinian West Bank, but we are not exposed to the Palestinian response to occupation and do not know to what extent this affects the girl. In the first scene in the yeshiva all are wearing religious garb, it is Shabbat. Rabbi Meltzer says "Sometimes our boys have to pray in strange places. For instance, in a tank, or in an armored personnel carrier. Even at the bus station, where the mind is set on the big question: When will the bus arrive, when will it leave? But the heart…" He sighs volubly. "…the heart is in Jerusalem."

He pauses and then continues: "Of course their prayer is wanted and welcome. But a Jewish soul yearns to return and pray in the very home of the *Shekhinah*." After another sigh and pause he says: "My father, G-d rest his soul, had a few students who wanted to go up and pray at that "place." They were considered crazy and he was considered 'the crazies' rabbi'." There is murmuring amongst the students at this. "But today," he continues, "there are a few hundred boys and they are not considered so crazy. Neither is their rabbi." He leans forward for emphasis, speaking softly. "That's it, my friends. This is the process. When there will be tens of thousands of boys wanting to go and pray at the Temple Mount, then we won't be considered crazies anymore, but, as they say, 'The Norm'."

He is inspiring.

The "home of the *Shekhinah*," the "place" that he is referring to is the Second Temple, its ruins built over by a succession of mosques with the name of Al Aqsa, the third holiest site in Islam. A more visible landmark, the Dome of the Rock, also occupies the site, known as the Temple Mount.

Is it crazy to want to destroy the Muslim sacred site and build the third Temple there? I can't answer that question, but clearly, whatever theological justification there might be in Judaic religion and history, it is now a highly charged political question. In Christian Zionist fantasy films like *Left Behind* and *The Omega Code* it is the "norm" as Rabbi Meltzer says (we look at those films later in this chapter). Religion plays a deep part in this however, and in some commentaries on the film the fictional Rabbi Meltzer has been compared with the real-life Rabbi Meir Kahane, a man so extreme that his political party was outlawed in both America and Israel. He is held responsible for much of the religious support given to the occupation and settlement of the West Bank, but there is another religious leader who

Meltzer might have been modeled on: Zvi Yehuda Kook, the leader of the Mercaz HaRav yeshiva in Jerusalem, founded by his father Abraham Isaac Kook. This father and son team matches Meltzer and his father perhaps a little better. Indeed, why else did the screenwriters give Meltzer the first name of Zvi?

A little later in the film we are back in the yeshiva, this time with the rabbi and congregation in casual clothing. Behind the rabbi we see a tapestry that covers the ark; he leans on the *bima* to deliver another lecture. He says: "We abhor the word 'war.' Killing is not our job. What are we? Militarists? Militants? What are we, battle-lovers?" The camera cuts to his class, young men wearing the *kippah*, and in the background there are bookshelves of holy texts. He tells them: "People feel that the most moral thing is to talk about the value of life, about bereavement, about peace." We cut to a close-up of his face, the tapestry in the background showing a seven-branched candlestick on either side of him. "That's the moral shield against the evil, ugly side of war." He pauses. What are the students, what are we, to think of this? What is he preparing us for? He continues:

> Maimonides says: "Let him not think of his wife or children, but erase their memory from his heart and go to war." A man must remove all private matters from his mind. What will happen to him, what will happen to the other. Now he is not a private person. He's part of the community of Israel. He who continues to be engrossed in his private matters will be afraid. But when a man goes to battle, when he is completely exalted with the ideal he is fighting for, he is so full of it, full of determination, of bravery, that it removes all fear from his heart. Whoever is not willing to give his life, whoever does not know that sometimes the dead lion is more alive than the living dog, will stay a dog.

The rabbi speaks persuasively, his intensity is below the surface. Why should we think him crazy at all? Earlier in the film a security officer confides this about the rabbi: "This Rabbi Meltzer, what makes him dangerous is not that he's a fanatic. On the contrary. The man's completely sane, he's brilliant. ... what two years ago seemed crazy is now finding its way in through the back door. The line, between the normal and the abnormal, has moved." So it is with all real innovation in the religious sphere, and those that bring it about are considered transgressional, antinomian, or crazy to start with. But is this a religious or a political question here? A young man called Pini in the film, a man like Danny and

David, succumbs to the idea of martyring himself for the goal that the rabbi appears to be setting out, though Meltzer denies it to the security forces at the end of the film. Pini is as lost and confused as the characters Channon, Danny, or David in films we have looked at, and like Channon, Pini pines for the girl he cannot have – in this case the daughter of Meltzer – but unlike Channon who had real religious faith, we find nothing more than craziness.

But what of Zvi Meltzer? He is the one we would compare to Sabbati Zevi. At the end of the film the head of the security forces tells Meltzer: "They're out of your control, Zvi. Understand that. For years you have been feeding them "Temple, Temple, Temple," finally a few students go ahead and do something about it." Meltzer denies that this was his intention, but what else are we to make from his sermons and his reference to Maimonides, one of the few Jewish writers to endorse the concept of the "just war"? What has happened here is that which could be religious has become political. Danny attempts to kill a celebrity Jew, but kills a fellow activist instead; he dies as atonement. David merely imagines violence against strangers and his "messiah-hood" implodes into incest. Pini becomes a terrorist and dies for nothing at all. All are crazed by their warped interpretations of Judaism.

Supernatural Craziness

Der Golem

A golem in Jewish folklore is an animated being created from matter such as clay, and is similar to an uneducated stupid person who acts as a slave, carrying out orders. This myth was given shape in the sixteenth century by the story of a rabbi in Prague who created a powerful golem to help defend the Jewish ghetto against attack. The film – the full title of which is *The Golem: How He Came into the World* – is a silent semi-horror movie made in 1920, and has some similarities in style with *The Cabinet of Doctor Caligari*. It depicts a world of crude beliefs and moralities, and its monster, the golem, is a clear forerunner of Frankenstein, King Kong, and the Hulk – and possibly even Tolkien's Gollum. The rabbi in the story is an astrologer who makes the golem after predicting a calamity for the community, but the golem itself, once it has served its purpose, turns on its masters. One can read this story as part of the Judaic reservations about learning and science: to command the forces of nature is to open the door for calamity and corruption. Bernheimer tells us:

Set in the sixteenth century, the story follows the creation of a golem (unformed mass) by Rabbi Judah Loew to protect the Jews after they are exiled. In this 1920 classic, Wegener remained true to the legend, drawing on the most famous version of the medieval folktale, *The Golem of Prague*. The formula for creating a golem first appeared in the sixth century in the *Sefer Yezirah*, and the first tales concerning its creation centered on Rabbi Elijah of Chelm but later shifted to Judah Loew ben Bazalel (1513-1609). The renowned rabbi had indeed successfully defended his people from the hostile clergy and government of Prague, well known as a centre of occult activity, which is what drew Emperor Rudolph II to the city from Vienna.[78]

Scholem tells us:

> It is to Hasidism that we owe the development of the legend of the Golem, or magical homunculus – this quintessential product of the spirit of German Jewry – and the theoretical foundations of this magical doctrine. In the writings of Eleazar of Worms, the most faithful of Jehuda's disciples, discourse on the essence of Hasiduth are to be found side by side with tracts on magic and the effectiveness of G-d's secret names, in one case even in the same book. There one also finds the oldest extant recipes for creating the Golem – a mixture of letter magic and practices obviously aimed at producing ecstatic states of consciousness. It would appear as though in the original conception the Golem came to life only while the ecstasy of his creator lasted.[79]

Gertel's objection raised earlier about *A Stranger Among Us*, that it did not properly place Hasidism in context, is all the more true of *The Golem*. As Scholem says the original Hasidic concept of the golem as a production of spiritual ecstasy – and having no life of its own beyond the ecstasy of the mystical adept – was long lost. The film has, therefore, much more to do with Jewishness of a middle-European type, than it has to do with Judaism. I have included consideration of this film in this section on deranged Judaism not because I don't value the film as a classic, but precisely because its status as a classic of German expressionism can prevent us expressing reservations about the distorted picture of Judaism embodied in it. From the opening of the film we see Rabbi Loew as an astronomer, astrologist, alchemist and magician and nowhere do we catch any sober glimpses of Hasidic Judaism in sixteenth century Prague.

The film opens as Rabbi Loew examines the heavens by telescope – he looks as mad as Rabbi Ezrael in *The Dybbuk*, but as the film unfolds we fail to discover any moral beauty in him or his actions. Loew, it is true, saves his community in this fable, but in real life we would have to place him with Saul Naumann in *Bee Season*, or the rabbi in *Pi*, because they have perverted or misunderstood the goals of the Kabbalah.

Der Golem is a film of *shtettl* Judaism, and like *The Fiddler on the Roof*, serves as a good reminder of the threat that Jewish communities lived under in Europe over long periods of time. The Emperor, based in Prague, has just issued this decree:

> DECREED: AGAINST
> THE JEWS
> We can no longer
> neglect the popular
> complaints against the
> Jews. They despise the
> holy Christian
> ceremonies; they
> endanger the lives and
> property of their fellow-
> men; they practice black
> magic. We decree that all
> Jews shall leave the city
> and all territory in sight
> of the city before the
> month is ended.

The decree is signed by the Imperator (Emperor), who sets his seal on it. It is under these circumstances that the golem is brought to life by Rabbi Loew, using incantations and Star of David magic amulet placed on the huge clay effigy's breast. The manner in which the golem saves the Jewish community is bizarre and even more bizarre, or just plain amusing, is that the first three tasks undertaken by this powerful creature are to hew wood and fetch water – perhaps a reference to Joshua's conquest of ancient Israel and the fate awaiting the conquered – and lastly to go shopping. It has to be said that the purveyors of the various necessities listed by Loew need some coaxing before they will supply this new servant of the rabbi. But the golem's real service takes place when Loew visits the Emperor as a court magician. (Note that Prague really was a centre of alchemy and learning in the fifteenth and sixteenth century, host to luminaries of the day such as astronomers Tycho Brahe and Johann Kepler, the painter Arcimboldo, and the alchemists Edward Kelley and John Dee.)

The Emperor asks what manner of magic the Rabbi will show him on this day, and Loew replies: "I will show you our people's history, and our patriarchs. And if you value your lives, let no one speak or laugh." He conjures up a scene of people on the march in a long column over hills. In the foreground appear the historical figures of the Hebrew Bible including Moses undergoing the Exodus from Egypt, but slowly, one by one the courtiers start to smile and then laugh. Despite the warning they become hysterical with laughter, pointing derisively at the scene apparently projected on the wall of the palace. The rabbi summons up destructive powers that begin to shake the structure of the building, then the golem awakes and people fling themselves from the windows. "Save me and I will pardon your people," pleads the Emperor. The rabbi summons the golem who props up a falling balcony and so saves the Emperor's life. The Jews are pardoned. It is, to be honest, a childish sort of story, and does not reflect well on Loew or his golem or Judaism or its mystical branch the Kabbalah.

The Jews celebrate their reprieve in the synagogue with the blowing of many *shofar*, but meanwhile the golem runs amok. This part of the story is not so different from the Frankenstein myth, but does have a happier ending: the golem takes a liking to some children playing, and a little girl plucks the Star of David magic amulet from its breast. It falls down dead and is carried back into the ghetto from which it had broken out.

The film has an odd implication that we need to point out: why would the rabbi magically project a scene from the history of his people as court entertainment? And why prohibit them from laughing at it? This implies a fear of ridicule and at the same time an exaggerated self-importance in demanding that the audience watch a history that is not theirs and do not in fact express ridicule. Does this not smack again of the Jewish narcissism that runs through *The Believer*? We have to say that if the whole golem adventure is crazy in the first place, then this makes suspension of disbelief – in the plot, that is – all the harder.

The idea of the golem lives on however: in the film *Inglourious Basterds* Hitler rants about Jews killing his soldiers, one of them known as the "Bear Jew" which he refers to as a "golem." His officers assure him that the man cannot be a golem but Hitler rants on. I doubt if this scene has any historical basis – the rest of the film certainly does not – but the golem as a symbol of Jewish resistance clearly still resonates.

Simon Magus

Simon Magus is set in a nineteenth century German Jewish community in which the village fool – named after the first century Samaritan Gnostic Simon the Sorcerer (or Magus) – is drawn into Christianity because of the ill-treatment he receives at the hands of his fellow-Jews. Simon is made to join the women and children in the synagogue because he is simple and therefore not considered a fully adult male according to the Jewish elders, and becomes a tool in village politics over a proposed railway station. In the end he saves them from the false accusations of ritual baby-killing, a trick used by the Christians to draw on the ancient prejudice against Jews. Ironically, early Christians were accused of just that by Romans intent on vilifying the emerging new faith. Prejudice, it seems, has a limited but eminently recyclable stock of images to draw on.

The film opens with footage of Jews forced to leave on carts; there is suffering in a mother's face. Simple wooden houses have signs on them such as "Moved to Waldemarsgasse," "Moved to Kegelhosstrasse, Bressau," or simply "Amerika"; in this and other elements we find a similarity with *The Fiddler on the Roof*. On the last house there is a sign: "Moved to Hell." It is the home of our protagonist Simon, and as he emerges we see that it is the most broken-down of shack dwellings imaginable. We found in *The Believer*'s Danny, *Song of Song*'s David, and *Time of Favor*'s Pini young men whose struggle with their faith makes them crazy in different ways – two of them dying in bomb blasts of their own making. Even to non-Jews they are believable characters, where Rabbi Loew of *Der Golem* must stay confined to the mythical realm along with his creature. Simon occupies something of a middle ground: he is on the one hand believable from a secular point of view as a schizophrenic or simply rather disturbed personality, but on the other hand there will be some quite unmaterialistic magic in the wake of his passing. In any case there is much Judaism of a quite realistic kind to be encountered in the film, pitted here against a German Romantic sensibility as embodied in the local squire.

Simon's Jewish community – clearly under siege in some way as the opening suggests – is down to ten men, the *minion*, or minimum necessary to hold religious meetings. If one of them is lost they will have to buy a Jew's time from a town some twenty miles away, or all travel there for the Shabbat. Simon does not count. He has his place as an emptier of latrines, and his "magic" is tolerated to some degree when he demands coins for the protection of crops and to prevent him from cursing them.

The central plot concerns a railway however – a symbol to the traditional Jews of encroaching modernity, and an incomprehensible and terrifying manifestation for Simon. The story has considerable charm and plausibility compared to the other films in this chapter – leaving out the magic of course. Furthermore the story is one of confrontation between the Hebraic faith of tradition and the Hellenic-inspired Romantic movement gaining ground in the German-speaking world that encloses this tiny Jewish community. In *The Quarrel* this confrontation was acted out between Chaim the novelist and Hersh the rabbi; in *Simon Magus* it is acted out between the squire Count Albrecht and the local Talmudic scholar Dovid Bendel, who has a plan to rescue the village from its decline by purchasing land from the squire for a new railway station. Dovid visits Count Albrecht, interrupting his poetry reading, and is not in the first instance much encouraged. He is challenged by the squire as to his reading habits, to which Dovid replies that he reads Talmud, Torah, nothing else.

"What else should I need to read?" Of poetry he knows little, and is of the opinion we found expressed at the beginning of *Yentl* that men should read religious works, while women, if they can read at all, should read poetry.

"Goethe, Schiller, Dante, Byron, Petrarch, Heine," presses the squire. "Have you heard of these people?"

Dovid has not, but is clearly an intelligent man, so the squire agrees to sell the land for the railway station at a price of twenty marks, a pittance, but has a condition. Dovid must read the squire's book of poetry; then read one book a week from his library; and engage the squire in one hour's conversation a week. In this deal he has competition from a ruthless Christian businessman Maximillian Hase, but the squire is less interested in Hase's superior cash than Dovid's superior intellect.

Simon meanwhile is increasingly angry with his community which quite naturally looks down on him as simple – or worse – and continue to insist that he prays with the women rather than the men. His approach to the Torah is unconventional to say the least. Simon is plagued by "voices" that he hears, which, before long, we discover are that of the devil. In several imaginative renderings Satan appears to him to demand transgressive actions, including the urinating upon three boys sleeping in a hay loft, a punishment for when they earlier threw stones at him. All four are beaten by the rabbi, though it has to be said that Simon gathers many more strokes of the birch than the boys. In another appearance the devil tells him that the Jews are the filth of Europe and commands that he should join the Christians instead.

Hence he appears in the local church where the priest tells him, on being offered a few miserable coins: "The love of Christ is not bought with gold but with purity of heart." He then proceeds to tell Simon the story of Simon Magus, the Samaritan religious figure who converted to Christianity, was baptized by Philip the Evangelist, and whose later confrontation with Peter is recorded in Acts 8:9-24. Our Simon's conversion is not however religiously illuminating of either Judaism or Christianity, but instead he becomes noticed by Maximillian Hase. Simon will be an ideal dupe by which to bring down the entire Jewish community.

It is Passover and the village prepare for it. Hase prepares something else: he "borrows" a baby, pacifies it with laudanum, and places it in a box. He charges Simon – now amply fed at Hase's table on the finest chicken dishes, and consummately loyal to "Christianity" – to smuggle the box into the synagogue where the Passover Seder will be celebrated. As Simon sings along with the congregation in Hebrew, in an agony of betrayal, a torchlit mob passes the squire's mansion, and then break into the synagogue using axes. The assembly is terrified, but Jewish custom requires them to offer hospitality to anyone who appears.

"Sit, Herr Hase," invites the rabbi, managing to hold down his alarm. "Eat."

But Hase has something else on his mind. He directs his henchman Buchholz to examine what is in the stewpot. "Human flesh?" he demands.

"It is lamb," protests the rabbi.

"Search the room!" demands Hase. Tension mounts after the box is discovered; it is slowly opened … but Simon has placed a rabbit in it, instead of the baby.

"They've changed the baby … into a rabbit," Hase says hesitantly. It is of course a pun – "Hase" means rabbit in German. The squire enters with a knowing eye as to what has been going on, so Haas and his gang leave, but not without first setting Simon's hovel on fire.

And so the film ends with a magical passing away of our holy fool. We don't see his dying, but we are aware that his spirit in its lingering on earth passes by all the principal characters in turn. Simon's last footsteps are blown away – he leaves no trace. Yet in that passing through the community he bestows magic blessings on them all. The barman's glass magically fills with beer; Dovid finds a wife; and the squire find love in a young Jewish woman who has a feel for poetry in a locale that is otherwise a barren flea-pit to any cultured man of the German Enlightenment. We can now perhaps label the film as magical realism, and in that reframing of our perceptions of it the film takes on something rather poetic. If there is a Plotinian moral beauty in the film it all takes place in this magical ending.

The Jewish Millennium

Millennial beliefs involving the Apocalypse, the coming of the Messiah, and portents of related future events originating mostly in the Book of Daniel are important in Judaism. Films such as the *Omega Code* and *Left Behind* embody crazed Christian versions of these ideas, but we find in the films *Kadosh* and *Pi* reminders of its Jewish origins.

Steinberg distinguishes between traditionalist and modernist interpretations of Judaism, particularly over the very concept of "Israel." For the traditionalist the faith in Israel, as he puts it, has four elements: the Election, the Covenant, the Mission, and the Vindication to come in the "end times."[80] The Election is a simple idea: Jews are the Chosen people. The Covenant is the agreement between Israel and G-d. The Mission is described like this:

> Israel lives not merely to know G-d and do His will but, by preachment and example, to communicate His truth and way to the nations, so that blind eyes may be opened, the prisoners come forth from dungeons, and in the end all men be induced to form one band to do the right with a perfect heart. [81]

For the traditionalists the goal of Israel, then, is the deliverance of mankind. The reward is that the children of Israel, so long dispersed and reviled, will return to their ancient land, their Temple will be rebuilt and Judaism universally recognized. The modernist rather fudges all this. But here is the point: these doctrines have leaked into Christianity and have been turned back on the Jews in a rather bizarre concoction. In my book *The American Cinema of Excess* I devote a chapter to films of the Apocalypse and Armageddon, all of which are lurid Christian imaginings based on Judaic writings and the Apocalypse of John. In the *Left Behind* films series we learn at one point that the "world's greatest religious scholar" is a Jew, that he has drawn on "456 messianic passages" in the Bible, and that all this points to Jesus being the Jewish Messiah after all. [82] Central to the filmic narrative here is the rebuilding of the Temple – which betrays a bizarre Christian obsession with the very architectural drawings of the building – and the certainty of the conversion of all Jews to Christianity at the End Time. The comforting conviction that all Jews must return to Israel before the Second Coming of the Messiah is matched only by the certainty that they will all convert – which betrays a Christian arrogance. The two *Omega Code* films follow a similar set of ideas. Should we imagine that the original *Left Behind* series – based on the popular books by Tim Lahaye – were period pieces of the 2000 millennium, it is worth pointing out that the film was reprised in 2014 with Nicolas Cage in a lead role.

We saw that Reb Saunders in *The Chosen* believed that only *after* the emergence of the Messiah should Israel be reborn. Nevertheless the basic millennial idea was clearly part of his belief system. In *Pi* we saw that the group of Hasidic Jews which kidnaps Max also believes in the millennium, in the run-up to the year 2000 CE – though this date has no significance in the Jewish calendar. Similarly in a film called *Kadosh* – looked at in later chapters – one of the characters drives around Old Jerusalem bellowing about the expected arrival of the messiah in the run-up to the year 2000. Also at one point in the film a rabbi addresses one of his congregation: "Meir, don't you feel, don't you feel we're on the verge of a new age? That something is coming? Are you making ready for it? Do you pray? Do you fast? Do you meditate?"

Summary

The premise of this chapter is that when a faith practitioner, a believer, has great personal energy and intensity, they are likely to challenge the constrictions of their faith. As Judaism is so bound up with Judaic Law, we can understand this as leading to antinomianism rather than heresy. Is that antinomianism the crucible in which the new is forged? Is Judaism fructified by all its great mystics and their possible transgressions on the path to new insights and new directions for their faith? If so, the transgressional must have moments of religious beauty. But we are forced to conclude that perhaps film can only take us so far in a search of it. Danny Balint in *The Believer* is tangled up in the ugliness of neo-Nazism, and carries out acts of violence that are the antithesis of the Jewish faith. David Cohen in *Song of Songs* is hardly more appealing when his violence remains in his imagination, or when his incestuous feelings towards his sister are acted upon, though both young men have a certain beauty in the intensity of their unbalanced struggle. When the young Danny challenges his rabbi there is great potential for him as an inspired trailblazer for new religious insight. When David challenges the teacher of the Talmud in the seminar room he speaks for millions of bored students who want more than the dried flakes of an ancient creed, who want something intensely alive. But neither do more than act destructively. Perhaps the modern filmmaker simply has not the religious imagination to comprehend the razor edge along which the great spiritual teachers of Judaism, or any other faith for that matter, dance, their fiery inspiration narrowly averting the chaos of destructive ramification. Yet despite all that, a study of these films can be rewarding, if we "labor" at them in the way suggested by Kierkegaard.

5. Secular Judaism

Preamble

In the last chapter we looked at films where protagonists exhibit various forms of extreme behavior in their pursuit of Judaism, or in their struggle to reject it, amongst which were some films with a largely secular or political context. Here we look more explicitly at the nature of the interaction between the secular world and the world of Judaic faith.

Jewish secularism has two sources: firstly the European humanism of the seventeenth and eighteenth centuries that gave rise to the so-called Enlightenment Jew, and secondly the shock of the Holocaust. The term *Haskalah* is used for the Jewish Enlightenment, a movement amongst Jews that was a response to the pervasive influence of the Enlightenment in general. Moses Mendelssohn – perhaps following in the footsteps of Spinoza – was a leading figure in this movement which later led to Reform Judaism. Whatever the impact on Judaism itself, the growing secularism of European culture and the rise of scientific materialism have led many Jews to cease the practice of their faith, and so, generations on, what often remains is a Jewish identity eviscerated of the Jewish religion.

We look at the films of Woody Allen as a prime example of this, showing how religion can run dry – and in doing so lose all its beauty. We also return to the struggle between the protagonists in *The Quarrel* and between the secular and Hasidic worldviews in *The Chosen*. In any sphere of human endeavor its original impetus and creativity may land up flowing through constrictions laid down by the tradition as it grows. Innovation is endless in religion as elsewhere, but tradition is a mixed blessing: it can nurture and protect the grandeur of the original vision and guide new developments, or it can obscure the source and stifle originality. For millions of confirmed atheists and secularists the latter is all they see.

I have characterized the filmmaker Ingmar Bergman as a "chronicler of exhausted Christianity": the same dynamic of exhaustion can operate in any faith.[83] While the work of such filmmakers often represents a personal journey through the collapse of their own faith, their films became cultural landmarks because they have picked up on the zeitgeist, and so speak to the inner struggle of millions. Such films are interesting because we can learn about anything through the portrayal of its negation, but also because it is necessary to say where these films go wrong. Yes, they capture the zeitgeist of the waverers unable to grasp the solid core of their own religion and seduced by a secular world that declares religion an illusion, and yes, this is a large constituency. But such films often pivot on errors of comprehension both about the nature of religion and about the basis of the secular dismissal of it.

Woody Allen's Crimes and Misdemeanors

Introduction to Woody Allen

Woody Allen says "… the only religion that I feel I can write about with any kind of accuracy is the Jewish religion. I have no feel for the details of Christianity."[84] But we will see that Allen cannot in fact write about Judaism with any kind of accuracy either; instead explores the space *vacated* by the Jewish faith. He does so much as the Ingmar Bergman he admires treats Christianity – and in *Crimes and Misdemeanors* he even uses Bergman's cinematographer Sven Nyquist.

In writing on a film by Allen called *Deconstructing Harry* – which dramatizes a series of short stories – Elliot Gertel suggests that it is the most imaginative of his films. He adds that the short stories "contain within them all the stereotypes of Jews and wholesale mockery of Judaism that have been the stock in trade of Allen's previous work." [85] I am not sure that Allen intends mockery exactly, but his Jewish stereotypes are certainly constructed to reinforce secular prejudices against faith.

In *Hannah and her Sisters* Allen's lapsed-Jewish persona has full reign as he undergoes an existential crisis in which he says: "I just felt that in a Godless universe I didn't want to go on living." But the search is shallow, his suicide unsuccessful, and he finds redemption in a Marx Brothers' film. At one point he turns to the Hare Krishnas whose exuberant devotions attract him. "What makes you interested in becoming a Hare Krishna?" he is asked, to which he replies: "I'm not saying I want to join, but I know you guys believe in reincarnation." He is therefore handed a small book but he can't be bothered to think it through, research it further, or speak with anyone on the subject. Allen has simply scored a comic point against religion; that will suffice: the mere mention of reincarnation invites all secular ridicule. In another comic moment he is debating the existence of G-d with his mother and demands: "If there's a G-d, why is there so much evil in the world? On a simplistic level, why were there Nazis?" His mother refers him to his father: "Tell him Max." His father replies: "How the hell do I know why there were Nazis? I don't know how the can opener works."

The scene in the film where Mickey attempts to grapple with religion is titled "The Big Leap." Johanna Petsche has this to say about the scene and about Allen:

> The "leap of faith" is a central motif in both *Hannah and Her Sisters* and *Crimes and Misdemeanors*, and indeed the caption for this sequence is "The Big Leap." The concept was explored at length by Soren Kierkegaard (1813-1855), one of Allen's favorite philosophers, who argued that the transition from a life without faith to a life with faith could not possibly occur as a rational transition, but as an enormous "leap of faith." In his treatise *Fear and Trembling* Kierkegaard discusses the biblical story in which G-d tests Abraham by commanding him to sacrifice his son Isaac. Kierkegaard argues that Abraham's obedience and total trust in G-d is unintelligible to prudential and moral reason and thus is absurd: "[Abraham] believed by virtue of the absurd, for human calculation was out of the question." This series of scenes perfectly reveals Allen's contemptuous view of religion as irrational and unsubstantiated as he depicts Mickey's seemingly effortless, off-the-cuff rejection of his Jewish roots and his erratic attempt to subscribe to Catholicism and later to the Hare Krishna faith because, as Mickey explains, "I got off on the wrong foot with my own thing." Much of the humor of the sequence comes from Allen's play on his own "Jewishness" as he taps into the well-established view of himself as the epitome of all things Jewish[86]

Allen may represent the end-point of the Enlightenment Jew, but does not represent Judaism; neither is his nihilism explored in depth as in Bergman. The American writer on culture Allan Bloom insists that American nihilism is an empty nihilism, because it has no high-culture basis. He says "American nihilism is a mood, a mood of moodiness, a vague disquiet. It is nihilism without the abyss." [87] Bloom applies this idea to Allen's film *Zelig*, but Christopher Lasch, another American writer on these themes who is equally skeptical of Woody Allen, could easily have had *Crimes and Misdemeanors* in mind when he wrote: "The confessional form allows an honest writer like Exley or Zweig to provide a harrowing account of the spiritual desolation of our times ... [but] the narcissist's pseudo-insights into his own condition, usually expressed in psychiatric clichés, serves him as a means of deflecting criticism and disclaiming responsibility for his actions." 88

Given all this, it is perhaps surprising to find that another Allen film, *Shadows and Fog*, has attracted serious theological attention. Paul Nathanson's analysis concludes by saying "*Shadows and Fog* can be considered a characteristically (though not uniquely) Jewish response to anxiety generated by 'the death of G-d'." Nathanson attempts to show that the power of the film lies in its serious depiction of the situation of modern secular men and women, "for whom, as virtually all philosophers and theologians make perfectly clear, the central problem is precisely meaninglessness." 89 But the story of Max Kleinman, played by Allen in *Shadows and Fog*, is a meaningless dramatization of the "small man" buffeted by forces he cannot understand or withstand, rescued by a deus ex machina ending as unsatisfactory as that in *Hannah and her Sisters*: instead of watching a Marx Brothers' film Kleinman joins a circus. Tackling the *problem* of meaninglessness is precisely what the film does not do, it merely *presents* meaninglessness. Its vaguely Jewish context gives us no glimpse at all into the mysteries of the Judaic religion, or the unique way in which its "struggle with G-d" can be a struggle with meaninglessness, for example in Ecclesiastes. Allen's work, to the extent that it engages with religious themes, is better understood as a presentation of Judaism run so dry as to be no longer present at all. It can nevertheless be instructive.

Introducing *Crimes and Misdemeanors*

Allen tells us that "*Crimes and Misdemeanors* is about people who don't see. They don't see themselves as others see them. They don't see the rights and wrongs of the situation."90 The film centers on Judah Rosenthal, a successful ophthalmologist – and in America this means being surrounded by the cocoon of wealth and privilege – who decides to murder his inconvenient mistress. Allen contrasts Judah with Cliff, a documentary filmmaker played by Allen himself, who does do the right thing, more or less, and is therefore the loser (of the love interest in this case). Judah has a rabbi client called Ben, who is actually going blind, but is the only one with faith – blind faith.

The film begins with the opening of a new ophthalmology wing at which Judah is speaking. "I'm a man of science," he says from the podium. "I've always been a skeptic, but I was raised religiously and when I challenged it, even as a child, some of that feeling must have stuck with me."

There is a flashback to two men in *tallit* reading the Torah in a synagogue, the seven-branched candlestick between them.

"I remember my father telling me, 'the eyes of G-d are on us always.' The eyes of G-d," he repeats. "What a phrase to a young boy. And what were G-d's eyes like? Unimaginably penetrating and intense I assumed. And I wonder if it was just a coincidence that I made my specialty ophthalmology."

Here at the outset is the jarring note that is the leitmotif in Allen's work: a reference to Judaism that is quickly deflected into something comprehensible to the materialist outlook. It is a thinking in bad faith that emerges again when Judah discusses the outrageous inconvenience of his mistress's demands with his mobster brother Jack. We anyway have to swallow the implausibility of siblings entering ophthalmology on the one hand and organized crime on the other: given the same Jewish family background that is unlikely. But even more absurd is this speech delivered by Judah to Jack:

> There is a fundamental difference in the way we see the world. You see it as harsh and empty of values, and pitiless, and I couldn't go on living if I didn't feel with all my heart a moral structure, with real meaning and forgiveness, and some kind of higher power, otherwise there's no basis to know how to live. And I know you well enough to know that a spark of that notion is inside of you too.

This is all very well, but the speed by which this outlook is swept away as Judah decides that the convenient offer from his brother to dispose of the mistress is after all the right option, is shocking. To give Allen his due he has his protagonist briefly go through the motions of anguish at least. And what does Allen provide as a religious backdrop to this conversion of Judah's from feeling the existence of a "moral structure" in his heart to abandoning it? The story of Abraham and Isaac. Allen may have been a fan of Kierkegaard but has not "labored" under the weight of its story as we see in *The Believer*. It certainly gives us no insight into the death of Judah's conscience, dramatized on a dark night with thunder and lightening.

The pressure of his terrible decision is so intense that he hallucinates Ben, the rabbi he knows as a client.

"What choice do I have?" Judah asks of him.

"Give the people you've hurt a chance to forgive you," says Ben, meaning Judah's wife Miriam.

"Miriam won't forgive me."

"It's a human life," pleads Ben. "You don't think G-d sees?"

"G-d is a luxury I can't afford," Judah tells him earnestly.

"Now you're talking like your brother Jack."

"Jack lives in the real world. You live in the Kingdom of Heaven."

"Could you sleep with that? Is that who you really are?" asks Ben.

"I will not be destroyed by this neurotic woman," insists Judah.

"But the Law, Judah," whispers Ben. "Without the Law it is all darkness."

This is the key word: darkness. It is the rabbi who descends into darkness – understood in ophthalmological terms – while Judah, once the murder is done, does *not* descend into darkness – understood in moral terms. Judah survives the amputation of his conscience with no ill effects.

In the final scene Judah tells Cliff that he has been thinking of a story, a murder mystery, with very strange twist. Cliff, as a filmmaker, is interested. Judah explains, effectively telling his own story but in the third person:

> After the awful deed is done he finds himself plagued by guilt. Little sparks of his religious background which he rejected are suddenly stirred up, he hears his father's voice, he imagines that G-d is watching his every move. Suddenly it's not an empty universe after all, but a just and moral one, and he's violated it. Now he's panic-stricken, he's on the verge of a mental collapse, one inch away from confessing the whole thing to the police. And then, one morning he awakens. The sun is shining and his family is around him. Mysteriously the crisis has lifted. He takes his family on a vacation in Europe and it comes to pass that he is not punished. In fact he prospers. The killing is attributed to another person. … Now he's scot-free back to his protected world of wealth and privilege.

"Yes, but can he ever really go back?" Cliff asks, pondering the story.

"Once in a while he has a bad moment but it passes," says Judah.

"Tough for someone to live with that. Very few guys can live with that, something like that on their conscience."

"This is reality," is Judah's response.

Cliff thinks that the character in the story should turn himself in because then the story would take on a tragic dimension.

"In the absence of a G-d he is forced to assume that responsibility himself," says Cliff. "Then you have tragedy."

"But that's fiction. That's movies. … I'm talking about reality."

What is astonishing about this is that Judah "awakens" to a guilt-free world; he has an epiphany in reverse that wipes out his conscience, the organ of the human soul that connects us to others and to G-d. Judah's insight is that *this is reality*. But for the religious person it is not, and it is a religious question, *re-ligare*, to be joined again, which is inverted in its usual course here: Judah's trajectory is to be sundered not joined.

The Seder Meal

In *The Dybbuk* we had a glimpse of a Jewish moral universe more intensely visualized than perhaps in any other of our films here. Each protagonist, whether living or dead, was accorded moral rights and obligations through the love by which each was held in the other. Such love and such moral structure are not known in Allen's film; sex replacing love, it seems, and "this is reality" replacing morality. But Allen is an artist, and he is nothing if not thorough in setting out the dilemma he wants to explore, so at one point in the film he has Judah visit the old house where he grew up in order to debate his situation with his elders – in his imagination. He looks round the house and then stands in the doorway of the dining room where he daydreams an extended family group celebrating the Seder meal, the Passover. As he turns to look into the dining room we hear a sung prayer, perhaps the Seder Kiddush. It is his father, Sol, who is singing from his prayer-book, wearing the *kippah*.

'Come on Sol, get on with it, I'm hungry,' complains one woman. Judah stares, rapt at this product of his memory and imagination.

"Do you mind?" says Sol.

"It's nonsense, anyway," the woman continues. "Putting everyone through this mumbo-jumbo. Bring on the main course."

"I apologies for my disrespectful sister…" Sol says, but she interrupts:

"This is the twentieth century. You have young boys sitting here…" This is true: we see them, presumably Judah and his brother, also wearing *kippahs*. "Don't fill their heads with superstition," she admonishes.

Sol mocks her in turn: "The intellectual, the schoolteacher," he complains, "spare us your Leninist philosophy just this once."

"You're afraid if you don't obey the rules G-d's going to punish you?" she asks.

"He won't punish me, May, he punishes the wicked."

"Oh, who, like Hitler?"

Sol objects to this. "May we're having a Seder." He doesn't see why Hitler has to be dragged into the joyous occasion of the Passover celebration.

"Six million Jews burned to death and they got away with it," she says.

Sol presses her angrily: "How did they get away with it? How?"

"Come on Sol, open your eyes. Six million Jews and millions of others, and they got off with nothing."

"How could human beings do such a thing?" asks another at the table.

"Because might makes right," insists May, turning to him. "Until the Americans marched in and stopped them."

"I don't like this talk at my Seder," repeats Sol, offended.

"Okay, Okay," she says. "Alright."

But the others want to take up the theme, and Judah looks on. It is all in his mind, and here Woody Allen has constructed a clever way to dramatize on film the inner workings of Judah's conscience – until its expiration that is.

"This is interesting," comes a woman's voice.

"You know, wait a minute," says May, "there's this joke about a prize fighter who enters the ring, and his brother turns to the family priest and says 'pray for him.' And the priest said 'I will, but if he can punch it will help.'"

"So what are you saying May," asks a man in a hat. "You saying you challenge the whole moral structure of everything?"

"What moral structure?" May asks indignantly. "Is that the kind of nonsense you use on your pupils?"

"Do you not find human impulses basically decent?" he asks. As he wears a hat and not a kippah, we can perhaps take him to represent the humanist at the table. Others are clearly enjoying the debate.

"There's basically *nothing*," she declares.

"She's such a cynic, my sister," Sol comments, "a nihilist. Back to Russia!" Perhaps by this he is remonstrating that without the human decency of the Americans in permitting her entry she would have suffered under yet more pogroms in the Old World.

A man in a white *kippah* declares: "Well, listen, I happen to agree with May when it comes to all that mumbo-jumbo."

"Why do you say that?" asks Sol, indignantly. "You come to every Seder, you pray in Hebrew …"

"Yes," says the man, "I'm going through the motions. It's just like any ritual, it's a habit."

The man in the hat returns to the discussion: "What are you saying May, there's no morality anywhere in the whole world?"

"For those who want morality, there's morality," she says. "Nothing's handed down in stone."

The woman sitting between the man in the hat and the man in the white *kippah* intervenes: "Sol's kind of faith is a gift. It's like an ear for music or the talent to draw. He believes, and you can use logic on him all day long, and he still believes."

"Must everything be logical?" queries Sol.

Judah takes this moment to enter the fantasy. He asks, hesitantly: "If a man commits a crime, if he kills, then what?"

Sol responds to his son: "Then in one way or another he will be punished."

"If he's caught, Sol," says the man in the white *kippah*.

"If he's not caught, a black deed will blossom in a foul manner," says Sol sternly.

"Ah, you're relying a little too heavily on the Bible, Sol."

Sol will not have any of this. "Whether it is the Old Testament or Shakespeare, murder will out."

"Who said anything about murder?" asks Judah.

"You did," answers Sol.

Judah stares at the assembly. "Did I?" he whispers.

There is a pause, broken by May: "I say if he can do it and get away with it and he chooses not to be bothered by the ethics, then he is home free."

There are murmured objections, but she adds: "Remember, history is written by the winners. And if the Nazis had won future generations would have understood the history of World War Two quite differently."

Sol excuses her: "She is a brilliant woman, Judah, but she has had a very unhappy life."

"And if all your faith is wrong, Sol, just what if?" asks the man in the white kippah. "If?"

"Then I'll still have a better life than all those who doubt," answers Sol.

"Wait a minute," says May, "are you telling me that you prefer G-d to the truth?"

"If necessary," says Sol, "I will always choose G-d over truth."

Critiques of Woody Allen

Allen tells us that existential subjects are the only ones worth dealing with, and in *Crimes and Misdemeanors* this involves the different characters' understanding of what the nature of "real life" – a phrase that crops up a lot in the film – actually is. But Allen doesn't really pose this as an open question, because he has already decided: it is empty. He told an interviewer once: "at best the universe is indifferent. At best!"[91] This is Allen's philosophy, a post-Judaic nihilism of apparent sophistication, and in this world Judah not only remains undiscovered as the instigator of murder, but so pretty much does his conscience.

Allen's film is well received, yet is exceptional in filmmaking in that its protagonist gets away with murder, not only judicially, but psychologically. Very few films care to present such a scenario, *Taxi Driver* being another such rarity. In Allen's case we can perhaps best understand the film as pursuing a nihilism that may have common ground with Bergman's, but differs sharply in not being truly anguished. Instead we have a New-York-Jewish-comedy-of-manners, which by definition does not ask of the audience that it seriously engages with existential questions.

Bernheimer says: "There are two stories told in tandem in *Crimes and Misdemeanors*, a complex morality tale that ranks as the cinema's most rigorous exploration of Jewish values and ethics as well as Woody Allen's most ambitious, accomplished, and thoroughly Jewish film to date."[92] We are faced here with almost complete veneration of Allen's work as a "rigorous" exploration of Jewish ethics, contrasted with Gertel's insistence that Allen's work represents nothing less than a "wholesale mockery" of Judaism. I lean more to Gertel than Bernheimer on this.

Other Dialogues across the Divide

The Seder meal scene in *Crimes and Misdemeanors* is perhaps Allen's best attempt at a dialogue between faith and secularism, in which a gift for faith is compared to a gift for music or drawing. However we have already seen superior debates in other films so far discussed, including *The Chosen*, *The Quarrel*, *The Jazz Singer* (both versions), *A Stranger Among Us*, and *The Believer*. I devote a whole chapter of my book *Luminous* to films of dialogue between open-minded secularists and faith adherents, suggesting that at their best they can illuminate faith better than one-sided proselytizing.[93] They ask questions of religion that must be asked.

In this section we look at the film *Holy Rollers* which shows how a young man simply loses touch with Jewish faith and morality in the encounter with the modern world, and at the film *Little Jerusalem* where Judaism has to compete with the philosophy of Immanuel Kant. In later chapters we look at the films *Left Luggage*, *The Pawnbroker*, *Kadosh*, *My Father My Lord*, *A Price Above Rubies* and *Arranged*, all of which present different facets of the secular-Judaism interaction.

It is also worth mentioning here that the film *Hannah Arendt* – about the life of the Jewish philosopher – is a good portrayal of the classic Enlightenment Jew. Her emancipation from the faith of her ancestors is so complete, and her intellect so brilliant, that here perhaps we find the true end-point of the movement started by Moses Mendelssohn. The film follows the controversy over her report for the *New Yorker* on the war crimes trial of the Nazi Adolf Eichmann. She made perhaps not only a political mistake in suggesting that Jewish leaders across Europe were too acquiescent in the face of the Nazis, but possibly also a factual one; at any rate that conundrum is what the lesser mind of Danny Balint struggled with. But her secularism surely stood her in good stead when she perceived in Eichmann nothing more than banality – the "banality of evil" as the expression then became, perhaps an enduring contribution to the debates in the aftermath of the Holocaust. But we see in her a modern mind, confronted as Danny was, with the horrors of the Holocaust, and we find not a shred of religious instinct in her engagement with it. Hers is a Jewishness with the Judaism vacuumed out.

Holy Rollers

Holy Rollers is another film set in a New York Hasidic community, this time with its characters employed in the garment district. It is a father-son drama in which the wayward boy – known as Schmuel to his religious community, Sam to the outside world – loses direction, his faith, and his liberty, the film ending with him imprisoned in a federal boot camp for drug smuggling. The young man's character is too vaguely drawn and his loss of faith too little anguished for the film to be particularly instructive about Judaism, but none the less some moments are worth mentioning, and there are glimpses of Hanukah and Shabbat observances, and a traditional Jewish wedding. The choice facing the young man is spelled out early in the film in the religious school where the rabbi is teaching a class with Sam in attendance. The rabbi says:

"They heard Ha'Shem's voice moving in the garden with the wind of day. The man and his wife hid themselves from Ha'Shem among the trees of the garden. Ha'Shem called to the man, he said: 'where are you?'"

He pauses for a moment and then asks: "Does Ha'Shem *know* where Adam was hiding? Schmuel? Schmuel?"

Sam cannot answer but another young man replies: "G-d being G-d knew where Adam was hiding, but the question is for Adam to answer."

This appears to satisfy the rabbi, who nods. "All men must answer this," he insists. "They must know where they stand in relation to Ha'Shem's presence. Either you move closer, or further away."

This sets us up for Sam's choice – which is clearly to move further away from G-d's presence. His journey is not informed by a critical mind or a desire to pursue the question of faith in his own way, or through any intensity of conflicted values as in *The Believer* or *The Song of Solomon*. It is simply weakness. He falls in with a neighboring Hasid who concocts a scheme for drug-running from Amsterdam, the religious garb of their community providing the perfect cover, a scenario apparently based on a true story. At no point does Sam object to any of this on moral grounds, but instead is driven by a desire for "geld" – something he is chastised for by the rabbi. Just like in *The Dybbuk* Sam hopes that money will help him secure a girl; his first *basherte* has rejected him.

Towards the end, in a Jewish district of New York, Sam is on the run after his couriers are busted at the airport. We hear the rabbi's voice again: "They must know where they stand in relation to Ha'Shem's presence. Either you move closer, or further away." This is perhaps true of the dynamic nature of the human mind, that it does not bear stasis but is perpetually either moving towards or away from things. If so, then secularization means we are moving en masse away from G-d and the films in this section document that.

Little Jerusalem

Little Jerusalem gives us a rare glimpse into the lives of a Sephardic Jewish group, as distinct from the Ashkenazim who populate most of our dramas here. Indeed the only other exception to the Ashkenazi predominance amongst our films is found in *Live and Become* which deals with Ethiopian Jews, known as the Beta Israel community.

Laura, of a Tunisian-French family, is resisting the Judaic tradition of her family through the study of philosophy. She lives with her mother and her sister Mathilde and her sister's husband and four small children in a typical high-rise apartment of the Paris *banlieue* of Sarcelle, a Jewish quarter appropriately called "Little Jerusalem." The film opens with a view of Jews standing by water, performing the *Tashlikh*, the symbolic discarding of sins for the New Year, just as we see at the start of *The Quarrel*. They appear to be throwing things into the water as they recite the sacred text and shake the hem or tassels – *tzitzit* – of their garments. A woman withdraws: it is Laura.

Her first revolt against Judaism is a curious one: she declares that from now on she will take a walk every day at seven in the evening. We later discover that the inspiration for this is Kant, as explained by her professor in the philosophy classes she attends. The great philosopher "religiously" kept to this routine, she has learned.

Laura's sister is called Mathilde who is conventionally married and committed to her faith. Mathilde is skeptical of the philosophers:

"You are wasting your time. You've been raised in the truth of the Torah. Why study these philosophers?"

"Their thoughts contain truths too," counters Laura.

"You're wrong," insists her sister. "Philosophers are like archers. They take aim and hit the bull's eye. But they pick the wrong target. The right one is just next to it. It is Ha'Shem. And we're trying to reach Him."

Unlike Sam in *Holy Rollers*, Laura is perhaps not so much turning away from Ha'Shem as seeking Him by other means. The whole secular world seems full of such seeking, a thirst for religion accompanied by the certainty that anywhere but religion is the place to slake it. Laura begins an affair with a Muslim man from Morocco who was noted in his country for being the first to write about women Sufis. "We are both mystics," he tells Laura at one point, but this idea is lost in the film as it is modernism that claims the young woman, not mysticism. The relationship between the sisters is touching however, and the anxiety that the married one has for the younger unspoken-for female is clear: "It hurts me to see you move away from Ha'Shem," she says. But Mathilde is dealing with her own problems; her husband has been unfaithful. Both women attend the ritual baths and in a moving scene the *mikveh* woman gives advice on sex to Mathilde with Laura listening in (I detail this later in the chapter on Family Judaism).

The Jewish community as a whole also has problems: its synagogue is torched, and the Jews have to conduct their rituals in a temporary shelter. In the dark and confusion at the time of the ruined synagogue the Torah scrolls are removed from the ark and kept safe for their new makeshift deployment. It is in some of these scenes in their temporary synagogue that we see the clearest differences from Ashkenazi tradition, and become aware of the influence of North Africa on the Sephardic Jews.

Laura's rejection of Judaism will mean a move away from her Jewish family and community and we wonder what her life will become without this support. She is serious – indeed the whole film is a little over-serious – but she has the same integrity as her sister. She might become another Hannah Arendt; she might marry and have children with a Muslim; or she might return to the fold. But for now her life will be deeply shaped by the attractions of the secular world.

Summary

We can know the beauty of something when it is lost. We can mourn its passing, we can see the gap where this beauty once stood. We can also see it vividly when the old coexists with the new, when there is a dialogue between Judaic tradition and the secular Jews who have abandoned it. That the gulf is deep is perhaps best shown in the Seder scene in *Crimes and Misdemeanors*. The faith of Judah's father Sol is dismissed by his sister May, but not by the film. His moral certainty that "a black deed will blossom in a foul manner" has a beauty that contrasts well to the ugliness of the film's ending, one that draws quite the opposite conclusion. But the criticism of Woody Allen, that his films are a "wholesale mockery of Judaism" stands because characters like Sol are isolated, and characters like his son Judah have so profoundly lost faith, not only in Judaism, but also humanism, that we learn little of the beauty they abandoned. In *Holy Rollers* there is again little we can learn from the journey of weakness in the protagonist Sam, even if there is redemption to come under the strict discipline of the boot camp. It is in *Little Jerusalem* that the struggle – this time between a religious sister and one who is abandoning the Jewish life at all levels – is the more interesting. But there is a beauty wherever there is honesty of debate across the divide, because, whether moving towards Ha'Shem or away from Him, He is somehow recognized.

6. Holocaust Judaism

Preamble

If the trials of Job are the classic test of faith in the Hebrew Bible; if the testing of Abraham echoes through Jewish history to the point that young Danny Balint believes that the whole Jewish people were permanently scarred by what happened at Mount Moriah and that the Jews still live in terror of it; then what of the test posed by the Holocaust? The shock of G-d's apparent abandonment of His chosen people reverberates to this day. *The Quarrel* is a good dramatization of this shock to faith, while the films *The Diary of Anne Frank*, *Left Luggage* and *The Pawnbroker* give widely varying insights into the same issue. There are of course many Holocaust films focusing on Jews and Jewish life but few of them make much real reference to Judaism. Eric Michael Mazur – editor of the *Encyclopedia of Religion and Film* – says: "If few Holocaust films feature characters living Judaism-filled lives, even fewer capture the diversity of modern European Jewry." [94] We will see for example that the Jewish family at the centre of the film of *The Diary of Anne Frank* have been Americanized and even de-racialized to become a typical post-war American family with merely the one-off celebration of a quaint, possibly European, custom, *Rosh Hashanah*, to indicate difference. Abram's point, that the Jew in cinema has only recently been allowed his or her "otherness" is well illustrated by the film, no doubt constructed in such a way as to allow the average American to relate to an entirely foreign world and circumstance.

Schindler's List, as a more recent treatment of the Holocaust, grants Jews their ethnicity, as does *Adam Resurrected* in a very different way. However both films subtly evade the reality of the Holocaust by refusing to grant what Hannah Arendt insisted upon: the banality of its evil. Both of these films have Nazi camp commanders whose random violence over their captives, however shocking, lacks this grit of reality. In any case neither tells us anything about the religious life of the Jews undergoing annihilation, or how the Holocaust impacted on their faith.

The Holocaust above all evils is the trigger for the classical question as Mickey enquires in *Hannah and her Sisters*: if G-d is good, then why does he permit evil? If I break my leg I am set back, if a friend is murdered I am devastated, but if millions of my kith and kin are incinerated – "holocaust" means "total burning" – then do I not call into question my most fundamental beliefs? At the dawn of the European Enlightenment, the beginning of the modern humanist sensibility, a whole new word was needed for this issue and in 1710 the German philosopher Gottfried Leibniz came up with one: "theodicy", meaning questions over why a "good" G-d permits evil. In his era it was the huge loss of life in the Lisbon earthquake of 1755 that prompted the fiercest skepticism regarding the goodness of G-d, and led to the ridiculing of Leibniz's optimism in Voltaire's novel *Candide*. However long before Leibniz had coined the term Jewish people had contemplated the problem, though Steinberg tells us that to many people Judaism seems to make a variety of incoherent responses. He disagrees:

> We are looking, let us remember, for an acceptable theodicy, that is to say, for such an explanation of evil as will reconcile the fact of it with the existence of G-d. But quite obviously no theodicy can be a cover-all, big and adaptable enough to be spread over any and all theologies. To the contrary, each must be relative to some particular G-d-idea. But Judaism, promulgating no single authoritative envisagement of G-d, very naturally has no single official theodicy to propound. [95]

Modern atheism, such as held by the popular science writer Richard Dawkins, tends to protest when religion becomes "vague," or "flabby" as he puts it. [96] The idea that there is no "single authoritative envisagement of G-d," as Steinberg says, is rather foreign to atheists, and is perhaps even annoying as it makes atheist arguments harder to pursue. What many of our films show at the very least is that Jews are comfortable with debate both on the nature of G-d and on the subject of theodicy.

We can usefully return to the Seder scene in Woody Allen's *Crimes and Misdemeanors* to contemplate this further. We may recollect that Sol, a religious Jew, and his sister May, an atheist, are arguing over the moral structure of the universe. "Six million Jews burned to death and they got away with it," she says, to which her brother responds: "How did they get away with it? How?"

His retort is not taken up by the others at the Seder table, but it is a good one. From one point of view the Nazis "got away with it" because they were not stopped in time – this is how May sees it when she insists that it was only the mightier force, that of the Americans, that ended the power of the Nazis. But from another point of view history's judgment on the Nazis was perhaps more thorough than on any other perpetrators of historic crimes. The Nuremberg trials executed ten principal members of the Nazi leadership, and jailed many more; Israeli forces later pursued others such as Adolf Eichmann and delivered retributive justice; post-war Germany made reparations to Israel for half a century afterwards, including the delivery of German-made nuclear submarines and other armaments. Laws against anti-Semitism were passed in most countries in the world, a unique legal recognition of the enormity of the Holocaust and the unique group targeted for destruction by the Nazis. All of this is, however, human justice. What a theodicy argues is that there is a divine justice, or rather a divine balance from which we can argue that G-d is good. In Woody Allen's Seder scene in *Crimes and Misdemeanors* it is a question of "the whole moral structure of everything". May will have no truck with this concept. At the centre of this film is the idea that May expresses: "For those who want morality, there's morality," she says. "Nothing's handed down in stone."

This, in a nutshell, is the problem with humanist morality: it seems to be elective. You can choose it if you like, rather like any other consumer option, or reject it. Joshua Rosenberg rejects it … and nothing happens to him. For a religious Jew – or the follower of just about any faith tradition – this makes no sense at all. The whole essence of Judaism is that there is a moral structure to the human universe, that it pre-exists our elective efforts, and that it is the creation or domain of the Almighty, Ha'Shem, G-d. You cannot choose to live within or without of this structure: you can only choose to act by it or against it; to move closer to G-d through observing it, or further away from Him by violating it. This was the choice of the young Hasid in Holy Rollers, as his rabbi made clear to him.

Having said all this, the Holocaust is the world's single most powerful challenge to any theodicy of goodness, justice or moral structure. No Jewish theodicy can ignore it. In this section we look at some films that explore this theme – including *The Devil's Arithmetic* where exposure to the reality of the Holocaust creates more faith in a young woman rather than less – but first it is useful to return to *The Believer*. I suggested earlier that Danny Balint was struggling with the Holocaust from a particular point of view: it left him seeing the Jew as weak and feminized, and in this inner turmoil over the issue he turns to violence as the answer.

The Believer

After Danny Balint and his gang are convicted of assault in a kosher restaurant, they are given the choice between thirty days in jail or sensitivity training. They choose the latter, which involves listening to the accounts of Holocaust survivors in an encounter-group kind of setup. An elderly man tells them how he and his family tried to get past Nazi soldiers in a hay-cart, but were discovered, with the result that one of the soldiers impales his three-year-old son on his bayonet and lifts him up with it so the blood would fall on the father's face. "The soldiers were laughing," added the man. Danny falls into a reverie in which we see the scene enacted in black and white. When the man finishes the story Danny is the first to respond.

"What did you do?" he asks brusquely. Neither he nor any of his gang evinces any sympathy for the group of elderly Jews. The other survivors are offended and demand: what could he have done? Danny is enraged.

"The sergeant's killing his kid! What could he have done? He could have jumped the guy, gouged his eyes out, grabbed his bayonet…"

"They would've shot him on the spot. He would have been dead in two seconds," interjects a woman, equally angry. "Who are you to judge?"

"So he's dead?" says Danny. "Big deal. He's worse than dead now. He's a piece of shit!"

The argument rages, then over the Holocaust itself and Hitler.

"Hitler was real," adds another old man quietly. "G-d created him to punish the Jews for abandoning the Torah."

Danny keeps insisting that the man who witnessed his son's death should have done something, to which one of the women respond:

"What would you have done if you had been there?" she asks.

"Not what *he* did," Danny insists. "Just stand there and watch?"

"How do you know?" she asks. "You've never been tested like he has. Here in this rich, safe, stupid country, it is so easy to imagine oneself a hero."

Danny has nothing to answer this with, and so leaves, telling the group leader that they have nothing to learn from the Holocaust survivors. The narrative of the film shows us otherwise however. Later in the film Danny is in a reflective mood and visualizes, again in black and white, the scene where the little Jewish boy crawls out from a hay-cart and is held in the arms of his father. Danny is in the middle of repairing the Torah scrolls vandalized in the synagogue by his gang. Is his religion beginning to change his certainties? We cut to the Nazi sergeant holding something aloft on his bayonet – we are spared the actual details. The Nazi now is Danny and he is looking up at his victim. It is after this vision that Danny binds the *tallit* to his waist, and which is later discovered by the fellow gang-member that he shoots.

In the next return to the hay-cart scenario, Danny is on a New York street and spots a small Jewish boy with *payot* and *kippah*, who turns to look at Danny. It triggers another monochrome vision, a continuation of where we left off, in which Danny is still holding the child aloft on his bayonet, blood now on his hands. His face is grim, triumphant, and from his motions we gather that he casts the dead child off his weapon, like hay off a pitchfork.

In the synagogue at the end of the film where Danny sits knowing that a bomb will go off, he is listening to Jewish prayer and singing and returns once again to the hay-cart scene. The Nazi officer kicks the body of the child towards its father. But suddenly the father is Danny, and he lunges at the sergeant, bringing him to the ground. He imagines another officer with rifle raised, hesitating over whether to shoot. Is this the turning point? Does Danny now realize that there would have been no hesitation? That any resistance would have meant instant death? He is grappling with this in the synagogue – we hear a shot. Some resolve forms in him, and we have already described the outcome: he saves the congregation from his own bomb and stays to die in its blast. He may have resolved something in him, yet in his welcoming of death we cannot be sure: does he permit himself to be destroyed as atonement for his violence to date? Or because it is better to be dead than "a shit," as he put it?

We can read *The Believer* as a set of reactions to the Holocaust from Jews who remain under the spell of Judaism. It is of course a common refrain: why didn't the Jews *do* something? As mentioned earlier, Hannah Arendt was pilloried for suggesting, however obliquely, that Jewish community leaders cooperated too easily with the Nazis. In the film *Sunshine* there is disbelief that one of the Sonnenschein family could stand there in winter and watch his father beaten, hung by his wrists from a post, and hosed with cold water until he froze to death, encased in ice, a scene memorably committed to film. How could he not intervene? For each survivor such horrible questions hang over them, adding to the impossibility of recovering from the experience, something that those spared such experiences cannot understand. Indeed how can anyone spared this fate answer the Jewish woman who said: "Here in this rich, safe, stupid country, it is so easy to imagine oneself a hero." No wonder that many Holocaust survivors – including such famous novelists as Primo Levi – committed suicide long after the events.

The Diary of Anne Frank

The Believer was made at a time when realistic films about the Holocaust were long common fare, though even then it spares us the actual sight of a child impaled on a bayonet. Kathryn Bernheimer tells us that *The Diary of Anne Frank*, released in 1959, was the first film to break a fifteen-year taboo on mainstream cinema renditions of the Holocaust. She says: "*The Diary of Anne Frank* is a sensitive but sentimental and woefully inadequate drama that marks Hollywood's first tentative steps that would eventually lead to fuller portrayals of the century's greatest horror." [97] At the same time we should bear in mind that Nathan Abrams documents how the Jew, at first a hook-nosed stereotype, then more respectfully treated, had mostly disappeared from film by 1935 following the Jewish high watermark of the 1927 film *The Jazz Singer*. Jews only slowly made a come-back, but before that "Gentiles playing Jews became the norm."[98] This was certainly the criticism of Millie Perkins as Anne Frank in the 1959 film, and is also a criticism of Paul Newman as Ari Ben Canaan in the film *Exodus* of 1960, though Newman had a Jewish father. The Hays Code, a protocol for limiting the depiction of screen violence more formally known as the Motion Picture Production Code, fell into abeyance in the late 1960s, so by the time of the production of *Schindler's List* in 1993 or *Inglourious Basterds* in 2009 it had become normal to graphically depict the most horrific of Holocaust events.

Whatever the criticisms of *The Diary of Anne Frank* made half a century after its release, I would suggest that the film remains valuable. Here is a movie that tells the horror of the Holocaust in an important manner, that of a family waiting and waiting, hoping against hope, pinned into a tiny space while war rages around them, only for a small mistake to send them to their deaths. From the outset we know that only Anne's father Otto survives from the group comprising the immediate family, that of the Van Daans, and a dentist called Dussel. In the roughly two and a half hours of its telling this fact is at the back of our minds right up to the point of listening to D-Day radio broadcasts, including the voice of Churchill, when salvation was only months away. We have become an intimate part of this Jewish extended family group and the knock on the door that spells the death of all but Otto is horribly shocking. In some ways this kind of shock works better on us even now, despite all the realistic screen renderings of Jewish murders by the Nazis, or perhaps because we have become more broadly desensitized to screen violence since the demise of the Hays Code.

The cruelty of their deaths – including Anne's – is infinitely multiplied by their long survival; indeed each scene that passes, each little drama of the group imprisoned in their attic rooms, adds to our hopes for their survival. To see a Nazi officer shoot a Jew for the most trivial offence at point blank range in a European street is shocking; to "live" with Jews for four years and see them arrested works in quite a different way.

The value of the film for our exploration of Judaism is slight however. As Abrams' investigation shows us, the "Jew" at that time in cinematic history was an assimilated figure. Not a single Shabbat is celebrated in the entire film, and only "an invented Hannukah scene" as Bernheimer describes it remains in the film as a reminder that they have a different religion to mainstream America.[99] Even then, as Bernheimer points out, the dentist Dussel is presented as an assimilated Jew, unable to comprehend the threat of anti-Semitism, and unfamiliar with any Judaic ritual. An

American audience could readily identify with him as he is lost over the correct observances at Hannukah. In real life, Bernheimer adds, the dentist confined in the attic with the doomed young Anne ("Hitler's most famous victim" as she characterizes her) was a Hebrew scholar "whose religion meant everything to him, according to his widow."

The Hanukkah scene is not without poignancy however, though the prayer read by the father would be entirely acceptable to Protestant Americans, more inclined to the Old Testament than the New:

> Praised be thou, our Lord our G-d, ruler of the Universe, who has sanctified us with thy commandments and bidden us kindle the Hannukah lights. Praised be thou, our Lord our G-d, ruler of the Universe, who has wrought wondrous deliverances for our father in days of old. Praised be thou, our Lord our G-d, ruler of the Universe, that thou hast given us life and sustenance and brought us to this happy season. We kindle this Hannukah light to celebrate the great and wonderful deeds wrought through the zeal with which G-d filled the hearts of the heroic Maccabees 2000 years ago. They fought against indifference, against tyranny and oppression and they restored our Temple to us. May these lights remind us that we should ever look to G-d, whence cometh our help.

None of the men wear the *kippah*, and, apart from the mention of the term "Hannukah" it could have been any Christian-based festivity such as Thanksgiving – even the absence of a turkey would have an obvious explanation. Anne and her father are keen readers of books, and we learn early on that Anne's choice is Dickens' *A Tale of Two Cities*. What the father reads we never learn, but we have no reason to believe it is the Torah, the Talmud or the Midrash.

Not only is Jewishness erased from the film – other than as an identifier for an oppressed group that the Americans magnanimously liberate – but so is Judaism. Instead we are invited to observe the developing teenage relationship between Anne Frank and Peter Van Daan, with all the pitfalls of young love in a confined space that the relatively innocent screenwriter of the 1950s could conjure. It is Mom and apple pie. Jews and Judaism are whitewashed from the story – as far as is possible – yet still, perhaps even that romanticized youthful encounter helps convey the real shock, the blow to the stomach, of Anne's perishing in the film's finale.

Left Luggage

Michael Mazur's point about Holocaust films failing to present "living Judaism-filled lives" is most obviously true regarding *The Diary of Anne Frank*, but it was an observation made in the context of the film *Left Luggage*. Mazur says: "Unusually, *Left Luggage* (1998) juxtaposes a dysfunctional family headed by secular survivors and a Hasidic family, the Kalmans." Omer Bartov has this to say about it:

> Jeroen Krabbé's *Left Luggage* (1998) attempts to examine the reactions of survivors' children in two very different milieus, the completely secular and the deeply orthodox, in early 1970s Antwerp. Based on the novel by Carl Friedman, the film is about betrayal and coercion of religion and its ability to heal and hold together what would otherwise fall apart. Well-meaning and occasionally sensitive, *Left Luggage* is concerned once again with the heroism of the fallen, the courage that emerges from the layers of repression and pretence, and the truth that is concealed under self-deception and obsession. It is also a kitschy and at times ignorant film, which only reinforces the sense that even as it addresses the attempt by individuals and communities to forge ahead as if the catastrophe had never happened and the world that was lost is still within reach, it simultaneously reflects the total eradication of the past and the inability of the present to reconstruct it faithfully, if only as a cinematic image.[100]

As I commented earlier Bartov is something of a "glass-half-empty" critic of film and television, but here his analysis is spot on. The film is focused on Chaya Silberschmidt, a philosophy student working in various jobs that she quits. She is played by as maddeningly an English actress in this film as all the actors and actresses are in *Sunshine*; in both cases it works against any real portrayal of Jews. Worse, the actress who plays Chaya has a twenty-first century British young woman's pout, at odds with the 1970s Dutch Jewish setting, though clearly in a lineage with the very mild version of the female teenage pout of the American actress in *The Diary of Anne Frank*. Chaya's father is convincingly played by Maximilian Schell, as was his role as David Malter in *The Chosen*. Also convincing is the portrayal of the "uncle" Yacov Apfelschnitt in a rare screen outing by Topol of *Fiddler on the Roof* fame. Mr. Silberschmid is the Holocaust survivor who keeps trying to dig up his memories of the life before the Nazis – literally. It is the "left luggage" of the film title, a suitcase with his treasured possessions –

mementos of a pre-occupation life – buried in haste as he fled the Nazis, and which he is trying to locate in the concrete jungle of modern Antwerp.

The kindly Yacov is more helpful to the young Chaya than her own parents, who, as Bartov indicates, have swamped their traumatic memories of the Holocaust in obsessive behavior. Chaya has lost yet another part-time job, and her philosophical studies have led her to take an interest in a Marxist youth, quite realistic for the era. However, unlike Laura's philosophy lessons in *Little Jerusalem*, we are not so sure that Chaya's studies really absorb her. Yacov has a new position for her to consider: as nanny to a very traditional Hasidic family. The warmth of Topol's acting is a strength of the film, and he is believable as a man who both understands the secular world of Chaya's rebellious youth and the sacred mysterious world of the Antwerp Hasidim. Also believable and possibly the best part of the film is Isabella Rossellini as Mrs. Kalman, the traditional Jewish mother who rather reluctantly offers Chaya the job of au pair. (Although Rossellini is not Jewish perhaps Italian ancestry helps to convey the centrality and benignity of traditional family life.) Chaya has applied even more reluctantly, her initial reaction to Yacov's offer being: "No way. I am not going to work for those idiots." It is the children who change her mind, above all the educationally subnormal Simcha, who becomes her main charge.

Mr. Kalman is openly contemptuous of Chaya on their first encounter, assuming her to be promiscuous – which by his standards she is – and immodestly dressed. "Gomer" he calls her, an allusion to a biblical woman whose father was Diblaim, a name apparently meaning "double layers of grapecake," and who gave herself entirely up to sensuality. Whatever the origin of the name or the freight it carries, Mr. Kalman intends it disparagingly.

Although Mrs. Kalman is clearly stressed by the many obligations placed on her to look after her children and run the family home for a traditional Hasidic male, she conveys an old-time certainty about her faith and her role within it. Here certainly is another Jewish woman who exhibits the "classical quality of Yiddishe *chen*" as Gertel puts it. The young Chaya – quite charming in her own secular positivity – will not be persuaded of the Jewish faith however, and it is her vision of the world that we are left with as the Jewish community close ranks over the tragic death of the little Simcha. Secularism has liberated Chaya from the sexual restrictions of her culture, liberated her from religion, and, above all, liberated her from burdensome consciousness of the Holocaust.

Holocaust Judaism

The Pawnbroker

We turn now to a film where a man cannot free himself from the Holocaust at all – to the point where death would be a blessing. Bernheimer tells us: "*The Pawnbroker* was the first American film to feature scenes set in a Nazi concentration camp and among the first to deal with the horror it so harrowingly re-creates."[101] Released only five years after *The Diary of Anne Frank*, its ambience is not at all "mom and apple pie," but rather that of the psychological thriller. Its Jewish director Sidney Lumet later made *A Stranger Amongst Us*, looked at earlier. The 1960s saw perhaps the most Freudian of cinematic eras, giving us some very dark portrayals of near-psychotic individuals in the grip of existential turmoil. In the case of Ingmar Bergman such individuals were often Freudianized in their despair at the loss of faith; in Hitchcock the dynamic was more of horror; others were influenced by the Theatre of the Absurd tradition of Pinter and Beckett. *The Pawnbroker* is the sum of all these influences, and so becomes an utterly different treatment of the Holocaust to *Anne Frank*, its protagonist Sol Nazerman persisting in a kind of living death, where Anne Frank was so prettily and poignantly – and briefly – alive.

Nazerman runs a pawnbroker's shop in seedy Manhattan, a setting given great vibrancy through the jazz soundtrack of veteran music producer Quincy Jones. Women sweep stoops, the Metro thunders overhead, the streets are full, and seedy indeed are many of the characters that walk them. Those that enter the shop are lost souls, as we see them through Nazerman's eyes, and in turn we see him through their eyes: a tragic figure, incapable of warmth, and locked behind the bars that serve him as protection from burglars. His assistant Jesus Ortiz will eventually die in a botched robbery he conceives with petty criminals, a robbery on the very pawnshop where he calls on Nazerman to be his tutor, to teach him the world of money and valuables.

At one point Ortiz – of Latin American extraction and therefore presumably Catholic in his faith asks Nazerman about the numbers tattooed on his forearm. As in *The Believer* where Danny has flashbacks to an event under the Nazis, Nazerman has flashbacks to the concentration camps, the difference being that Nazerman's memories are his own. With this already established in the film we can imagine that Nazerman's reaction to the restless inquiries of the hot-blooded young man will be oblique to say the least.

> ORTIZ: Is that a secret society or something?
> NAZERMAN: Yuh.
> ORTIZ: Yeah, well what do I do to join?
> NAZERMAN: What you do to join? You learn to walk on water.

It was indeed a miracle that Nazerman survived, but on the other hand much in him has not. He is effectively played by Rod Steiger, who we saw in another Jewish role earlier as Reb Saunders in *The Chosen*. Later on Ortiz asks about the secret of the success of "you people." Nazerman enters a tirade:

> First of all you start off with a period of several thousand years during which you have nothing to sustain you but a great bearded legend. You have no land to call your own, to grow food on or to hunt. You have nothing. You're never in one place long enough to have to have a geography or army or land myth. All you have is a little brain. A little brain and a great bearded legend to sustain you and convince you that you are ... special.

His bitterness flows out as he describes how poverty drives the Jew to buy a cloth at one price, divide it and sell it at a marginally higher price, over and over again for centuries. "You are a merchant," he says grimly. "You're known as a usurer, a man with secret resources... a Jew, a Kike!"

At another point Nazerman in his bitterness calls all the races on earth "scum." Ortiz is shocked.

> ORTIZ: They are all children of G-d are they not?
> NAZERMAN: You believe in G-d?
> ORTIZ: I don't know Mr. Nazerman. But you believe in G-d. And I make book on that.
> NAZERMAN: I do not believe in G-d, or art, or science, or newspapers or politics or philosophy.
> ORTIZ: Ain't there nothing you do believe?
> NAZERMAN: Money! Next to the speed of light which Einstein says is the only absolute in the universe, second only to that I rank money!

But there is still some moral structure to the universe for this man who survived the camps. Through flashbacks we learn that his wife did not survive, for she was forced into the "Joy Division," forced into sexual servitude to Nazi officers, while he in turn was forced to watch. Nazerman's business is not totally honest, as he money-launders for a local gang boss, a confident Afro-American whose distaste for Nazerman is palpable; it is the distaste of the living for the dead. But after an exchange with this man Nazerman realizes that the money he is laundering comes in part from brothels, and he baulks at that. He refuses further deals, and is badly beaten. He does not care: they would do him a favor by killing him. The gang boss simply laughs at him and tells him he will die at a time not of his own choosing.

However it is the young assistant, Jesus Ortiz who dies in the bungled robbery at the end of the film, and in some small way we imagine that Nazerman's emotional defenses are penetrated by this tragedy.

At this distance the mannerisms of this "psychological" type of film may be as clumsy to us as the mannerisms of the sanitized *Anne Frank*. Despite that *The Pawnbroker* gives us some glimpse of how the Holocaust must leave its survivors emotionally scarred, and how all talk of G-d or faith is bitterly turned away from. Money was the only thing left to Nazerman, but even then he goes through the motions mechanically – he merely lives out a stereotype that he himself mocks when he declared his people in thrall to nothing more than a "bearded legend."

When May Rosenthal in *Crimes and Misdemeanors* so confidently scorned any notion of a moral structure to the universe, she did so as one who had made some accommodation to the events of the Holocaust. Perhaps she married, had children, and participated in life, albeit in a cynical way. Nazerman does not wish to participate at all, and in dramatizing such a life we see how the horrors of the camp kill its inmates long after the event.

At an even greater remove, in a bizarre film called *Everything is Illuminated*, a young Jewish man called Jonathon Safran Foer from the second generation of Holocaust survivors appears to be emptier still of life and emotion. The film is empty too of any reference to the Jewish religion, but its surreal comedy leaves a disturbing impression. The "psychological" treatment of Sol Nazerman had a certain realism to it, but the "post-psychological" treatment of Jonathan is surreal. Nazerman lives through a crisis – the death of Ortiz – and there is hope for some bud of humanity to blossom again in him. Jonathan appears only as a cipher, living, not in *his* past, but in that of ancestors he never knew except through the photographs and other artifacts that he collects about them. He will never change. As with *Adam Resurrected* – where its Jewish protagonist survives the Nazis by clowning to the point of acting as a kind of dog to the camp commander – it seems that our cinematic endeavors to come to terms with the Holocaust are becoming less effective rather than more with the passage of time.

The Quarrel

May Rosenthal, Danny Balint, Sol Nazerman and Jonathan Safran Foer are cinematic representations of the Jewish response to the Holocaust. The responses are as varied as one can imagine, though all represent a turning away from faith. Danny symbolically repairs the Torah as he imagines himself firstly as a Nazi brutally murdering a child and then as the father of the child in a futile attempt to fight back. He represents a strange kind of hope for Judaism, where Sol Nazerman's re-humanizing – if at all – may have no religious element in it. May Rosenthal is brusquely efficient at banishing the demons of both faith and doubt, while young Jonathan – every bit as mechanical as Nazerman – remains unfathomable. The Silberschmidt parents in *Left Luggage* exhibit various obsessive behaviors. Cinema has many more cameos along this spectrum of response to offer.

Just occasionally the response is a deepened faith, so we return now to a key part of the film *The Quarrel*, concerning Chaim, the secular novelist, who encounters his boyhood friend, the deeply religious Rabbi Hersh. The Holocaust has prompted opposite responses in them, and in a park in Montreal they talk through their differences. They are sheltering from the rain in an old garage and the Rabbi speaks:

> What is it, really, that separates us? We look at people, you see their potential for good, I look at people, the *same* people, I see their potential for evil. You believe that if people would only follow their reason that would be in the best interests of everyone. I believe that if people followed their reason it would lead to disaster. … The wise men of Athens. Ever since the Greek philosophers people believed that reason alone could lead to morality. How could this be? Reason alone is amoral. To the most moral Greek it seemed perfectly reasonable to take a newborn baby that was unhealthy and put it outside to die. In other words reason is a tool. … So, how do we protect ourselves if reason fails us? By relying on something higher than reason. If a person does not… If there is no Master of the Universe, then who is to say that Hitler did anything wrong?

These words, the flow of them, the feeling, come easily to Hersh because he had rehearsed them countless times in his imagination when in the concentration camp thinking his friend was dead. Hersh had always been the more religious of the two, and had followed the principle enunciated by Reb Saunders that to have eyes for the world is to forfeit one's life. But the circumstances of the Holocaust changed him:

Holocaust Judaism

> You accused me of hiding in my room from the temptations of the world. You were right. I spent most of my youth with my eyes on the ground, so I wouldn't be tempted. But then in 1941 a young German soldier grabbed me by my Jewish beard, and pulled my head *up*, and forced me to look up into his eyes, and I saw the World there. And I haven't put my head down since.

He now sees the Nazis as the "real" face of the world. He cannot believe in the secular values of Chaim, a man who makes the world his primary reality, because however fine the world may be at this moment "Nazis" of any kind can rear up again. The "world" is a place of betrayal, cruelty, emptiness. He begs Chaim to return to his faith in the most moving of terms. Chaim replies with depth of feeling: "*If* I were to return to G-d it would be for the sake of your passion." He adds that "it is a blessing to share this day with you." Then he pauses, and says: "But, there is another chapter to your story." He tells of an old Lithuanian woman he met in Paris who smuggled Jews to save their lives, but was an atheist. Her belief was not in G-d but in human beings, risking her life to save Jews and Jewish texts from the Nazis. Chaim has faith, Hersh has faith, that is what matters, not what that faith has as a starting point. The difference in their paths is now visualized in their disagreement as to how to head back in the woodlands of Montreal Park. All paths lead to the same place, Chaim says as he strides off in the opposite direction to Hersh. Both are equally lost, but do of course arrive at the Chalet du Mont Royal.

As Bartov says, "The dispute between Chaim and Hersh centers on two related issues. One is faith: does the Holocaust teach one to trust G-d or to rely on man? The second is betrayal: the betrayal of G-d by man, the betrayal of man by G-d, and the betrayal of one's fellow human beings." [102] Our interest here is also to ask this: how has the Holocaust changed Judaism? We may recall that Scholem records a change in Judaism after the Exodus from Spain. The religion became less this-worldly and more other-worldly; more specifically it became more Messianic. But the outcome of that, a messiah in the form of Sabbatai Zevi who not only failed to usher in the Kingdom of Heaven, but even failed to remain a Jew, was hardly positive. And after the Holocaust, given the modern setting, it is not surprising that it is secularism that many Jews like Chaim turn to, not messianic fervor.

The Devil's Arithmetic

We finish this section with a film that takes a modern young woman a little like Chaya Silberschmidt in *Left Luggage* but whose exposure to the legacy of the Holocaust turns her towards her faith rather than leaving her a secularist outsider. Hannah Stern is a young Jewish woman growing up in 1980s New York whose patience for tradition runs thin during the family Seder. Her aunt Eva is fond of her and tells her she looks like a family member called Chaya whose identity is something of a mystery. Those present at the Seder read appropriate verses relating to the departure from Egypt but Hannah refuses when it is her turn. The father pours 'the cup of Elijah' and asks who will open the door to let the prophet in, a symbolic moment in the Passover festival. Children enthusiastically offer to do so but Eva turns to Hannah who reluctantly gets up at her aunt's behest to carry out the ritual. As the family sing Hannah goes through the door and is magically transported to a Jewish home in a Polish village in 1941. Her confusion is explained by her recent illness and recovery but the next day Nazis arrive to drive the Jews out and to a concentration camp, perhaps Auschwitz. Hannah, now called Chaya, witnesses 'first hand' the cruelties of this and when her new-found cousin Rivka is selected for execution she saves her life by switching places with her. She then magically returns to her modern life, lying on pillows surrounded by anxious relatives. 'You drank too much honey,' is the verdict. However Hannah thinks only of aunt Eva and her safety and when her aunt approaches she calls her 'my Rivka'. Her aunt is stunned. 'How do you know?' she asks in wonderment. 'How?' she demands, as Hannah reveals the whole story. They then ask the question together that all Jews must ask, 'how could the Nazis have done this?' Hannah agrees with her aunt that only G-d can answer the question. And more: that Hannah now knows how to talk with G-d: 'so quietly that only G-d can hear me.' Fully recovered, Hannah can now fully participate in the Seder, the prayers that Jews give to G-d for their deliverance.

Summary

How can one possibly find religious beauty in films made in the wake of perhaps the ugliest event in world history, the Holocaust? Danny Balint is no beauty – his struggle to reconcile the pull of Judaism with the pull of militaristic self-defining merely ends in self-destruction, while most Holocaust films do not touch on Judaism anyway. But we cannot contemplate this religion, and the filmic treatments of it, without considering the impact of the Holocaust on this faith. Where the Spanish Exodus provoked messianic fervor, the Holocaust has wreaked largely secular bitterness, and the film character who most epitomizes that is Sol

Nazerman in *The Pawnbroker*. His namesake Sol Rosenthal in *Crimes and Misdemeanors*, in contrast, retains his faith. Mr. Nazerman believes only in money and the rationalism of Einstein, while Mr. Rosenthal sets faith above rationalism. Somewhere in the middle Chaim Kovler is bitter, but acknowledges the position of his friend, tells him that if he returned to Judaism it would be for his sake. But it is Chaim's friend Hersh who we really need to understand.

Hersh has not rejected the lessons of the Holocaust. He no longer looks down to avoid the "World" but stares it in the face. He has not turned to surrealism or to obsessive behavior to mask the pain of the Holocaust. What he has rejected is the modern world, and in particular he has rejected the "return of the Greek" in Western culture. "The Greek" was as much rejected by early Christianity as it was traditionally by Judaism, but returned triumphant, first in the Renaissance and then in the modernist project of the Enlightenment: seminaries which taught only the Scriptures became Universities full of "Greek" topics in which theology now lives on only as a relic, its practitioners excused the scientific rigor demanded of the other disciplines. Hersh rejects scientific rationalism and he rejects art, the Romantic. We must not forget that "Roman" – with the emphasis on the second syllable – is the German word for "novel." Fiction, for the German-speaking world, is Romantic, full stop. Hersh rejects precisely such made-up tragedies of the Greeks and the Romantics because he has faced the real tragedy of the Holocaust. Nothing, he insists, will satisfy the tragic imaginings of the Romantics, because they desire only the passing, not Ha'Shem, not the Lord, not G-d. In terms of Kierkegaard's three "existence-spheres" Hersh has understood that after the Holocaust the middle sphere, that of the moral, faces the overwhelming failure of all theodicy. Where Chaim retreats to the first sphere, the aesthetic, Hersh has made his home in the third: religion.

The Devil's Arithmetic agrees with Hersh. The film in effect was saying: 'You only have faith in your G-d when things go well with you? Here is a girl who gives her life for another in the concentration camps. Does not such a thing give meaning to the world even in its darkest hour?'

7. Israel Judaism

Preamble

The Holocaust changed everything for the Jews. We saw in *The Chosen* that liberal Jews like Reuven Malter's father lobbied hard in America for the establishment of a Jewish homeland, and in the 1980 version of *The Jazz Singer* the cantor father says "Harry Truman was a wonderful man. Without him we would have been nowhere." This is a debt that many Jews feel to the American president who backed the creation of the new state of Israel. As the Jews in *The Chosen* watched the first broadcasts from the liberated concentration camps the momentum behind the founding of modern Israel grew, despite opposition from the Hasidim and other Jews who regarded Zionism as theologically incorrect. By now we have seen enough films to know that it would not be quite right to say that Hasids regarded Zionism as a "heresy," even if some used that word on their placards, it was more of a debate with strong views on both sides, as expressed by Reb Saunders and Professor David Malter, and was anyway largely settled after May 1948 when the fledgling State – amidst bitter fighting on the ground – declared its existence.

So how did the founding of Israel impact on the religion of the Jews?

The Roman Expulsion created the "portable" religion of the Jews, still apparent in the ark and Torah scrolls that can be so easily moved – as we saw in *Fiddler on the Roof* and *Little Jerusalem*. The Spanish Expulsion created messianic fervor that, according to Scholem, fed into Hasidism. The Holocaust created the bitter atheism of Sol Nazerman. But the founding of Israel has been a complex phenomenon so far in terms of the evolution of Judaism, and perhaps we don't yet have the distance from it to say anything conclusive.

For some commentators Israel has become the article of faith that has replaced G-d in the religious life of many Jews, while Yad Vashem, the Holocaust memorial museum a little west of Jerusalem, has become the third Temple. In *The Chosen* we see the beginnings of this shift. But films set in Israel shows something different, that while secular and Holocaust Judaism, as explored above, have deeply shaped Israel, the original beauty of Judaism also lives on, particularly in Jerusalem. We first look at some films of Israel history – *Masada, Exodus, Kippur* and *Waltz with Bashir* – none of which touch much on Judaism, and then films of Jerusalem Judaism: *The*

Body, *Ushpizin*, *Kadosh* and *My Father My Lord*. We then complete this survey with a remarkable film about Ethiopian Jews in Israel: *Live and Become*.

Israel History

Preamble

In *The Believer* Danny arrives at the Ansche Chesed synagogue in Manhattan and banters with an old class-mate about Abraham and Isaac. This degenerates into an accusation that Danny is a Jewish Nazi. He counters this by accusing his friend of being a Zionist Nazi.

"The Zionists are not Nazis," his friend protests.

"They're racist, they're militaristic. They act like storm troopers in the Territories."

A woman butts in: "And you hate them because they're wimps or because they're storm troopers?"

"They don't have extermination camps," the friend adds forcefully.

"They have Sabra and Shatila," Danny tells them, Torah in hand, *kippah* on head.

Is this a plausible conversation in the vestibule of a synagogue? I don't know, but perhaps part of Danny's inner conflict lies in his perception that the Jews in Israel have behaved like any other occupying force aiming at constructing an ethnic dominance. The film goes no further than this, but if Henry Bean, the director of the film, became more religious in the making of the film, no doubt this was an issue he must have thought about a great deal. What Jew does not?

We will see that *Waltz with Bashir* is an entire film devoted to the question of Sabra and Shatila, though the question of guilt and atonement are examined within a psychological framework, not a religious one. Before that we look at *Masada*, a film that dramatizes the effective end of Jewish sovereignty in Palestine and *Exodus* which dramatizes the effective beginning of modern Israel, plus a mention of the somber Israeli war-film, *Kippur*, which documents aspects of the Yom Kippur War, a war sprung on Israel on the Day of Atonement. All of these historic events frame the Jewish religion, have changed it in one way or another, and are part of the fabric of Jewish culture.

Masada

Masada is a TV mini-series released in 1981 comprising a total of 394 minutes of viewing time. It dramatizes the last stand of the Jewish people against the forces of the Romans in 73 or 74 CE in the ancient fortification of Masada overlooking the Dead Sea, built by Jewish kings and fortified by Herod the Great. The siege of Masada, according to the Jewish historian Josephus, ended in the mass suicide of its 960 rebels, and symbolizes the end of the Jewish inhabitation of their ancient land. From this time until 1948 the Jewish people mostly lived on as a diaspora. After the founding of the Israeli Defense Force (IDF) out of various militias involved in the war that established the state of Israel, the IDF held initiation ceremonies for its new recruits at this historic monument.

Masada opens with stunning aerial views of the fortification and a narrative explaining its historic significance. We see IDF recruits arriving for their swearing-in. "Part of their ceremony here," says the narrator, "will be the recounting of that moment in history which still echoes resoundingly today: the stand of 960 Hebrew men, women and children against the 5,000 men of the Roman tenth legion."

It is stirring stuff as you can imagine, produced for an American audience sold on the idea of the little guy standing up to the bullies of imperial might. After the real-life introduction the film series settles into its historic re-enactment, beginning with the sacking of Jerusalem in 70 AD. A few survivors escape, taking with them the only religious symbol they have: the seven-branched candlestick. On the way south they pass through Hebron, the site of the tomb of Abraham and the other patriarchs and matriarchs of the Jewish religion. Meanwhile the Romans are systematizing their tax collection across the province of Palestine, as they termed the land.

There is a synagogue scene in which a priest, covered in a *tallit*, prays aloud from a scroll in front of a seven-branched candlestick, located on a mountain near Hebron, where Eleazar, leader of the Jews, plans a raid on the town. A pact with the Romans fails and the Jews work their way south in the direction of Masada, encountering the Essenes on the way. These are keepers of the sacred scrolls, the scriptures, and are considered along with the Pharisees and Sadducees as a "sect" of the Jewish faith or philosophy. They were perhaps the equivalent of later Christian monastic sects, but, since the Diaspora, Judaism has for obvious reason not given rise to a monastic tradition. Eleazar argues with them, telling them that their monastic life is at an end: they have to work and to fight. The Jews continue to pray with their ancient scrolls in their synagogue, but just how historically accurate any of this is uncertain.

The siege of the fortress takes an uneven course, but the outcome is in no doubt. Eventually Eleazar has to accept that the end has come, and that the Romans can be held off no longer. He speaks to the assembled Jews of the inner circle, knowing there is no escape, knowing that some can fight and be killed but many will be taken alive to become an ornamental triumph for Vespasian in Rome. He knows what the Romans will do to Jewish women and children, a fate not right even for the worst amongst them.

"I say we should not insult our own flesh by letting them touch it while we live," he says looking into the eyes of his wife Miriam. "To put each other out of their reach, that is what is possible," he concludes. Slowly the others concur. Eleazar consults with a kosher butcher regarding the killing of animals, who tells him that the kosher rule means "to kill without giving pain." He gives instructions: the sharp knife is passed once across the jugular and the carotid veins. "Like that," is how the animal dies, he shows in a gesture.

In thinking of themselves as the sons of light, perhaps they have been guilty of pride, Eleazar tells the greater assembly. The Romans will butcher, rape and enslave them; they represent the sons of darkness. "The Jews are to be servants to no man," he declares, "Only to G-d himself, and who is the only true and just Lord of mankind. Now there is only one way to stand before G-d and say 'I am free.'"

He has given them the choice: to take their lives as he will his, or fight the Romans in the morning and possibly live as slaves.

"Was it He who put it in your mind?" asks an Essene as he leaves. "I don't know," Eleazar replies.

According to Josephus they all choose to die except for two women and five children later found alive. However, the historical accuracy of all this is in dispute, as only twenty-eight bodies have been found by archaeologists at the site. Still, Masada stands as a foundational myth, regardless of its historical basis. I discuss this in *The American Cinema of Excess*:

> It is not until the third *Matrix* film, where "Zion" is almost overwhelmed by besieging machines, that we realize how uncannily the scenario echoes a much more ancient siege: the one at Masada. "Zion" is the name given by the Wachowsky brothers to the heavily defended rebel community, a name that caused difficulties for the film across the Arab world. Zion is only mentioned in *The Matrix*, but *The Matrix Reloaded* begins with the threat to Zion from tunneling machines and "sentinels." A quarter of a million of them, one each for every man, woman and child of the Resistance.[103]

The modern retelling of the Masada story in *The Matrix Reloaded* concludes in total victory over the "virtual" besieging hordes and no suicide. In general Jewish culture does not condone suicide in the way the Romans did, for example; we saw in *Yentl* that Avigdor's marriage prospects were dashed when it was discovered that his brother had committed suicide. In *Schindler's List* doctors in the Warsaw ghetto administer poison to help their sick Jewish patients commit suicide before the Nazis ransack the hospital. This rare example, if based on historical fact, would be another echo of Masada.

Exodus

Exodus retells a story about a ship carrying Jewish Holocaust survivors. In real life the ship Exodus brought these refugees from France to British Mandatory Palestine on July 11, 1947, only to be seized by the Royal Navy. Every single one of these desperate camp survivors were sent back to Europe where many were forcibly placed in the only available holding areas: concentration camps once used by the Germans. It does not take much imagination to understand the despair of these Jews. It was a scandal that shamed Britain and helped galvanize support for the new state of Israel. In the film version the Exodus becomes something very different: a ship used to take Jewish refugees from a British camp on Cyprus to Israel, where they successfully disembark – a fiction typical of the loose relationship to history that characterizes the entire film. The actor Peter Strauss who played the heroic figure of Eleazar ben Yair in *Masada* was Jewish, but the heroic lead in the film *Exodus* was played by Paul Newman, whose Jewishness is debatable. We saw earlier that Abrams is concerned about films with Jewish characters played by Gentiles, such as Millie Perkins as Ann Frank. Abrams tells us this about Newman: "It should be mentioned, however, that Newman, whose father, was, and name is, Jewish, was not by *Halacha* (Hebrew: 'Jewish law') Jewish, that is by Orthodox / Conservative standards, but was so by Reform and Reconstructionist ones, and is listed as such on major websites."

Bartov has this to say about the film *Exodus*:

> Perhaps the most successful and influential film ever made on the link between Jewish victimhood in the Holocaust and Jewish heroism in Palestine / Israel is Otto Preminger's *Exodus* (1960). Loosely based on the story of the refugee ship *Exodus*, which carried forty-five hundred Holocaust survivors from France to British-Mandate Palestine in 1947, and also on several other events related to the period, the film depicts the Jewish State's struggle

for independence through the perspective of two amorous relationships. [104]

Bernheimer makes this introduction to the film as her number nine Fifty Greatest Jewish Movies: "The most extensive film production to date at its release in 1960, *Exodus* introduced a radically new image of the contemporary Jew to a vast audience. A valiant, virile and victorious Jew – personified by the dashing Paul Newman – was proudly paraded before the American filmgoing public in full Technicolor, Super-Panavision splendor in this epic drama based on the biggest bestseller since *Gone with the Wind*." [105] The novel on which the film was based was indeed a bestseller, and it and the film version probably did more to cement in the American imagination a certain version of the events leading up to the foundation of Israel than anything else, a version in which the Palestinian side of the argument was entirely overlooked. Americans in the late 1950s were not that interested or supportive of Israel, but *Exodus* changed that dramatically.

If Paul Newman as Ari Ben Canaan personified the new Jew in film, then he personified a Jew stripped of all Judaism. As a film it has nothing of interest concerning the beauty of Judaism, but it is a useful reminder perhaps that not only was Israel founded on secular principles – as Reb Saunders objected to – but that it was sold to the American public on that basis. We will see however in the other films in this chapter that we can discover interesting facets of Judaism in what is now the homeland for the Jews.

Kippur and *Waltz with Bashir*

First we look at two films that deal with Israeli wars: *Kippur*, set in the Yom Kippur War of 1973, and *Waltz with Bashir*, set in the First Lebanon War of 1982. Both portray entirely secular worlds, the first aiming simply to show what it was like to serve in war conditions and the second effectively an agonizing over Israeli guilt concerning the Sabra and Shatila massacres. Both show ordinary Jews in a country where military service is compulsory – with only Israeli Arabs and the ultra-orthodox exempted – a world away from the Hollywood heroics of Eleazar ben Yair and Ari Ben Canaan in *Masada* and *Exodus*.

Kippur opens with two soldiers driving to the front in a private car debating the key issues of their lives. One recommends that the other reads *One-Dimensional Man* by Herbert Marcuse – we note that the recommendation is not for the Torah or the Talmud. Just as with Danny Saunders the call of the Jewish thought of Marx and Freud – as found in the work of Marcuse and the Frankfurt School – appears more relevant than the Talmud.

In *Waltz with Bashir* the guilt over participation, even indirectly, in the fighting that led to the Sabra and Shatila massacres is dealt with in a psychological and not religious manner. The film opens with an old friend calling up the film director, Ari Folman, and insisting on meeting him in a bar. He needs to tell him about a recurring dream where he is chased by vicious dogs, connected with his military service more than twenty years previous in the First Lebanon War. Folman's real shock is the realization that he has blanked just about all of it from his memory. Why did his friend call him, instead of a psychiatrist or psychotherapist? Because a film can be therapeutic. "Don't you have flashbacks from Lebanon?" asks the friend.

"Flashback" is a filmic term: we have encountered films here with flashbacks, such as in *The Pawnbroker*, to first-hand events, and in *The Believer*, to recounted events, both based on the Holocaust. But "flashback" as a psychiatric term means the irruption of suppressed material into the conscious mind, via dreams or daydreams, or which can be recovered by regression techniques. In a religious context there is more however: the flashbacks dealt with in this film are about guilt, and where there is guilt there is the possibility of atonement. We should note however that the modern secular mind, as in Woody Allen, has abandoned the idea of a moral structure of the universe in which guilt should mean anything, and further, we saw earlier that in the novel and film *Atonement*, the modern secular mind has also abandoned the idea of atonement. What then can we expect from *Waltz with Bashir*?

Ari Folman denies that he has had flashbacks. His friend reminds him that he was a hundred yards from the massacres. "More like 200 or 300 yards," responds Folman, and that night, for the first time in twenty years, he does have a flashback to the war in Lebanon. Folman is standing on the beach – probably in Beirut – modern high-rise apartments to his left, a palm tree blowing in the wind and rain, and the sea to his right. He stares into the night, the sky lurid with light pollution. In his mind Folman sees the flares that illuminated the massacres, flares provided by the Israelis. Yellow flares.

A psychiatrist advises him to visit a friend in Holland who would know details of the events that are surfacing from Ari's unconscious mind. "Isn't that dangerous?" Ari asks. "Maybe I'll discover things I don't want to know about myself."

This is a crucial idea. What religion in the proper sense, and psychotherapy in the proper sense, have in common is a search for truth, regardless of the danger to constructed self-image. Facing uncomfortable truths is the essence of these paths. Of course, Ari Folman's exploration of his own truth through this personal filmic story-telling is also a universal truth for Israel, and more widely for us all. His friend is comforting him however: "We don't go to places if we really don't want to. A human mechanism prevents us from entering dark places."

In a flashback set in the height of the fighting Folman is in charge of a Merkava tank transporting the dead and wounded. He had never seen an open wound or bleeding before and in the shock of this he is now "looking for a bright light, salvation." One soldier asks the other what they should do. "Keep shooting." he says. "Isn't it better to pray?" asks the first. "Then pray and shoot," answers the other.

As Folman interviews other veterans of the war the story is the same: repressed memories and guilt, yet the guilt takes a different shape for each combatant. At one point a soldier, just arrived for the fighting in Beirut, winds his arm *tefillin* on, being about the only acknowledgement in the film that this war was fought by Jews who had a religion. In *Ushpizin* we found a man who had turned to his religion as a path of atonement for his violent past. But for Israel as a whole, indeed for any nation as a whole, that may not be possible, simply because in the foundation and perpetuation of a nation war is a defining act. The Israeli historian Benny Morris has seen this more clearly than most perhaps, concluding that "the Zionist project is faced with two options: perpetual cruelty and repression of others, or the end of the dream." [106] On the same theme Moshe Dayan is recorded as saying in 1956:

> We are a generation of settlers, and without the steel helmet and the cannon we cannot plant a tree and build a home. Let us not shrink back when we see the hatred fermenting and filling the lives of hundreds of thousands of Arabs, who sit all around us. Let us not avert our gaze, so that our hand shall not slip. The is the fate of our generations, the choice of our life – to be prepared and armed, strong and tough – or otherwise, the sword will slip from our fist, and our life will be snuffed out.[107]

Ordinary citizens of Israel, like Ari Folman, may not be aware of these sentiments, the latter by a founding figure of Israel, the former by one of its key modern historians. But Folman's "amnesia" and the need to explore it are part of the fabric of his nation and a direct outcome of this history.

What role could the religion of Judaism have in the healing of past guilt, and the construction of a future that was not one of "perpetual cruelty"? For such a future must come about. Ironically, it is the son of Moshe Dayan, Assi Dyan, who plays rabbis in two of our films, *Time of Favor* and

My Father My Lord. In neither case does the on-screen Judaism pursued by these men suggest a way forward however. The films are partially intended as indictments of religion, but *Waltz with Bashir* is an indictment of war itself.

Jerusalem Judaism

Preamble

In this section we are interested in films that build a picture of Judaism in Jerusalem. In 70 CE large numbers of Jews were expelled from Palestine by the Romans, and many of those that remained or later returned converted to Islam in its early conquests, a whirlwind sweeping up from the Arabian Peninsula that left Islam's third holiest shrine built on the ruins of the Jewish Temple. But some remained Jews, continued to practice their religion, and lived alongside Muslims and Christians in Jerusalem, the city in the world with perhaps the greatest concentration of religious heritage. Indeed there is even a psychiatric condition known as "Jerusalem Syndrome" in which Jewish, Christian and Muslim visitors to the city are overcome by religious fervor.[108]

The films here give us glimpses of the physical Jerusalem with its characteristic buildings erected from Jerusalem stone, quarried largely on the western slopes leading to the city. The architecture is blocked out using dressed stone and simple arches; in a climate with a strong Mediterranean sun and low rainfall pitched roofs are the exception not the rule; we also have glimpses of the religious "architecture" of an ancient Judaism. We saw that *Ushpizin* is set in a yeshiva associated with the Breslov Hasidic group, meaning that its spiritual heart has been re-imported as it were: the *shtreimel* headgear originally from the Crimea, while Breslov itself is a town in the western Ukraine. In general the Ultra-Orthodox of Jerusalem, or Haredi, originate in Eastern Europe. The term "Haredi" and its plural "Haredim" derive from references in Isaiah meaning to tremble at the word of "G-d", hence the title of the film *Trembling Before G-d*, looked at below (Quakers acquired their name for similar reasons). The Haredi grew out of resistance to the "Jewish Enlightenment," a desire to retain tradition in the face of secular, atheist and scientific ideas that appealed to many European Jews, as we have seen. Jewish immigration into Jerusalem in the nineteenth and early twentieth centuries resulted in three branches of Haredi established there: Hasidic sects, Lithuanian-Yeshivish streams from Eastern Europe, and Oriental Sephardic Haredim. All lived on the principal of *halukka*, donations from diaspora Jews who donated via their congregations around the world. Generally the Jerusalem communities of Haredi are very family-oriented, live in gated communities, and shun many aspects of modern life. They have also been spared military service.

Mea She'arim is one of the oldest such settlements in Jerusalem, and was established in 1874 as a courtyard community. It is the setting for the films *Ushpizin* and *Kadosh*, while *My Father My Lord* is set in the Etz Haim Yeshiva located on Jaffa Road close to the Mahane Yehuda Market in downtown Jerusalem, not more than 400 meters away. *Eyes Wide Open* was also partly shot in Mea She'arim, but, because of the subject matter of the film it had to be done guerrilla style: apparently the filmmaker and his team were regularly chased out of the district, and so landed up building a similar-looking location in Jaffa. As we saw earlier *Time of Favor* was shot on the desert hills of Kfar Adumim, the shooting location halfway between Jericho and Jerusalem, as well as around the Temple Mount.

The Body

In *The Body* – a film mostly set in Christian sites in Jerusalem – Jewish practice is an aside to the main story concerning the possible discovery of the remains of Christ. While not as slick as *The Da Vinci Code* – into which territory it strays – *The Body* is more credible, and has the same idea at its heart: what if evidence is unearthed – in this case literally – that challenges a foundational myth of the religion? If the Resurrection is not literally true, then what happens to Christianity? The film gives us a few glimpses of Judaic practice and ideas, as contrasted to Christian ones, and also dramatizes an interesting encounter between Catholic faith in the person of the Jesuit priest charged with investigating these claims, and the scientific search for "truth" in the person of the female archaeologist.

In a key scene in a synagogue a delicate negotiation has to take place between the Jesuit and the rabbi of a large and vocal congregation. The tomb where the alleged bones of Christ have been discovered is raided by Orthodox Jews, who "attack any archaeological dig where they think bodies have been found," according to the archaeologist. This leads the Jesuit into an interesting debate on the Talmud in front of a full synagogue, the members of which are initially determined not to return certain remains. The negotiations conclude when the Jesuit insists that his translator tell the venerable rabbi that "the Talmud needs men, as much as men need the Talmud." It is a polite way of saying that the Talmud is fallible. Once understood by the congregation there is an uproar. We are only prepared for such a scene in a synagogue – who can imagine it in a church? – because we know that disputation on religious questions is central to the Judaic tradition. It is not a breakdown of order but part of the order. Once quiet is restored, the rabbi speaks and the interpreter gives the translation:

"The rabbi is right!"

"Which rabbi?" asks the Jesuit.

"You," says the translator.

Fanciful, you might say, but none the less I think it indicative of a beauty peculiar to Judaism, the possible generosity towards a theological opponent in debate. This generosity leads in this case to a compromise: the jar of historical importance will be returned to the archaeologists but they must in turn promise that the bones will not be disturbed until they are sure they are that of a gentile. This is the religious point in question: for the Haredi in Jerusalem it is a sin to disturb the remains of a Jew. Negotiating the fact that Jesus was not a gentile is avoided later in the film by launching into implausible action-adventure violence, naturally.

Ushpizin and *Kadosh*

Ushpizin and *Kadosh* are films set in ultra-Orthodox areas of Old Jerusalem, the first, as we have seen, a positive and upbeat view of such a religious life, while the second, to be explored further in the chapter on Gendered Judaism, is more critical. *Kadosh*, as a film that apparently delivers a harsh critique of Haredi life, particularly for its women, would not have secured the cooperation of the Mea She'arim community, and we see no immediately recognizable scenes indicating a courtyard community. More of the film than in *Ushpizin* is set in the synagogue, which makes its location of interest however. There are also many street scenes, all of which convey the sense of the Old City of Jerusalem and the palpable religiosity of it.

Monastic traditions of the various faiths – which are communities set apart from family and ordinary life – exhibit huge variation in the rules for living and spiritual practice. As mentioned before Judaism could not develop monastic traditions once it became a religion of diaspora. However, given that family is at the centre of the religious life in Judaism, one could not imagine a better arrangement than a courtyard community bound together within a yeshiva and led by an inspired rabbi. Such extended family units live and worship in close proximity and follow a common Haredi tradition with a unique religious philosophy, distinct from other such communities. *Ushpizin* demonstrates this vividly, and was filmed, as far as I understand, with the willing cooperation of the residents of Mea She'arim.

In relation to such communities I want to turn to a comment by Martin Buber on the teaching of the Ba'al-Shem Tov, forerunner of the Breslov Hasidism of the *Ushpizin* community:

> The Baal-Shem teaches that no encounter with a being or thing in the course of our life lacks a hidden significance. The people we live with or meet with, the animals that help us with our farm work, the soil we till, the materials we shape, the tools we use, they all contain a mysterious spiritual substance which depends on us for helping it toward its pure form, its perfection. If we neglect this spiritual substance sent across our path, if we think only in terms of momentary purposes, without developing a genuine relationship to the beings and things in whose life we ought to take part, as they in ours, then we shall ourselves be debarred from true, fulfilled existence. [109]

We may recall that Moshe's trial is to be sent two criminals, former acquaintances, to be his *ushpizin*, his guests during the Feast of the Tabernacles. According to Buber's presentation of the Baal-Shem's teaching all the people we meet contain a "mysterious spiritual substance." Hence Moshe's duty during Sukkot was to acknowledge this spiritual nature of his guests, develop a genuine relation with them and help them towards spiritual perfection. Malli was right that they had flunked this basic test when Moshe sent them away.

Buber's exposition goes further however. It is not just people that we have to relate to in this way but all things, including animals, the soil, the materials we use and the tools we make to work with them. This is a universe not really touched on in our films: the world of work, the world of the production of things. Hasidism may be a key flowering of the Judaic spirit, and in it we find many things of beauty, but the world of work is given a sacred dimension elsewhere: in the Protestant tradition. "Work" – as in the making of things – has never been truly elevated to the sacred in Jewish culture, despite the strong indications of its importance in the passage above, though its related activity, business, has. Hence the Jews are sometimes compared with the Quakers, Amish, Parsees and Jains, all religious minorities that became wealthy business people.

Once we are alerted to this idea we can see it in many films. In *Ushpizin* the courtyard communities do not make things or participate much in the world of work; instead they are kept by devout Jews worldwide who donate towards their upkeep. This is no different of course to the tradition in many faiths of such upkeep of the devout. In *Der Golem* we saw that the golem, once created, was immediately put to work in fetching water, hewing wood, and shopping. In *The Pawnbroker*, when the bitter Sol Nazerman describes the economic history of the Jews he describes the purchase and selling of cloth, not its making. And in the film *Schindler's List* there is palpable bewilderment amongst the Jews required to work in Schindler's enameling factory, turning out kitchenware and then armaments. More, I would say: it is the bewilderment of the film's director, Stephen Spielberg. "Work" is not natural to the philosophy of the Enlightenment Jew, as we can see in the writings of Hannah Arendt or Karl Marx. As Arendt says, "… the revolution, according to Marx, has not the task of emancipating the laboring classes but of emancipating man from labor; only when labor is abolished can the 'realm of freedom' supplant the 'realm of necessity.'" [110]

This is not a criticism, but merely a way of placing in context the religiosity of the Jerusalem Haredi. In the founding of modern Israel they encountered something entirely foreign: industrial capitalism, imported from Protestant lands that had invented it, based on a profound engagement with materials and tools. For the tension between these two worlds to be resolved, it would seem that a revisiting of the Baal Shem Tov's words is needed. In fact all of us probably need to rethink our relationship with the modern means of production by which we live, to rediscover the spiritual substance of materials, tools, the earth, and its animals. Indeed perhaps it is the genius and beauty of Hasidism that we need to explore in order to "overcome the fundamental separation between the sacred and the profane," as Buber puts it.[111]

My Father My Lord

My Father My Lord returns us to a theme begun in the Introduction of the story of Abraham and Isaac, and that to engage with this story we should be willing to "labor and be heavy laden" as Kierkegaard put it. We may well have found that working through the disturbing film *The Believer* left us heavily laden with issues relating to the story, and it would be a labor indeed to any religious Jew to contemplate Danny Balint's assertion that Isaac remained a *putz* all his life as a result of his near-sacrifice. It certainly framed Danny's whole issue of passivity in the face of violence. We also saw that Johanna Petsche could relate the story to the work of Woody Allen, again through the connection with Kierkegaard.

In *My Father My Lord* the place of the biblical Abraham is taken by Abraham Eidelmann, an aging ultra-orthodox rabbi, and that of Isaac by his young son Menahem. This Abraham is a typical Haredi, and in various sets during the film we can see that his *shul*, as mentioned earlier, is the Etz Haim Yeshiva located on Jaffa Road in Jerusalem, now defunct.

Abraham prays thus at the bed of his sleeping child:

Israel Judaism

> Blessed are You, Lord, Who teaches Torah to His people, Israel. ... My Lord, the soul You have given me is pure. You created it, You formed it. You breathed it into me, You guard it within me, and one day You will take it from me and restore it to me in life eternal. As long as this soul is within me I thank You, my Lord, Lord of my forefathers, Master of all creation, Sovereign of all souls. Blessed are You, Lord, Who restores souls to dead bodies.

Menahem has woken to this prayer and to his father caressing his brow, and smiles. A little later the boy is tested by his father on the way home.

> ABRAHAM: Let's see if you know.
> MENAHEM: The arm *tefillin* corresponds to the heart and the head *tefillin* to the brain.
> ABRAHAM: Good. Which do you start with? The arm *tefillin* or the head *tefillin*?
> MENAHEM: The arm *tefillin* and then the head *tefillin*.
> ABRAHAM: What's the blessing for each one?
> MENAHEM: The blessing for arm *tefillin* is "To put on *tefillin*," and for head *tefillin* is "The commandment of *tefillin*."

They are walking along golden-hued Jerusalem stone making up the walls of the neighborhood, and we catch glimpses of the perimeter wall of the Etz Haim Yeshiva. We will pursue the Abraham and Isaac theme shortly, but first there is another theme that runs through the film: that of our relationship to Nature. Menahem encounters three things that belong to the world of Nature and the Nature religions, and which are antithetical to his father's narrow Judaism. The first is an Alsatian dog, the second is a playing card with a picture of indigenous people on it, and the third is a collared dove, nesting on a window ledge of the yeshiva. What strange filmic coincidence is this however? There are dozens of possible birds to discover in California and in Jerusalem on a window sill, but it was the collared dove, if you recall, that also appeared on the window sill of Elly's hotel room in the film *Bee Season*.

The dog prompts Menahem's first discussion with his father. He has witnessed an old lady taken ill and stretchered into an ambulance, accompanied by an Alsatian which attempts to lie on the floor of the vehicle, all the time moaning softly. It is clearly aware that its owner is in trouble, and has to be removed by a neighbor. Menahem ponders this and then asks his father: "Do dogs have souls?"

Abraham replies: "Absolutely not. Why do you think so? Do you think dogs are like humans? ... They have no will. No sins, No commandments. Nothing."

Menahem, like children all over the world, exchanges playing cards in the playground of his school. One of them depicts natives with a drum. His mother Esther is disturbed by it and calls in Abraham.

"Is this idolatry?" she asks.

"It is idolatry," he murmurs. "It is."

Menahem asks: "They're worshipping an idol?"

Abraham is becoming angry now. "Menahem, I don't know if they're worshipping, but it is idolatry. Idolatry! It should be torn up."

He insists that his son destroy it and shouts at the reluctant boy to force him, so the mother intervenes, suggesting that they can buy him some toy to replace it.

"Reward him for not participating in idolatry?" Abraham is incensed. His response to the dog and the card represent two facets of the total rejection by Judaism of its predecessor religions, those of an animist, shamanic, Goddess, and polytheistic type; we would expect nothing else from a conservative rabbi.

The theme of Nature is further pursued by Abraham in Torah class. His lecture is on Providence and starts off by pointing out that the Jews learn modesty from the Torah, not cats. He continues, watched by his son who is listening carefully:

> Our sages have taught us that the Almighty has two types of Providence when watching over the world, General Providence and Personal Providence. In General Providence the Almighty takes care of all the species in nature, seeing to their continued existence as species and kinds, not as individuals. G-d doesn't watch over individuals in the animal and plant kingdoms. When an animal eats another one or a man steps on an ant, it's not because the Almighty decided that that ant should die just then. He instituted natural cycles in them, which proceed according to His decree and He doesn't take into account what happens to them as individuals. The Almighty provided Personal Providence for man alone. The Almighty decrees an individual's destiny and what happens to him every moment. But here, one must understand that by "man" they meant only the righteous man who worships G-d. G-d doesn't watch over those who don't observe the Torah, and, naturally, doesn't watch over

those who aren't Jews with Personal Providence. Only with General Providence. And the entire purpose of people who do not worship G-d in this world is to serve the righteous man (*tzadik*). And they were created on account of him, just like inanimate objects, animals and plants. As of themselves they would not have the right to exist, were it not for the righteous man, who is the purpose of all Creation.

The film's purpose with this lecture is clearly to set Abraham up for a hubristic fall. What he has declared is against all natural justice and is nothing less than an indictment of his faith – at least if understood at face value. A deeper exposition may uncover a truth in it all that is quite reconcilable with ordinary notions of justice, but that is not the trajectory of the film.

A little later, and still on the theme of Nature, Abraham carries out a bizarre act, one which would be incomprehensible if we did not know its origins in the Torah. He has spotted the collared dove that Menahem has lovingly observed, caring for two fledglings in the nest on the window ledge, which Abraham climbs up to with some difficulty. He even breaks a window pane in his effort to reach the bird, the purpose of which is to scare it away. He then prays to himself in Hebrew. Menahem is upset by this, telling his mother that the bird has two fledglings.

In response Abraham asks the boy: "Do you know the commandment of 'sending away the mother bird'?" The boy says nothing, so Abraham recites the *mitzvah* to him: "'If you come across a bird's nest along the way you must let the mother go and only then take the young.'"

Menahem asks "So what happens to the young ones?"

"They're there… And you return them."

This makes little sense to Menahem. The boy is concerned that if the mother does not return, the young ones will be abandoned. All his father can say is this: "We do everything that is written in the Torah without asking why, because those are the laws of the Almighty."

Abraham is referring to a Jewish law derived from the Torah called *shiluach haken*, which applies to Kosher birds, and requires one to send away the mother bird before taking her young or her eggs. The Torah promises longevity to someone who performs this commandment, but does it really apply to any nesting bird, as opposed to domesticated fowl? That is doubtful.

In these scenarios the filmmaker is pointing us back to the key idea in Scholem's characterization of Judaism that it is a conversation between man and G-d, a drama played out in the human realm, and that "the scene of religion is no longer Nature." In all the Nature religions the animals most definitely have souls, so an Alsatian or a collared dove – even if eaten for food – would be at the heart of their religious drama. Abraham rejects all of that, as does his heritage. He has a precise theology of that rejection, that of two kinds of providence, a General Providence, which looks after species as a whole, but not over individuals, and a Personal Providence for man alone. Even then this is for the *tzadik*, the righteous man, and all other men are there to serve him – a stance that the modern democratic mind finds unacceptable. Of course, all of the rest of Nature, including all the animals, is there also to serve the *tzadik*, and part of the purpose of this film is to show how mistaken that must be.

But how is Abraham in this film to be corrected? By making him an unwitting Abraham of Mount Moriah, where he will sacrifice Menahem his boy, his Isaac. We are prepared for this by a scene in Menahem's school, where they are re-enacting the Abraham and Isaac story on the blackboard. The children each have cut-out figures they are sticking to it; Menahem has one of the ram. On first viewing of the film one could miss this: he keeps failing to stick the ram in place, because there is some problem with the glue, or he is getting something wrong. It is an odd detail that only makes sense after the tragic unfolding of the film runs its course, but clearly if there is no ram then Abraham has to go ahead and sacrifice Isaac.

And so it goes. The family has planned a trip to the Dead Sea for a holiday, and on their arrival Menahem and his father join the men's part of the beach, Esther the women's. Menahem is drawn to the world of nature as usual, and captures a little fish which he places in a plastic bag. But when it is time for him to join his father in prayers he is late in putting on his sandals, and then returns to the fish because he is concerned that the water will leak out of the bag. The father prays with the men, and does not watch over his son. We do not know why but the boy enters the water again and gets into trouble and there is no one there to save him. His mother is separated from him by Jewish law; his father is praying, again to fulfill the law, and in that double abandonment the boy drowns. It is a harrowing ending to the film, and is clearly meant as an indictment of a rigid religious adherence in which new life, a young mind, the creatures of the natural world, and even plain common sense are all abandoned in favor of strict observance of tradition.

Shifting Tides

Israel Judaism

Preamble

We encountered a number of times the idea that Judaism became a "portable" religion after 70 CE, and we have seen a number of films in which the Torah scrolls are carried out of one synagogue for one reason or another, and transported to a new home. No consecration is needed: it might be a new purpose-built synagogue or it might be a temporary structure as in *Little Jerusalem*. As Steinberg says of the Torah: "Not only does every synagogue contain this book; it is primarily by virtue of its presence, together with that of a congregation, that a synagogue is a synagogue, that is to say, a place set apart for Jewish worship."[112] Rich Cohen provides a vivid history of how this came about through the leadership of a rabbi known as Jonathan Ben Zakai. He opposed those Zealots who resisted the armed might of Vespasian and who perished at Masada, because he could see that the Roman military machine would inevitably triumph. In a pact with Vespasian before he became Emperor he was granted safety in a town called Yavne and permission to open up a religious school. After the destruction of the Temple it was largely Zakai who forged the changes in the religion at that time. As Cohen rather colorfully puts it, Zakai had to solve the problem of how the Jews could pursue their faith without the Temple, without a place for the animal sacrifice, without the place for all ritual, without the home of G-d. "These were the problems ben Zakkai was determined to solve," says Cohen. "In doing so, he would free Judaism from its physical home – from sanctuaries and courtyards and altars – so it could live in the air, where it could never again be plundered. It was ben Zakkai who turned the Temple into a book."[113]

Cohen is a secular Jew however, and his take on this dramatic change in Judaism, while true to some degree, misses the real nature of religion. He says that the Jews became a "meta-people" not living in the world but in their texts. We have seen examples of this to some extent in these films, *My Father My Lord* being one example. Cohen says that after the Jews were exiled from their land by Rome they "exiled themselves from time." Again this is also true to some extent, but then any attempt to maintain an ancient tradition must resist at least some of the march of modernity. We have seen that in many films too. Most controversially Cohen says that the continued study of the Talmud and the Torah has made the Jew "batty": "The Jew is a traveler on a fifteen-hundred-year-flight with just these books. He's read them so many times that he's come to see patterns in them, secret meanings, eerie coincidences, signals and clues."[114] Certainly this makes us think of Max and his Hasidic friends in *Pi*. Finally he says that the outcome of the Diaspora is mysticism, and that "the brain of every Hasid is filled with butterflies."

Now, Cohen praises Scholem's *Major Trends in Jewish Mysticism* as a great book and part of the modern Jewish canon, but one has to balk at "butterflies." Reb Saunders is a vastly solid fictional creation based on many real-world Hasidic rabbis whose mysticism is more grounded in the moral universe of existence than any materialist of the Woody Allen kind. Saunders's brain is certainly not filled with butterflies, for how else could he subject his boy to silence for the sake of his spiritual development and then at the end of the film ask in all humility whether what he did was right?

One might say that Cohen has yet to find the opening instructions on the box of Judaism. But Cohen's thesis about the "portable" nature of Judaism is cogent, and in the film *Time of Favor* we have seen the rumblings of a religious movement to reverse that, to rebuild the Temple in physical, non-book form. I included the film in the chapter on crazed Judaism because the rabbi in the film was accused of being crazy, and his pupil Pini carried out a crazy act of suicide bombing. Perhaps Rabbi Zvi Meltzer did have butterflies in his brain – as much as Rabbi Abraham Eidelmann did in *My Father My Lord* – but that would be to deny them their truly serious, if misguided, intention.

The *political* ramifications would be immense if Pini's ideas take hold of more ultra-Orthodox Jews, and any ensuing violence would be ugly. Intrinsically however there is no reason why the inner beauty of a religion should not be expressed in the outer beauty of architectural structures, and there are plenty of magnificent synagogues round the world to prove it. The modern country of Israel, founded as a secular state, is however a strange kind of place for a religion to undergo change. If a return to a Temple-orientation is one tide of change – and for world peace we may hope that this tide is stemmed – there are other tides in ebb and flow in this volatile new country. This is because it is the one place where all Judaic traditions meet: Ashkenazi, Sephardic, Mizrahi and the Ethiopian Jewish tradition also known as "Beta Israel". Our next film centers on that tradition.

Live and Become

Shlomo Sand in his controversial book *The Invention of the Jewish People* suggests that Judaism was a proselytizing religion until the rival religion of Islam swept through the Arabian Peninsula, the Maghreb, east Africa and the Levant. Sand sets out to challenge many myths about Jewish history, including for example the Exile of CE 70. We already saw that archaeologists have found only a tiny proportion of the supposed 960 bodies at Masada that Josephus insisted died there in a mass suicide. Historians today point out that little or no evidence exists for much of the religious history of the Holy Land, including that of the life of Jesus, and no conclusive remains have been found pointing to the Hebrew figure of King David either.

Not all of Sand's ideas are accepted, but it is clear that many non-Jews adopted Judaism as their faith throughout history. Indeed in *The Big Lebowski*, as I pointed out, a principal character is Jewish by conversion. In the film *Everything is Illuminated* the Ukrainian guide's dog is named "Sammy Davis Jr. Jr." and we learn that Sammy Davis Jr. himself, the Afro-American singer, converted to Judaism. Whole nations or parts of nations converted, either voluntarily or under edict.[115] One group of Jews who clearly converted to Judaism at some point in their history come from Ethiopia and are known as "Beta Israel." Their history is contested, but in 1984 and 1985, organized under the name "Operation Moses," many of them immigrated to Israel under difficult circumstances, their numbers now around 100,000. They had been persecuted in their own country, in which place the term "Falasha" originated, used as a derogatory reference meaning "wanderer" – an ancient and universal insult leveled at the Jew. Amos Elon praises Israel – then still reeling from the cost of the Lebanese War – for the airlift of the Ethiopians: "Few others would have gone to such trouble at home and abroad to import 14,000 destitute Africans, many of them illiterate, at a time of economic crisis."[116] He goes on to report: "The simple faith of the Ethiopians touched many a heart, 'It is impossible not to love them,' a doctor at one of the hospitals was reported as saying." Elon adds another interesting insight: "They were welcomed as Jewish *people* rather than of the Jewish *faith*."

The film *Live and Become* centers round a little boy caught up in this flight to Israel in Operation Moses in the 1980s. As a black child in a white Israeli middle-class family attending primary school – despite the broadly warm welcome his people receive – he is the subject of considerable racial prejudice. The twist to the story is that he is not – in the first instance – Jewish at all. He is born Solomon to Christian parents, but when his mother falls sick in the refugee camps she makes him go with a Jewish woman who has just lost her child. "Go, live and become," she urges him, convinced that otherwise he will die as she will. On arriving in Israel he is renamed Shlomo. We follow his life into adulthood and finally to reunion with his mother who survives after all.

When the bewildered young boy joins his adoptive family for their first supper the father says: "I want to be frank Shlomo ... we're not religious people." But he knows that the Falasha have "always defended the Torah" and out respect for the boy's tradition he produces *kippahs* for Shlomo, his step-brother and himself, in preparation for prayer before the meal. The boy just says, "That's nice, but not tonight," for he knows nothing of Judaism. A little later the father drops him off at Hebrew school, where the rabbi asks the usual questions of the class. Where did we receive the Torah? – Answer: on Mount Sinai. Who brought us the Torah? – Answer: Moses. The rabbi turns to Shlomo who is unable to hide from his gaze.

"Who is the founder of our religion?" he asks.

"Jesus," answers the boy, and in his confusion, as all the class turn in shock to stare at him, he elaborates from his rather muddled knowledge of his own faith. At several points in the film Shlomo turns and prays to the moon suggesting that his Christianity was anyway intermingled with older animist beliefs, as is common across North Africa.

The film is historically accurate concerning the difficulties facing Beta Israel in its new homeland. At one point the boy is summoned to Jerusalem for a "medical exam," going with his adoptive father and finding themselves at a place with the nameplate "Ritual Bath of the Jerusalem Rabbinate." Doctors there are attempting to take a drop of blood from each male's penis, as a way of "conversion", a symbolic circumcision. Once they discover this they escape from the compound with other Falashas, outraged at this deception pursued because of popular suspicion that they are not "proper" Jews. There are national demonstrations against this move, after which such attempts were dropped.

The boy's difficulties are continuous, despite the loving foster home and a range of benign authorities. Above all he longs for his mother, and is conscious of the fraud he is perpetrating. He even gives up at one point, goes to a police station and confesses to the desk sergeant that he is not a Jew at all, but the kindly policeman thinks that this is merely a reference to the popular suspicion against Falashas in general, and will not hear a word of it. Instead he encourages the boy to think of becoming a policeman when he grows up: the force needs more Jews like him.

Shlomo's one anchor point is an ageing fellow-Ethiopian called Qes Amhra. In Qes – a true Ethiopian Jew – we catch glimpses of how the Judaism of Beta Israel, while true to its original character, also absorbed some African spiritual elements. He is wise, as a rabbi should be, but indisputably African; he dances as an African and not as an Eastern European; he leads a community that is equally Jewish in Israel as any other group, but knows that politically and economically some are more equal than others – to use the Orwellian phrase. He officiates in a small synagogue filled with the smell of *challah* baking for the Shabbat, but he tells Shlomo that Israel has real Judaism but the real smell of the *challah* has gone – it was "the best bread of the week." He adds: "In the land of the Torah nothing smells anymore," no doubt a reference to industrialized food production that is overwhelming Arab tradition in Israel as much as Jewish.

Live and Become is a film of general beauty, telling the story of a non-Jewish boy in Israel who misses his Christian mother and the smells and moon of his own country. The particular beauty of Judaism is conveyed in two ways in this film: firstly through moments of Judaic practice and observance, and secondly because the film itself has a strong moral structure. It avoids no difficulties or controversies; Israeli society is portrayed warts and all; Shlomo himself is conflicted and does not always behave well. But he has great integrity, and we know this partly through his actions and partly because the actor who plays the adult Shlomo conveys this integrity well.

One of the more religiously beautiful moments comes when Shlomo's fledgling and rather mixed-up Judaism wins the day against conventional theology. Shlomo has put himself forward for Torah debate in the hope of doing well with the family of the girl he loves. Ahead of the event he is coached by Qes, who listens to Shlomo recite from the Torah. "No, that's not good," he says. "*Interpret*, Shlomo, don't repeat like a parrot. Interpret. Put some Shlomo into it. Let's start again." This is good religion; good Judaism. Unless each interpretation, each *Midrash*, contains something of its interpreter, what good is it?

The congregation gathers in the synagogue, Shlomo and his opponent are seated to face the audience, the rabbi is present. The father of Shlomo's would-be girl is the one who poses the very loaded debating question: "what color was Adam?" There is tumult in the audience, then hushed by the rabbi, amidst calls of "white, he was white". Shlomo's opponent is the first to answer.

> Adam was created in G-d's image. And the beautiful color chosen was white. We were all white in the beginning. After the flood, Noah and his sons emerged from the Ark. Noah cursed the descendents of his son, Ham, along with his grandson Canaan: "Cursed by Canaan, the lowest of slaves will he be to his brothers." Genesis, Noah, 9-25. Kush, Ham's eldest son, inherited another curse: some of Ham's descendents would have black skin. And so it was: Kush became black and from him were born the "Kusheems," the black people of Africa. The descendants of Ham became slaves and black.

There is much applause. "Kushim" is a derogatory Israeli term for black people, its origin is in the biblical land of Kush, which is today's Sudan – where some believe the Jewish Falashas came from. Now it is Shlomo's turn and he hesitates, saying "Are Adam and G-d the same color, white?" There is a long anxious pause. He begins tentatively again: "Michael said…" But Qes in the audience shakes his head and puts his hand on his heart, indicating that Shlomo must put himself into the argument. The young man begins again:

> No. In the beginning was the Word. G-d created Earth and us, giving life to the Word. G-d believed in Man, in each one, entrusting him with the Word, on condition that each give a different, marvelous and profound life to the Word in interpreting it. As for Adam, his name comes from "adama," "earth" in Hebrew. G-d created Adam with the earth, from clay and water. He gave him spirit, something marvelous like the Word. That's how Adam was born. Adam is the color of clay: red. Like the Sioux. Red in Hebrew is "adom." So you see, Adam is neither white nor black, he is red. But does he feel alright, alone and red in this new world? That's when G-d thought of Eve. But Adam did not understand what G-d wanted, what He was expecting of him. What was he supposed to do on Earth? What was he supposed to become? Why all these trials? But he knows he can't go back, he knows he has no choice, that he's here because G-d wills it, and he must become, and G-d is disguised as the moon, and watches over and protects him.

There is a pause as the audience digests this unorthodox account. Qes nods. Slow applause breaks out which then becomes thunderous; even his opponent claps in appreciation. Sara's father is the only one displeased, and as they leave many of the congregation shake Shlomo's hand, but Sara's father says that the boy is of the devil. "How dare you compare G-d to the moon!" He is right of course; the idea smacks of idolatry and animism. But Shlomo has spoken with the conviction of someone who does, admittedly, see the world in a slightly different way to the Jews of tradition, but in a way authentic to the African experience, and, more to the point, authentic to his own experience. One can object on theological grounds, but when faced with the integrity of that conviction religion must flex its boundaries a little or die.

Summary

Israel has a complex history. Judaism clearly lives on in Jerusalem in traditions mostly owing, it seems, to Eastern Europe, though the influx of Mizrahi and Ethiopian Jews bring other influences. Certainly the film *Live and Become* suggests that African Jews are contributing to the religiosity of

Israel Judaism

Israel in potentially fruitful ways. But perhaps the most beautiful image I take from our set of Jerusalem films is that of the courtyard community devoted to the religious life, as seen most vividly in *Ushpizin* but also in some of the other films here. In the next chapter we look at *Kadosh* and *Eyes Wide Open* which dramatize the difficulties that women and gay men may face in such ultra-Orthodox Jerusalem communities, and we should not avoid contemplation of such issues. Jerusalem has a filmic beauty however which, in the golden light that tinges the native stone of the Old City, gives Judaism a color and luminosity very different from that portrayed in often dark and candle-lit scenes of the East European *shtetl* films, or those set in New York.

8. Gendered Judaism

Preamble

In the films we have seen so far we have glimpsed a religious world almost exclusively defined by men. The Kabbalah was "made for men by men," as Scholem tell us. The wife and daughter of Reb Saunders are feisty enough but are confined to traditional women's roles, while Malli, the wife of Moshe, is religious enough, but takes her lead from her husband, and in *The Quarrel* the entire drama is between two men. Family is of the highest importance throughout – and is the subject of the next chapter, Family Judaism – which means that heterosexual relations sanctified by marriage are centre stage. Sex is far from a taboo subject, but so far only under the conditions of the imperative for children and the continuation of the Jewish race. In this chapter we look at films exploring the difficulties facing women, homosexuals and lesbians in traditional Jewish communities. We then find something of a contradiction in these films: in the very moments where the injustices faced by these people are most apparent within Judaism, the beauties of that religion are simultaneously made rather visible.

The problem for all ancient faith traditions, and especially so for monotheisms with their reliance on textual sources, is: how do you update it? While all faiths change, the pace of change demanded by the encounter with progressive humanism since the eighteenth century creates massive contradictions, and nowhere is this more apparent than in the area of gender and sexuality: we saw this in *Yentl*, looked at earlier. In this chapter we look at *Kadosh*, which dramatizes the difficulties modern women face in traditional Judaism, as does *Price Above Rubies*. We then turn to the documentary *Trembling Before G-d*, which deals with gay and lesbian Jews in Israel and America, while *Eyes Wide Open* explores homosexuality in an Orthodox Jerusalem setting.

Kadosh

Kadosh (meaning "sacred") juxtaposes glimpses of traditional religiosity with the theme of the patriarchal oppression of women. The film opens with Meir, a married Talmudic scholar, praying: "Thank you for your compassion in rendering my soul to me. You are the source of all trust."

Gendered Judaism

Steinberg describes the morning ritual, following a man's first prayers:

> Then he rises, and with each act in the process of getting up recites an ordained blessing: on washing his hands and face, prescribed as his first duty; on setting foot on the ground; on attending to his bodily needs; on donning an undergarment adorned with the fringes commanded by the Torah. So he refers his every move to G-d and fulfils the instruction that a man shall be strong as a lion and fleet as a deer to do the will of his Father who is in Heaven. [117]

Thus we watch Meir dress in religious fashion as he continues with his prayers which include thanks that he was not created a woman. This sets the tone and is part of what has attracted considerable criticism for emphasizing only the negative aspects of the Jerusalem Haredim, the religious community portrayed in the film. Meir proceeds to strap on the *tefillin* or phylacteries, one on the head and one on the left arm so as to be near the heart. He kisses his wife Rivka goodbye; it is clear that he loves and respects her. On the way out he touches the *mezuzah* – a little box fixed to the doorframe containing the sacred scroll – and kisses his fingers almost as lovingly as his wife. As he arrives in the (fictional) Guithaym Yeshiva, prayers are being half-read, half-sung. The room is banal and un-ornamented but well lit.

Rivka and her sister Malka can only peer at them through a screen, rather as Yentl did from the bars on the synagogue balcony from where she gazed with longing on the Talmudic scholars. Malka asserts that she won't get married. "Of course you will," responds Rivka. "We all do." The prayers continue, and to the untrained ear have a commonality with the sound of Arab Muslim prayer: very beautiful. Malka loves Yaakov, a musician, but we discover that a husband has been chosen for her, Yossef. She has to choose between tradition and love. In the next scene, back at the *yeshiva*, Yossef prays volubly for G-d's love and for the ability to study Torah, his voice reaching shouting pitch, while Meir sits through the racket immersed in his scripture.

"I beg of you," shrieks Yossef, "for you alone can hear my prayers."

Clearly the filmmaker is being a little sarcastic in the presentation here. Yossef wails and dances. Meir repeats with quiet dignity: "Blessed is our Eternal G-d, whose word has created all." Then there is silence. Then they debate whether making tea is forbidden – as "cooking" – on the Shabbat. These details are serious to them, and within the rigorousness of their approach to scripture there is much warmth amongst the men.

Once back at home Meir is told by Rivka that she can see the suffering in his heart: she has not been able to give him children. "You think we live in sin," she mourns, aware that without children their marriage remains unsanctified. "It's been ten years," he acknowledges. "But I will never leave you." It is the same tension in their marriage that faced Moshe and Malli in *Ushpizin*: the ordinary desire for children made more acute by scriptural injunction. He kisses his yarmulke before making love to her. Do etrogs help? Does such a kiss bring good luck? In Rivka's case no.

Kadosh introduces for us the particular nature of Jewish millenarianism in the run-up to the year 2000: the messiah is expected, as commented on earlier in the chapter on Crazed Judaism. Yossef drives through the streets proclaiming it over a megaphone. "Join us at eight tonight to enjoy one another's company," he shouts, "to pray, and to love one another." This love is religious love. His singing is not reserved for the yeshiva now, but broadcast over the streets. No one seems to mind. Back at the yeshiva they watch a Hassidic wedding on TV with a dancing rabbi in a *shtreimel* who moves just like Reb Saunders in *The Chosen*, arms in the air. All of this is Judaism, the beauty of it, even if the intention of the film is skeptical. The musician boyfriend Yaakov and Meir meet up and they sing:

> The Messiah will come
> We'll study the Torah.
> We'll live in Jerusalem
> In Jerusalem we'll study the Kabbalah.
> We'll live in a world of peace and brotherhood.
> Everything beautiful, everything perfect.
> It's not that bad studying the Torah.

How did that last line creep in? Is it more sarcasm from the filmmaker? I am not sure.

We mentioned in *Little Jerusalem* how Mathilde and Laura are advised by the *mikveh* woman in the ritual bath house (and we return to that scene in the chapter on Family Judaism). In *Kadosh* Rivka is told by the *mikveh* lady that sometimes women are barren because they have not obeyed the purity laws, so Rivka prays that she has properly observed the seven days of separation, that her body is to be purified. "For it is written," she says, "'I have sprinkled you with water and made you pure.'"

We return to more singing in the yeshiva: it is exhilarating, masculine. Meir's rabbi takes him aside, as we saw earlier, and says: "Meir, don't you feel, don't you feel we're on the verge of a new age? That something is coming? Are you making ready for it? Do you pray? Do you fast? Do you meditate?" Meir assents. "You know our laws," the rabbi continues. "The only task of a daughter of Israel is to bring children into the world. To give birth to Jews. And to enable her husband to study the Torah." A woman's place is in the home, her only joy in raising children. Meir is pulled between the force of love and loyalty to Rivka and the increasing pressure on him from his rabbi. In the *yeshiva* Meir is reminded: with the production of children they will vanquish the "others," the godless and the secular government – the one feared by Reb Saunders and his Hassidic followers.

"Sterility is a curse," declares Meir, who has become increasingly distant from his wife, unwilling to try further for a child. Marriage might be a sacred commitment but he is beginning to accept the pressure on him that declares him released from that bond on account of her sterility. She goes to the Wailing Wall and kisses it, retreating backwards in reverential fashion – she is facing divorce and her sister is facing a forced marriage to Yossef. Rivka is trying anything within the Jewish religious sphere to have her marriage blessed with child. Malka on the other hand plans to lose her virginity to Yaakov, and let Yossef repudiate her on the wedding night; these two women are made desperate in a man's world.

In Yaakov we find the modern Israeli counterpart to Kierkegaard's poet, singing of Romantic love in a night club. He cannot be the husband of Malka because he is not part of the Haredi world, instead he represents the secular Jew whose spirituality is drawn to the mysticism of the Kabbalah perhaps, and to the world of aesthetic musical beauty, a product equally of the Enlightenment and the New Age.

Rivka eventually receives a letter telling her that a woman without a child would be better dead, a text copied from the Talmud; it must be from the rabbi of Meir's synagogue. She feels that Meir is ashamed of her; even her mother is ashamed of her. Women don't study the Talmud, says Malka, furious, so they cannot find any way to contradict the men. She is enunciating an important truth: the Talmud is so big as to ensure that almost every injunction is open to debate, but when only men debate it what justice can there be for a woman? "That way they can do as they like with us," she adds. A woman, she complains, "cannot even hand a man a cup if she is menstruating." She is beginning to alarm her sister when she declares that she would like to stand in the synagogue and hold the Torah in her hands like a man (like Yentl perhaps). "You're mad," is the reply, but the real contradiction lies in the wedding dress she has been trying on. Malka is as conflicted over her forthcoming wedding as Yentl was, but a part of her clearly enjoys the significance and ceremony of the dress.

And so the wedding takes place, Yossef wearing the *shtreimel* to dancing and singing, the veiled bride walking around him accompanied by her mother. "Enter joy and elation," they sing under the traditional wedding canopy, the *chupah*. Once the ceremony is complete the men sing and dance

— as if in victory. That night Malka cuts her hair off as required by tradition and Yossef prays: "let my wife put forth sons to study the Torah."

Rivka's doctor then suggests the unthinkable: could Meir come for a sperm test? The clash between secular medicine and religious custom is total. Malka returns to the ritual bath for complete immersion, twelve times for the twelve tribes of Israel. She is unclean. Yossef is loudhailing again "... at the dawn of the year 2000 we will bring about deliverance."

At this point in the film we have perhaps the best shots of Meir's *yeshiva* showing the ark of the Torah scrolls as we hear singing. Again to the untrained ear its simply sounds Mediterranean, Levantine, Arabic. Beautiful. But the rabbi is forcing the issue: "You have the marriage contract?" Meir attempts to use the words of Ecclesiastes, that a man should live with his wife all the days of his life. But ten years are up and the rabbi is adamant that he must take a new wife.

"Sarah was barren, and our father Abraham did not abandon her," Meir comes back with.

The rabbi is unmoved: "A woman's life is in him who makes use of her."

The singing continues in the background, its beauty contrasted with the ugliness of the planned betrayal. Finally Meir gives in and raises the marriage contract – looking a little like a passport – to his lips. The rabbi takes it and kisses it too. But the religious respect shown here is clearly intended by the filmmaker as contrast with the disrespect for Rivka – for all women. The secular humanist world is not forgiving of this.

Rivka is cast out. The room that she rents is bleak and speaks of a secular world, though for countless young people it is the beginning of an adventure, one's first room on leaving home perhaps, alone, facing a new city to succeed or fail in material terms and in "relationships"; goodness knows, modern Israel has a thousand opportunities for a woman in business, in a university, anywhere. But to others it says this: all real community is now ended, you are sundered from your roots. Rivka stops speaking, even when Meir comes with a bottle of wine to celebrate the festival of Purim. He prays, but she is alienated from him. What in the world is he doing there? She retreats into her silence, wounded. Malka meantime makes love to Yaakov, is found out as being no virgin, and is driven out of her home by Yossef's belt. "Slut!" he shouts at her. So the two sisters, their lives and feelings apparently of no significance to their religious menfolk, lie together in the bleak room that Rivka has been forced to rent.

"There's another world out there," says Malka. "It's so big. Our world isn't all there is, Rivka."

Her sister responds: "I heard people singing a song outside: 'Put your hand in mine, I'm yours and you're mine.'" It is a popular secular song, the call of the poet, not the priest. Malka is suffocating in the Orthodox world, but Rivka just intones: "G-d of our fathers, for the psalms I have sung before you to soothe the pain of my child-bearing and to give me strength. That we not weaken, neither I nor the child I bear, before the day of my deliverance. When my time comes on the bed of deliverance in your mercy safeguard me from all pain and sorrow, Ease my deliverance. Let the child come painlessly and calm."

Is she going mad?

That night she goes to Meir, not yet remarried we assume, and lies with him. In the morning she is dead, we don't know how or why. But it is the Romantic ending to love, as Kierkegaard shows, the ending of the poet not the priest.

Kadosh then is a film of two worlds: the beauty of traditional religion lived by men of spiritual ardor, and the awkward sharing of it with women who are its casualties when the strictures of their religion cut across their needs.

A Price Above Rubies

A Price Above Rubies can be compared with *A Stranger Amongst Us* as portraying the religious-secular divide in a Jewish gemstone community in New York. Unfortunately *A Price Above Rubies* is mostly a cheap sop to popularism with some glimpses of genuine Judaism, where *A Stranger Amongst Us* is mostly genuine in its respect for the religion of the Jews with just a few cheap concessions to the mainstream.

Nevertheless *A Price Above Rubies* can be instructive not so much of a Judaism lost, but more as to how it is lost. The protagonist Sonia Horowitz is married to a devout Hasidic Jew and has a young child; her father was the finest gemologist in the State. Like Yentl she wants out of tradition; like Rivka tradition seems stacked against her; like Mathilde and Laura she is seen in the *mikveh*, though without any instruction we are aware of. Like Chaim in the *Chosen* she is drawn to the Romantic notion of the creative arts, but really the propaganda in this film is rather weak on art – in this case sculpture – rather the propaganda is more about sex as the ultimate value. Sonia is played by the actress Renée Zellweger, which I mention here only because of her well-known role in *Bridget Jones's Diary*, and her convincing portrayal of pouting resentful modern womanhood. She is feisty but wears the perpetual air of a little girl about to burst into tears.

We join the film some way in where her husband's brother Sender is about to introduce her to the gem trade – a move that brings condemnation from her sister and the wider community: a woman has no place in this man's world. Like Yentl, Sonia sees a "male" role as her fulfillment however; the bond with her child and her role as a mother mostly as a hindrance. Sender asks her about a stone and its mount and she proves to have as much expertise in this field of masculine learning as Yentl did in the Talmud. Sender is bemused, asking why she did not go into the gemstone business. She says her parents wanted her to marry a great scholar and live a decent spiritual Jewish life. "Did you marry a great scholar?" asks Sender provocatively: he must have known his brother well enough. "Well that I am not qualified to answer," she answers sulkily. She swallows as if this brings her pain. "But I know I married a *tzadic*."

"A holy man?" sneers Sender. "Don't you think our Mendel is a bit young for this distinction?"

"Age has nothing to do with it. Either you're born with the heart of a *tzadic* or you're not."

"And your heart?" asks Sender pointedly. "Is it in you heart to be the wife of a *tzadic*?"

The pouting, near-tearful, conflicted young woman cannot answer the key question of the film, though we quickly realize the answer is no. Her discomfort with traditional life leads her to seek advice from the rabbi that her husband serves, who praises Mendel's work: to fill the souls of children with the love of Torah, in his opinion, and that of G-d, is the greatest *mitzvah*. She just nods, but cannot speak until the attending scholar is replaced by the rabbi's wife.

"I don't know where my body ends and my soul begins," she tells the rabbi. "I felt ever since I was a very young girl like there was a fire inside me." It has been getting hotter. Now every touch burns her, she is on fire. "I have no soul," she declares in desperation. It is a bizarre confession.

"You have a soul," insists the rabbi with passion. "The Almighty gave every one of us a soul."

"Maybe," she says, "but if I do it wasn't G-d that gave it to me."

This is inexplicable to the rabbi, but for some other inexplicable reason the rabbi is inspired by Sonia's strange confession to make love to his wife that night; perhaps twenty years have passed since he told her she was beautiful.

We can certainly accept that Sonia is rebelling against her Hasidic tradition, and we can understand the lure of creativity and success in the business world. We could accept that Sonia has existential doubts. But can the film carry the metaphysics of it all? It has an hour left to do that.

Sonia takes the job of gem buyer offered by brother-in-law Sender. He then rapes her, at least that is one interpretation made by commentators on the film, another would be that it was casual sex, as she seems not to object.

This is after Sender tells her that he had realized at a young age that a conscience would be of no use to him: he is clearly far along the path that Judah Rosenthal only enters when he has his inconvenient mistress murdered.

As it becomes clear that she will have to leave her Jewish family behind her, her husband Mendel asks what it is that she wants.

"I don't know. Mendel, if I knew ..." She pauses. "Mendel, I just want something beautiful."

"But Sonia you have it right here. You have a home, a child, a husband who loves you more than anything in the whole world," says Mendel. He is wearing a *kippah*.

"Yes," she says. "In this world, maybe. But what about the other world? The world of the spirit and the Torah and the Talmud? What about that world? Do you love me more than that, Mendel? What about G-d? Do you love me more than you love G-d, Mendel?"

"Sonia, that's a terrible thing to ask," is all he can say. She withdraws her hand, held up to now in his. It is a terrible thing to ask, one could say, or one could say more metaphysically that it is a category mistake: these are different kinds of love.

She retreats across the kitchen. "You're a good man," she tells him, "and this life is good, but it is not *beautiful*." We see their infant child behind him in a high chair.

"But goodness *is* beauty," says Mendel with a calm conviction, lovingly. The baby stares up at him.

"No," insists Sonia. "Beauty has goodness in it, but beauty can also be *terrible*."

"Is that what you want?" asks Mendel puzzled. He hesitates. "That things should be terrible?" he asks. "Is that what would make you happy?"

Again the film has set us up for a metaphysical enquiry. Is this a reference to the poem "Easter, 1916" by William Butler Yeats in which the refrain is found: "All changed, changed utterly: A terrible beauty is born."? The phrase "a terrible beauty" was later used by historian Peter Watson for his book *Terrible Beauty: A Cultural History of the Twentieth Century*; [118] indeed "a terrible beauty" is one way to look at not just modernity and its wars, but perhaps our very life on this planet. There is enough in the Hebrew Bible that meditates on such a theme. But in the twentieth century "a terrible beauty" is also a deeply Romantic idea. Sonia has succumbed to it, but the film simply moves from this potentially meaningful exchange between her and her husband on this theme to sex on a table with her husband's brother. We learn nothing more about a "terrible beauty."

Through her work for Sender Sonia meets and develops a relationship with Ramon, an Afro-Latin sculptor, who she regards as a *real* artist. To the ordinary cinema-goer it might be convincing, but to anyone brought up in a genuinely bohemian background it rings false. The ambience, the nude modeling, the sculpture itself is typically of the avant garde that is co-opted by the mainstream and commercialized decades later. Thus portrayed, decades out of date, our long familiarity with it means that it carries no shock of the new, nothing transgressional in it at all and in this case offers no answers of any depth to Sonia's existential question.

She leaves her child and community behind, and so we are left with little hope for her. Many women – and men – have sacrificed their lives – and children – to art, but we are left dubious that Sonia will fare any better with art than with religion. Her existential anguish does not have the abyss behind it, we could say, just petulance, and without the abyss her art will mean little either.

If you doubt that the film becomes mere sexual / art propaganda against religion and fails its own metaphysical challenge, just consider this. At the funeral of the rabbi we discover that the his wife – the *rebbetzin* – is grateful to Sonia. Sonia's bizarre and incomprehensible confession to the rabbi, described earlier, stoked his long-forgotten ardor into lovemaking and in the midst of which he passed away; his wife tells Sonia that his last words were "I love you." It was the first time in twenty years he had said it. "You took a man away from his people for ever," says the *rebbetzin*, "but for one night you gave back a wife her husband."

One act of love-making means more to her than her husband's continued life, companionship and religious inspiration? Clearly it in was not in the *rebbetzin's* heart to be the wife of a *tzadic* either.

Arranged

Apart from *Little Jerusalem*, *Arranged* is the only film discussed in this book where traditional Judaism rubs up against traditional Islam. *Arranged* – as the title suggests – is about arranged marriage, in this case of two women, one Jewish and one Muslim, who work in a secular school. The film is set in the Ditmas Park area of Brooklyn some two miles away from setting for *The Chosen* and not far from the setting of *A Price Above Rubies*. Although the restrictions of traditional religion form part of the women's difficulties, *Arranged* effectively reverses the polemic of *Kadosh* and *A Price Above Rubies*.

Nasira, a young Muslim woman, and Rochel, a young Jewish woman, undergo an induction program in the school where they are about to teach. Nasira introduces herself as born in Syria, coming to Brooklyn when she was five. Her father was a *hafiz*, a scholar of the Koran, who now owns a gas station; she chooses to wear the *hijab*. Rochel, who suggests they call her

"Rachel" if they find it easier, does not mention her Jewishness or any adherence to Judaism, in contrast to Nasira's open expression of her faith.

A little later Rochel has to meet the *shadchan*, the matchmaker woman engaged by her parents, who talks about the business potential and earnings of each male, and before long Rochel suffers the embarrassment of meeting her first terrified Jewish suitor. This goes badly. "If this is the best there is I'd rather wait," she says; he is definitely not her *bashert*. The idea of waiting any longer is met with doubt from the *shadchan* and family alike, however, as she is no spring chicken.

Perhaps the most instructive episode of the film is when Principal Jacoby, headmistress of their school, invites Rochel and Nasira into her office. She thinks the two women are her best teachers.

"You are both successful participants in the modern world," Jacoby tells them, "except for this religion thing. So what happens in two, three years, I lose you to the yeshiva, to the mosque-school, and then they marry you off? C'mon, we're in the twenty-first century here. There was a woman's movement you know, I went through it."

The young women are equally dumbfounded, a reaction the head had not expected. In embarrassment Jacoby then offers them some money to buy designer clothes. They refuse. "Have a drink, enjoy yourself, you are too serious," she says, only making things worse. Afterwards the young teachers are equally stunned, and agree that they had not seen this coming, the event marking the beginning of a friendship, this time not one across the religious-secular divide, but across the Judaism-Islam divide. It is a common sentiment in many interfaith circles of course that participants of different religions have more in common with each other — even despite historical religious antagonisms — than they have with secular-minded people. It is not so common to find this explored in film however, and here is the value of *Arranged*.

The two women later meet in the park, both still thinking about the lecture they endured from their headmistress, who they agree was both ignorant and arrogant. As this is America they reflect that they could sue the principal and retire on the proceeds, or at least educate her a little. They do none of those things of course, but are able to support each other not only in the face of secularism, but also against the immediate pressure to take unsuitable offers of marriage.

The call of the modern world is strong however, and its messenger turns out to be Rochel's cousin who left the Jewish community with no regrets. She invites Rochel to a party. "Step into this world for a minute and see how it feels?" she says. The bass and drum music is throbbing, deeply sexual. Rochel won't shake hands with a boy. After a while she does dance with him, but he is too familiar for her liking. She looks on at everything, detached, sees dope smoking and suddenly finds she cannot cope with any of it: it is the shock of the religious person suddenly thrust into secularist world. She reads the Torah on the train on the way home; we are perfectly persuaded that nothing she saw at the party appealed to her. Looking back to *The Jazz Singer*, the version with Neil Diamond as the cantor's son, we may recall that his wife Rivka visits him in Los Angeles. She peers into his dressing room, a world of scantily-clad women, money-men and the trappings of stardom, to which she is as little attracted as Rochel is to the hedonism of her cousin's party.

Rochel becomes depressed about her marriage prospects but Nasira says: "G-d will show a way. We both believe that, right?" To help things along a little Rochel takes to wearing a wristband for good luck, however their headmistress spots it and rails against superstitious nonsense, how can they live so in the past? There is now a furious row about "choice." Rochel shouts that she has a choice! It is to be religious.

It is good to hear this said once in a while.

In a nice little twist Nasira plots a little matchmaking for a Jewish boy that Rochel likes, and visits the matchmaker who assumes from her looks that she is a Sephardic Jew. Rochel gets the Jewish boy she likes; Nasira also is lucky, so we conclude that matchmaking works, well, sort of.

Eyes Wide Open

Eyes Wide Open is a rather bleak portrayal of a married Haredi Jew, living in a Jerusalem district like Mea She'arim, who has a homosexual affair. Aaron has recently lost his father, and re-opens the family butcher's business in which much of the drama takes place. He has time for Torah study in his yeshiva. "He who dwells in abstinence is a sinner," reads the rabbi from the scripture, and the yeshiva followers nod in agreement; the pleasures one should not abstain from include wine. "G-d doesn't want a man to suffer. He shouldn't cause himself sorrow," continues the rabbi. But Aaron disagrees with this easy acceptance of life's pleasures. Loving G-d for him means a struggle with difficulties; to become a slave of G-d means loving the hardship. He is a man who does not smile much. The scene is intended to set us up for his forthcoming trial, but we can also take something else from it. The rabbi is a preacher, yes; he is enthusiastic about an idea in the Torah, yes; he speaks convincingly about it, yes. But when a student, in this case Aaron, contradicts him, he listens. The *manner* of his listening, if true to tradition, recommends that tradition to us. It is certainly how I conceive of the religious life: a deep listening to each other over questions of faith.

Let us turn to the drama of the film. Into Aaron's butcher's shop and into his life walks a young man called Ezri, a stranger looking for a yeshiva.

Of his past we know nothing. Aaron offers him his father's old camp bed in the room over the shop. Soon an erotic attraction grows, and perhaps the only time we see Aaron smile is when he is coaxed into the water of a stone cistern on the outskirts of Jerusalem to join the naked young man, where they wrestle and play in the water.

Ezri is then invited to join the Shabbat supper with Rivka, Aaron's wife, and their four children. Aaron touches the *mezuzah* on the way in and cheerfully leads the singing and clapping; he is still smiling. It is a classic celebration, undermined for us by Aaron's dishonesty. Whatever our views on homosexuality, this is also betrayal, or at least a moment leading to betrayal.

"You have a beautiful family," says Ezri to Rivka.

Ezri's rabbi calls at the shop and asks Ezri to drive him. In the narrow streets of Old Jerusalem the old man warns Aaron not to trust Ezri: he was thrown out of his old yeshiva. But Aaron defends him in an interesting way: "With all your knowledge and wisdom," he tells the rabbi, "you should understand this. G-d gave Ezri life and substance. And Ezri's way of worshipping G-d can only be accomplished by Ezri." Again, this is to me a deeply religious idea.

Later, on the roof of the butcher's shop Aaron attempts a kiss. Both are troubled by it. Aaron tells Ezri he must rise to this challenge; life is meant to be hard this way. "Why did G-d create lust?" asks Aaron. "For the catharsis of the soul." They look at each other. "We have a mission," adds Aaron. "The Lord didn't create broken tools. There is no such thing as 'broken'! Look what beauty, what complexity. You are a masterpiece. This is the challenge only we can overcome!" The young man does not look convinced … and perhaps we are not either. As in *A Price Above Rubies* we have a film here that sets its characters a metaphysical or religious challenge, but rather fails to follow through. Rivka slowly realizes what is going on, and finally asks Aaron what he wants, to which he says that he wants the be with her, his family. On the way to this resolution he and his shop are threatened by Jewish Haredi "heavies" who seem to police local morals. A window is smashed; posters are distributed saying there is a sinner in the neighborhood. Although the rabbi sends the heavies packing and addresses Aaron as "tzadic" or "righteous," the message is clear and is delivered in a slap. Aaron has transgressed the Law. All Aaron can say is that he needs the young man to feel alive. "I was dead and now I am alive."

That too is not so convincing. The homosexuality in this film, apart perhaps from the cistern scene, is not portrayed as particularly joyous or loving, and in the end is condemned by Aaron himself when he says to Rivka by way of a lame explanation: "It's the evil that took over me."

We might say that the film is brave and provocative, and that the subject needed an airing. It does also give many glimpses of Judaic practice, little details of life in a Haredi community in an unsparing and unromanticized way. But we probably need to be already convinced of the beauty of Judaism before we can find it in the details in this film, and we probably already need to be convinced that homosexuality is a genuine path before we can find its celebration here.

Trembling Before G-d

Trembling Before G-d is a film where Jewish religiosity is seen lovingly and respectfully, while critiquing that tradition: it exposes the agonies suffered by Jewish gays and lesbians because of the religiously-sanctioned prejudice they face. It is non-fiction however, structured around a series of interviews, and is arguably a *poetic* documentary because of interconnecting scenes showing elements of Jewish life and ritual in choreographed silhouette (a little like some scenes in *Fiddler on the Roof*). Once again, what comes over to an outsider to the religion is how intense the *struggle* is within the religion and with its G-d: this is conveyed, as in *The Quarrel* and so many other of our films here by the capacity to engage in passionate and at times angry debate, quite foreign for example to the sensibilities of British secular society. One is left however with the longing for Judaism, as with all ancient religions, to move more quickly on gender issues. The potential loss of the men and women in this film to their community is so unnecessary.

In *Kadosh* the women suffer mutely, but in *Trembling Before G-d* the gay men in particular, but also the lesbian women, engage vigorously with their tradition. The "other world" the big world of secular modernity is no more an option than it is for Rivka and Malka: the religion of these gays and lesbians goes so deep that the only option is to struggle with it, to struggle with G-d.

The film is based around interviews with gays and lesbians in different communities around the world, including in Jerusalem. The latter interviews help put the last film, *Eyes Wide Open*, into perspective: where Aaron was simply faced with more or less hostile elements within the Haredi community, a rabbi within such a community is shown in real life to be able to draw on another very Jewish, though partly secular resource: the psychiatrist.

The film opens with the proscription against homosexuality found in Leviticus 20:13, and the more obscure proscription against lesbianism in the *Shulchan Aruch*, Even HaEzer 20:2. The *Shulchan Aruch* is a Code of Jewish Law widely recognized, and contains within it the punishment of flogging for "women who rub up on each other" being like the "forbidden sexual actions of the Egyptians" mentioned in Leviticus 18:3. For homosexuality the punishment is death. Here we find again a startling contrast, not between the Jews and the Egyptians but the Jews and the Greeks: one only has to read Plato to find not just a tolerance of homosexual culture but arguments for its superiority.

"Even when you are sinning, you are with G-d," is the opening narration to silhouetted tying of the arm phylacteries and the commencement of bowing prayer. "When one falls, one falls right into G-d's lap, that's how one falls." This is how one homosexual comes to terms with his location in the Jewish faith. A woman then voices over the silhouetted images of women preparing candles and ritually washing hands: "I thought for a while: how can I be a religious lesbian? How does that go together? And I thought for a while: what if I am not religious? And it was almost like a physical revulsion, almost a physical rejection of that thought: it could not possibly be."

This real-life person is echoing what the two fictional women in *Arranged* knew: that secularists keen to solve their problems for them were entirely mistaken in thinking that leaving their religions was an option: their religions were simply too beautiful. On contemplating not being religious, what does one feel? An almost physical revulsion.

These opening moments set the tone for the film. The woman speaking about being a religious lesbian is shown in silhouette, the classical film or TV strategy for interviewing those who wish to protect their identity. It relates to the silhouette sequences which link all the interviews in the film, and which visually portray essential outer observances of Judaism. Collected together these sequences alone would form a significant short film of aesthetic merit pointing to the beauty of the religion. And here is a key thought about lesbianism from one of the interviewees: "It is more shunned by the Jewish people than by the Jewish law itself." This echoes Malka's point that the Torah and the Talmud are huge and in which all points of view are represented. Why take just one commentary as the ultimate arbiter of sexual conduct in this matter? The reality is that it is the community in its ignorance which shuns the homosexual and the lesbian, just as the community put pressure on Meir to divorce the wife he loved because she was barren.

A young man proudly wearing the *yarmulke* says simply: "I don't want to be a less-than Jew because I'm gay."

The pain of being something that is rejected so fiercely by tradition is palpable in each case, and it cannot be denied that *Trembling Before G-d* is a difficult film to watch, whatever one's views on homosexuality and lesbianism. In Jerusalem a rabbi with a mixed group of more and less outwardly-observant Jews is saying "Let us do this atonement ceremony for the sin of homosexual sex." They are attempting to atone for the sins of others; they rub ice-cubes over their arms and foreheads and blow the *shofar*, while gays and lesbians are attempting to change who they are with aversion therapies, prayer, diet, you name it. A Jerusalem therapist tells us of a rabbi who loves his wife, has had twelve children with her, but is gay and is always falling in love with his boy students in the yeshiva. Yet in fifty years he has never touched one, never given in to his true sexual longings. The therapist admires him as a truly religious man. But for a new generation that is not good enough: they want to be practicing gay or lesbian *and* be fully welcomed into the Jewish faith as practicing Jews.

We watch a lesbian couple make *challah* bread for Passover, we watch the lighting of candles, we watch the tying of phylacteries, we watch holy festivals, Jewish weddings, kissing of the Wailing Wall, religious dancing; we listen to Jewish music. There is tolerance and there is intolerance. It is not the point of this book to take a stand on the issue, but instead simply to point out that if you find the beauty of Judaism stirs you, then this particular film, despite the difficult subject matter, is more full of that beauty than many much easier films, and that beauty is at times unbearably moving. A young gay Jew dying of AIDS tells us how great Ha'Shem is, how grateful he is to Ha'Shem for the Torah, and for all his Jewish friends who celebrate the Jewish religion with him, and for the gift of having been made a Jew. Above all Ha'Shem has given him a soul; he seems not to be afraid of death. Indeed, what else is religion for, but to take away the sting of death? After all, is G-d not more available to us in the time of hard struggle than in the time of ease? *Eyes Wide Open* promises us some insight into that struggle but rather fails where this film succeeds.

"G-d wishes to learn from his conversations with humans," declares one interviewee. "It is all over the Torah. That's what the covenant is about!" It is not Judaism, he declares, if it is not *responsive* to the human condition.

Women in Judaism

I want to return to the particular problem of heterosexual women in the Jewish religion, which, in its origins, is patriarchal. The great Herodian structure in Hebron, the Cave of Machpelah, is also known as the Tomb or Cave of the Patriarchs, or the Ibrahimi Mosque, and according to tradition in both Judaism and Islam, Abraham, Isaac, Jacob, Sarah, Rebecca, and Leah, are all believed to be buried there. These are the patriarchs and matriarchs of the Jewish people, but "matriarch" gets left out in all of the varied names of the great fortress building: this symbolizes the gender imbalance.

In many of our Judaism films we find women of the modern era struggling with their role and identity within traditional Judaism. However, we also have many films where Jewish women are portrayed as content in their traditional roles, conveying what Gertel refers to as "the classical quality of Yiddishe *chen*, graciousness and understanding". As we saw he explained this quality as "knowledgeable and knowing, attractive and spiritual, devoted yet indomitable."

To the modern woman brought up in a feminist consciousness "indomitable woman" and "patriarchal religion" cannot co-exist. At the very least Margaret Miles is surely right when she makes this point about the films *Yentl* and *The Chosen*:

> *Yentl* is, however, a fairy tale, and *The Chosen* is a "realistic" film about the 1940s. Thus Yentl was somewhat more fortunate in her pursuit of learning than was Danny's sister who, when she tried to read a book, was first interrupted and teased by Reuven, and then ordered to the kitchen to cut vegetables by her mother. After Reuven learns that she is not a possible wife for him, Danny's sister is never seen again in the film. [119]

But is an "indomitable" Jewish woman one who seeks her own private fulfillment, as does Yentl or Sonia (in *A Price Above Rubies*)? Yentl, we saw, was firstly rather submissive for an indomitable woman, and secondly was prepared to risk the reputation and happiness of another woman, Hadass, in "marrying" her. Sonia, as we saw, had no idea of what she really wanted, other than some perhaps rather self-destructive desire to find something "terrible" in something "beautiful". Instead, should we not understand the "beautiful" that is sought by an indomitable woman more as a Plotinian beauty, i.e. something just, righteous, full of human warmth, and generous? When Leah, in *A Stranger Among Us*, compares Emily to Deborah, a female "warrior" in the Hebrew Bible, was this Deborah one who sought her own narrow ends, or that of the whole of Israel? Emily is after all serving the community, in which she is a stranger, as a "judge" – one who administers justice – and, despite and because of being armed, potentially risks her own life in the process. Emily is deeply taken by Leah, praised by Gertel for exhibiting *chen* or feminine charm and strength.

I cannot resolve this here. I suspect that the traditional role of Jewish mother leaves her with responsibilities and the exercise of power within the household that more than matches those of her husband in the world of work and Torah study. I suspect that there is potentially at least a balance to be had, one which *Kadosh* either deliberately overlooks, or simply could not find in the particular cases that formed the background to the film. However, if we had to judge by the films that are available, we would have to remain a little skeptical on this point. At the very least we have to wait for a film that dramatizes the indomitable spirit of the Jewish woman who adheres to the Jewish faith and who is at the same time a match for the weight of male tradition when it pitches against her. Avigdor tells Yentl that she already knows what is in the Torah. In one sense everyone does: the moral path is no actual mystery to anyone if they are honest enough with themselves. A film that has an indomitable Jewish wife who takes her studious menfolk to task for blind adherence to the Law – as in the blatant cruelty of what Abraham Eidelmann did with the collared dove – would set the record straight perhaps.

Summary

In this chapter we have considered a number of films where the weight of traditional Judaism works against women, and against gay, lesbian and transgender people. All traditional religion has to be held to account here in the light of the palpable advances in human rights of the humanist tradition. At the same time we have seen that the dilemma facing many protagonists is not just about losing their community. It is about losing their religion. Here the beauty of Judaism has been at its most poignant: who would care about losing something ugly? Of course faith and community are deeply bound together, but Rivka in *Kadosh* cannot face secular Israel with all the opportunities it offers to an emancipated modern woman; neither does her sister find a satisfactory solution. In *A Price Above Rubies*, however cheap many of its dramatic elements, Sonia's husband Mendel is more believable than her when he says the good Judaic family life is beautiful because it is good, where she declares a desperate desire for something "terrible." Did not the secular Nazis and the secular atom bomb provide enough "terrible" things to last that century and this? And the young women in *Arranged* are portrayed as deeply sane to resist the cocksure blandishments of secularism offered by the principal of their school. They *choose* religion, is what they tell her.

We have to say that the gay affair in *Eyes Wide Open* neither show us much joy in homosexual love, nor joy within the Jewish faith, but we could easily imagine a film with a similar narrative that did. It is, rather surprisingly, in the non-fiction film *Trembling Before G-d* that we find portrayals of both gay and lesbian love on the one hand and Judaism on the other that are equally filled with love and dignity. And a great deal of beauty.

9. Family Judaism

Preamble

Mystical Judaism, as we have explored it here, may draw some adherents and may be of general interest to others, but it is not the experience of most. Even less does the general population encounter the extremes of Judaism, the product of crazed Jews, whether ultimately constructive – as in genuinely pious and original rabbis, potential messiahs – or ultimately destructive. Loss of faith deriving from the Enlightenment or from the Holocaust tells us only of what is missing. The problems of gender – stemming from the clash of worlds where an ancient religion lives cheek-by-jowl with modernity – are all very difficult. Even more fraught are the multi-faceted problems of Judaism in Israel, a nation virtually under siege since its inception. But in one area the Jewish faith speaks to us all with simplicity and particular beauty: in the realm of the family.

Family life is one of the best things we know, and good family life surpasses all single pleasures known to us because it is perhaps the composite of all that is good. And, as Mendel Horowitz says of family life, what is good is beautiful. And of all good possible family lives Jewish family life has to be contender for the best. It returns us to Scholem's key remark that as Judaism turned away from Nature as the site of the divine it would now be the human community that would become the stage on which the drama between G-d and humanity would be played out, and this human community is above all an extended family. Within the family there are of course all kinds of tragedies and misunderstandings, and the rivalry between Abel and Cain epitomizes them. But in good times the Jewish faith is expressed most beautifully and in its greatest fulfillment in family life.

In *A Stranger Among Us*, Emily – the policewoman investigating the missing gem-worker – realizes in her first encounter with the Hasidic community that she is dealing with an extended network of family connections. She asks: "So you're all like a family?" The father of the missing man answers: "In a manner of speaking." This is another key to family Judaism: it is the extended family of tradition, not the nuclear family of modern times, in which the religion comes alive.

If we look at it another way, what does excommunication mean for a Jew? It means, amongst other things, exclusion from the *family* of Israel. Consider the following scenes from the Neil Diamond version of the *Jazz*

Singer. When Cantor Rabinovitch visits his son in California and learns of his son's divorce and new partner he realizes that Jess has rejected Judaism, rejected Israel. The old man tears his lapel as if mourning Jess's demise. His son has effectively excommunicated himself so is now as good as dead, but at the end of the film Jess takes his father's place as cantor in the Eldridge Street Synagogue in New York, where his father sits grim-faced through the recital. He has still not forgiven Jess and does not respond to his pleas for reconciliation. Afterwards Jess shows him a photograph of his grandson, named Chaim Rabinovitch. Initially this has no effect on the old man, so Jess just thrusts it into his father's hands. The old man stares at it, but still says nothing. Jesse gives up and walks off saying: "I guess if you don't have a son you don't have a grandson." His father further examines the photo. "Not so!" he says suddenly, clutching the photo close to his face, in time for Jess to stop and turn. "Mama's smile, your eyes." He kisses the photo and turns to his son. The bonds of family are too strong, the love of progeny too great, and so a man of the old faith has to accept his son again and abandon his more abstract principles.

Anyone who has watched the films discussed in the previous chapters will be struck by the many family scenes around the dinner table, whether the father is a rabbi or not, and whether the occasion is a religious festival or not. We complete this survey of Judaism on film by revisiting some family scenes in these films.

Festivals and celebrations

Steinberg tells us that the Jewish year "is adorned with many colors and much poetry." [120] He means the various festivals, many of which have appeared in our films, such as the Jewish New Year, Yom Kippur, the Passover and its Seder meal, and Sukkot, the Festival of the Tabernacles. Shlomo Sand tells us this on the subject of Hellenisation: "The temple that Herod was to build would be in a typical Greek architectural style; after its fall, even the Passover meal, the Seder, would take on the character of a symposium – i.e. a Greek feast." [121] I am not sure about this, but it cannot be denied in our films that the Seder meal is an opportunity for much debate. Perhaps it is simply a Mediterranean habit, to gather with wine and family, and discuss the great issues of the day and of eternity – certainly a custom that appears strange for example to the British with their nuclear families and dislike of talk about anything other than the weather. We saw that the Seder scene in *Crimes and Misdemeanors* was central to the film, and central to the moral problem that Woody Allen wanted us to consider. It was also a Seder meal that was interrupted by the anti-Semitic rabble in *Simon Magus*.

In *Left Luggage* the Seder meal is an important scene because the little boy, Simcha, thought educationally subnormal, has been coached to speak the appropriate prayer. It was potentially a good-humored family Passover meal, spoiled only by the father's insistence on correcting him over the first question. The father is referring to the telling of the story of the Exodus from Egypt, which begins with the youngest person at the Seder asking the Four Questions. This begins with: "Why is this night different from all other nights?"

In *The Devil's Arithmetic* the Seder becomes the crucible in which the modern Jewish woman – skeptical to tradition and leaning to all that secularism offers – comes to fully understand her G-d and the meaning of the Passover festival of deliverance. The Seder bookends the film and introduces for us the tradition of 'Elijah's Cup' and the ritual opening of the front door for him.

The Jewish New Year, *Rosh Hashanah*, also appears in a number of films: in *The Quarrel*, *The Diary of Anne Frank*, and *Little Jerusalem*. The *Sukkot*, the Festival of the Tabernacles, appears in both *Ushpizin* and *The Dybbuk*, marked with the holding of the "four species" including the etrog. The prayers in the synagogue in both films are rather beautiful: Moshe is being brought back to the path by his rabbi, while it was the setting for the solemn vows of Sender Brynicer ben Henie and Nisan ben Rifke regarding their future offspring. The festival of Yom Kippur, the Day of Atonement, is memorable in both versions of *The Jazz Singer* because of the utter beauty of the sung Kol Nidre.

Finally we witness the celebratory singing and dancing of the Hava Nagila in *Song of Songs* and the 1980 version of *The Jazz Singer*. In the former we are embarrassed by the young David's transgressional antics, while in the latter we are moved by the warmth of the community as it celebrates the birthday of the old cantor. It starts slowly as Jess comforts his old man and beckons to the little band to start playing. People start to clap, men get up to dance with each other, and then a circle forms. Faster and faster it goes, men and women together, unlike other scenes of more traditional communities where men and women dance separately. Okay, perhaps this is Jewish rather than Judaic, but in comparing the two scenes we can see what Jess is losing as he chooses pop music over sacred singing, and what David has lost when he wishes only to pervert all tradition.

Weddings

There are plenty of Jewish weddings in our films. Happy ones are found in *The Chosen* (though Reuven is a bit upset that Danny's sister Shaindela is now engaged), *Fiddler on the Roof* (though a fight breaks out), *Live and Become* (though Shlomo is not quite a real Jew), and *A Stranger Among Us* (though Emily must still feel the loss of Ariel). Unhappy weddings are found in *The Dybbuk* (featuring an unwilling bride who fails to go through with it), *Kadosh* (featuring an unwilling bride who does go through with it), and *Yentl* (featuring a groom who is really a woman).

Let us return to *The Chosen*, our first film, to look again at a Judaic wedding. We know that the advice and help of the Lubavitcher Hasidic community were sought in the making of the film, so we should imagine the wedding to be fairly authentic – even though real *shtreimel* hats were too expensive for this scene and dyed raccoon tails were used to make them instead. [122] The wedding is prefaced by a thought from Reuven Malter: "What a strange and wondrous household this was. I never realized how full the life of a rabbi could be. There were babies to be blessed and boys to be bar mitzvah'd and disputes to be settled. An almost endless procession of people came in and out to get advice from Reb Saunders. The really special events were the marriages."

Indeed, we then see such a marriage, accompanied in the beginning by sacred singing, as described earlier. A street seems to have been taken over for this event with perhaps fifty or more celebrants, and they form large concentric circles to dance, this time men and women separate. Reuven's secular reserve has to be broken to even handclap; dancing he is not up to. Danny dances in the traditional way, hands in the air, but Reuven resists, saying he doesn't know how to. The traditional cover is held over the groom, and more athletic dancing and handstands precede a slow tune and handclaps which is the cue for Reb Saunders to get up and dance solo. His movements are ecstatic, as we saw, his hands raised. Danny looks on with admiration.

What does it mean, this ecstasy? Reuven is clearly puzzled by it: his own father has never put on such a show. For such it is: a show by which the old rabbi blesses all the dancers. He sits down before long and claps vigorously, encouraging the increasing pace, as in the Nagila Hava. His dance is not long, but in it Reb Saunders condenses not just the Hasidic tradition of the Ba'al Shem Tov, but all Davidic dance, all sacred dance. It is a dance that reaches to the sky, somber at one level, blissful at another, movements of religious grace that have been lost in the spread of a more sexual dance sanctioned by secularism and materialism, a religious grace threatened with extinction. A civil marriage, whatever humanist equivalents are found, will mostly lack this special blessing.

Family Judaism

Sexual Relations

There are many religions, or branches of religions, in the world where a serious pursuit of faith means chastity. Not so in Judaism. Even for the most devout of rabbis the idea of celibacy would not only be bizarre but positively forbidden: it is a *mitzvah*, a duty to marry and have children. When Scholem discusses the emergence of medieval Hasidism as the second of his major mystical traditions, he comments on its emphasis on asceticism as one of its defining features. However he adds:

> There is one important respect in which Hasidism differs sharply from its Christian contemporaries: it does not enjoin sexual asceticism. On the contrary, the greatest importance is assigned in the *Sefer Hasidism* to the establishment and maintenance of a normal and reasonable marital life. Nowhere is penitence extended to sexual abstinence in marital relations. The asceticism of the typical Hasid concerns solely his social relations towards women, not the sexual side of his married life.[123]

In *Left Luggage* the Hasidic father of the family refuses the outstretched hand of the young woman babysitter. This is an example of what Scholem means by "social relations towards women": he is forbidden to touch a woman other than his wife. Similarly until she gets the point, Emily in *A Stranger Among Us* keeps extending her hand to male Hasids, to no avail of course.

In *Little Jerusalem* the *mikveh* lady gives advice on sex to the married woman Mathilde, her unmarried sister Laura listening in. Laura is the only one who has not covered her hair.

> MIKVEH LADY: Can we talk about your intimate moments?
> MATHILDE: (pauses) They're normal. I don't do things that the Torah bans.
> MIKVEH LADY: Such as?
> MATHILDE: (laughs in embarrassment)
> LAURA: Want me to wait outside?
> MATHILDE: (laughs again)
> MIKVEH LADY: Such as?
> MATHILDE: No, you can stay.
> MIKVEH LADY: I'll teach you to pleasure your husband, while respecting the Torah. You know you can be intimate in many ways?
> MATHILDE: (pauses) Yes, I know.

MIKVEH LADY: So?
MATHILDE: I'm afraid of losing my modesty ... of not respecting the commandments. And of moving towards my soul's evil inclinations. Aren't some things forbidden?
MIKVEH LADY: (sternly) Where does the Torah say they are?
MATHILDE: I was told.
MIKVEH LADY: Don't listen to others. It is written that, "if the evil inclination didn't exist, no man would build a house, take a wife or have children."
MATHILDE: But it is also written: "If the law is respected during intimacy, the divine is present."
MIKVEH LADY: Believe me, pleasure is authorized by Jewish law, and doesn't repel the divine. In fact, it reveals it. A devout woman must just keep her modesty, but modesty doesn't rule out pleasure. If your husband takes the initiative, you retain your modesty. You understand?

Between the three of them they sort out a matter of marital intimacy. The scene is beautifully played; in particular Mathilde's embarrassment, innocence, and determination to stay within the Torah are very well acted. It is of interest again to note that women may have less knowledge of the Torah and be at a disadvantage, not because of their religion, but because they have heard misleading interpretations of it. I have no idea if the women who officiate in the *mikveh* draw on the Holy Letter, the Kabbalist work that appears in *Yentl* and *A Stranger Amongst Us*, or whether they draw on a different text, but we are left in no doubt that sexual pleasure is okay. Of course, we should also note that limits are drawn: there is no real equality here if only the male initiates intimacies, as the *mikveh* lady says, and so we have to suggest that Judaic sexual law might need an update here and there.

Sex between husband and wife reveals the divine, we discover in Judaism, but this is in the context of creating the next generation of Jews. In a number of films we have seen that this obligation, or *mitzvah*, is taken so seriously as to become a burden on a wife, or even the cause of divorce if she proves barren. But under normal circumstances the progression of the generations is an expression of the Jewish faith as much as shared family ritual – for example the Shabbat – is its continued reinforcement within a generation. The practice of *tzeniyut* – modesty – is another *mitzvah*, as Gertel insists is well portrayed in the Hasidic community of *A Stranger Among Us*. When the policewoman at the beginning of her murder investigation appears in the office of the rabbi her bare legs are gently covered by a shawl so as not to violate the laws of *tzeniyut*.

The honorable place that the body, the sexual body, has in Judaism is clear from a remark by Steinberg: "The tension between body and soul which so harrowed first the pagan world and then the Christian is relaxed in Judaism. To the age-old question: which shall a man gratify, his flesh or his spirit, Judaism answers simply, 'both.'" [124] Steinberg also cites an ancient Jewish sage: "'He who sees a legitimate pleasure and does not avail himself of it is an ingrate against G-d who made it possible.'" [125] The point here is not to advocate indulgence through glut, but to sanctify the body in all its appetites, and no context does that more profoundly perhaps than marriage. As Steinberg puts it: "On all these scores, Judaism holds it to be a man's duty to marry and rear children. Conversely, it views voluntary abstinence from marriage as a triple sin – against the health of the body, the fulfillment of the soul, and the welfare of society." [126]

Nothing in Judaism is without debate however, and in her essay on the *Holy Letter* (the *Iggeret*) Evyatar Marienberg points out: the text

> [the text] fiercely attacks a relatively famous statement from one of the most prominent Jewish authors of all times, Maimonides (1135-1204), who said, "The sense of touch is a shame to us." The author of the *Iggeret* insists that sexual relations practiced in the appropriate manner are holy and clean. If done for the sake of heaven, "there is nothing holier and cleaner" than such relations. [127]

In *A Price Above Rubies* the wayward Sonia complains that sex for husband a *mitzvah*, a holy act. She asks: how can she enjoy sex when she knows he is thinking of Abraham and the Rabbi? Surely she is mistaken here, and Mathilde in *Little Jerusalem* is right, though needs the *mikveh* lady to help her out: it is absurd to suggest that husband and wife should think of Abraham or their rabbi while making love.

The Shabbat

Steinberg tells us this about the Shabbat:

> A delight and medicament to the observant Jew, the Shabbat is also something more; it has ever been a restorative of the vigor of Judaism and the Jewish group – so potent a restorative that there is a literal validity to the epigram of Ahad HaAm, modern philosopher of Judaism: "More than Israel has kept the Shabbat, the Shabbat has kept Israel." [128]

Family Judaism

Another key point about the Shabbat is that it is the central *family* event. We can observer this in many films. *Schindler's List* begins with a Shabbat scene of an extended family group. Two candles are lit as the prayers are recited by an elderly man holding the goblet and we hear the Hebrew of which this is the English version:

> Blessed are you, Lord, our G-d, sovereign of the universe,
> Who has sanctified us with His commandments,
> And commanded us to light the lights of Shabbat.

There is a wine bottle, and covered *challah* on the table, nothing else: this is the absolute minimum required for celebrating the Shabbat. All this fades out leaving just the two candles. This in turn fades to the guttering of the candles. The flame goes out; all highly symbolic.

Much later as the end of the war approaches, Schindler approaches a man grinding a shell-casing in his factory.

"How are you doing Rabbi? Rabbi?"

"Good, Herr Director," is his polite reply, having removed his cap.

"The sun's going down," says Schindler.

"Yes, it is," observes the rabbi, looking up at the skylight.

"What day is this? Friday? It is Friday, isn't it?"

"Is it?" asks the rabbi, uncertain.

Schindler leans into his face, aggressively, and asks: "What is the matter with you? You should be preparing for the Shabbat. Shouldn't you?"

For the American audience it was "Sabbath", rather than "Shabbat", but the rabbi is just bemused. Candles should be lit no later than 18 minutes before sundown, and Schindler understands this; also that a certain beverage is needed.

"I have some wine, in my office," adds Schindler. "Come."

So, some workers assemble, and candles are lit and turn yellow, one of the few color elements in the film apart from the famous scenes of the little girl in a red dress. The rabbi's singing of the Shabbat blessing is intercut with Germans frowning to hear it. The celebration ends with "Gut Shabbos."

There is nothing much more of Judaism in the film, beyond a scene with a rabbi wearing *tefillin* as an illustration of the Jews' arrival in Krakow, and a makeshift wedding in the camp where a woman, who is, obviously, not a rabbi, officiates. But why should there be? It had a different story to tell in its 195 minutes, and the near-bookending of the film with the Shabbat is very appropriate.

Family Judaism

As mentioned earlier the Shabbat evening in *A Stranger Among Us* is as romanticized as the barn-raising scene in the film *Witness*. However if we can put that criticism aside it is perhaps one of the best Shabbat scenes in the films we have considered. Emily has been wished "a good Shabbos" by the rabbi and the film then cuts to preparations in the kitchen. Emily has been set to work cleaning fish in a busy scene populated with perhaps seven adult women and five children. She manages to drop the fish to all-round hilarity and accompanying Yiddish music; a young woman helps a child break an egg into a flour mix for the *challah* bread. A much older woman prays before braiding the dough and placing three long loaves in the oven. Literally, "challah" is a *mitzvah* in the Torah which requires one piece of dough from each batch to be set aside for G-d, but the term now simply refers to this bread. Chicken is stuffed, salad is prepared, the bread is now baked, the kitchen table covered with dishes ready for serving, the dining table prepared with napkins and special goblets for the Shabbat wine, the "Kiddush cups."

The women light the Shabbat candles and sweep their hands in a ritual gesture three times towards their faces – taking in the "light" of the Shabbat, a way of internalizing the Shabbat spirit perhaps. They intone a prayer and wish each other a good Shabbat (in the film they use the alternative "Shabbos"). The rabbi, dressed in conventional *tallit* and *shtreimel* enters, flanked by two men in different costume, perhaps intending to convey Sephardic and Mizrahi rabbis respectively. The room fills with people to a total of perhaps forty in all. The rabbi, flanked by his more exotic counterparts, then holds the Kiddush cups and intones the Kiddush. Ariel is instructing a boy wearing *payot* and *yarmulke* on the Torah: he dips the boy's finger in honey and says: "So G-d's name will be sweet on your lips." The boy grins. This is all witnessed by a thoughtful Emily; nothing in her own life would have prepared her for this extended family-community meal – all we know of her own relatives is that she has a father, also a policeman.

A little later Emily has a small girl on her lap who feeds her something. Emily bends her head down sideways in an affectionate gesture to the child, and then kisses her. Ariel looks on in approval. How could all of this not stir something in the stranger among them?

Once food is eaten there is religious singing and dancing to vigorous handclaps. When the Western world looked on at Nelson Mandela he was so often dancing with friends and supporters, age being no obstacle to this, a mystery to Western families where Mom and Pop are "forbidden" to dance anywhere near their teenage children. The dancing becomes more athletic, as in *The Chosen* and *The Fiddler on the Roof*, and then mellows out to a circle dance in which there seems to be a determinedly international flavor: Ashkenazi, Sephardic and Mizrahi.

In *Little Jerusalem* it is a much smaller family, of African Sephardic Jewish descent, which celebrates the Shabbat. The group is a more realistic size in the modern world: a nuclear family of father, mother and four children, augmented by the wife's sister and mother. Even so there is a step-change here from the nuclear family in which Emily is likely to have grown up, in the inclusion alongside the *pater familias* of a step-mother and step-sister. They pass around the Kiddush cup, a silver goblet; the father and the little boy wear white yarmulkes, another boy a black one. Even the little girls drink the wine – very French you may say. "Shabbat Shalom" they repeat in turn. They boisterously sing and clap on the table. There is tension in the family, the nature of which becomes clear later in the film, but the structure of the Shabbat meal remains intact.

Finally we return to *The Believer* where Danny's girlfriend Rina sets a Shabbat table for him on his return. I commented on it earlier as a rather beautiful scene, this time for just two people. Danny spurns her, but we have to ask: what has drawn Rina to the rituals of a faith quite foreign to her own upbringing? Neither of these individuals is a good person in any ordinary sense: he has by now committed grievous bodily harm on complete strangers, attempted an assassination, and shot a colleague – at the very least that was manslaughter. She is the daughter of far-right parents equally committed to violence. But the Shabbat table is beautiful, she is beautiful, the evening light on her hair, on her dress, and on the candlesticks, glasses and wine bottle are beautiful. Beyond all of that the filmmaker seems to be saying: Shabbat is beautiful. Surely this is no Jewish narcissism which we suspect of being present elsewhere in the film: here is a celebration that we have seen in many of our films, a sacred mealtime with family, the outward rituals of which are all filled with grace. There is no reason on earth why anyone – including myself – who peers into the box marked "Judaism" should not find them beautiful.

Summary

In this chapter we have seen many example of how the Judaic faith touches on all aspects of family life. A set of forty-odd films dealing with Buddhism – which would equally be available to us – would not show us the same thing at all. The beauties of Buddhism lie elsewhere; after all, its founder abandoned wife and child in order to make the breakthrough that led to the new religion. Whatever lay Buddhists adapt in their religion to serve family, their faith is underpinned by celibate monastic orders. In contrast, Judaism,

Family Judaism

as a religion-on-the-move and without the possibility of the convent or monastery, had to integrate its deepest observances within family life.

The "color and poetry" of the Jewish Year, as Steinberg puts it, is much down to the festivals and the Shabbat, celebrated as extended family affairs. Returning to the film we started with, *The Chosen*, we must also acknowledge a Jewish wedding as something special indeed, when a Hasidic rabbi can dance so solemnly and ecstatically to bless a marriage.

Conclusions: The Beauty of Judaism on Film

There are secular people who are indifferent to questions of religion. There are secular people who study different religions much as non-artists study different art movements. There are those of one faith who study other faiths. There are angry atheists who have spent a lifetime studying the scriptures to refute religion. There are practicing and non-practicing Jews. Why should any of them imagine that one can discover the particular beauty of Judaism through the medium of film? I hope this book has answered that question in a way that is considerate to all the above constituencies. As I said at the beginning, just one film, *The Chosen*, is made so well as to embody all of what we are looking for. Nevertheless, some forty films later we have a far richer picture of Judaism and many scenes of Judaic practice or dispute that are vivid in the memory.

In bringing together some of the most religiously poignant, moving and dramatic moments from the films under discussion the sacred possibilities for Judaism on film are argued for. I have sought "the beautiful" throughout, and used it as prism by which to examine these films, but we could just as easily drop the term. Through film we have peered into the box marked "Judaism," one with no opening instructions, or at least we could say with fewer openings than other religions which are actively proselytizing. It is possible, and perhaps some would argue this, that we have looked only into a museum. Our survey of film may have been systematic, and the presentation structured in a plausible manner, but, as I said at the outset, we are unlikely to have gained a comprehensive view of Judaism in all its variety. Perhaps we have discovered next to nothing of contemporary Judaism. Perhaps we have only partaken in varieties of Hasidism as the main course, in a side helping of the Kabbalah, and in a garnish of randomly interesting things such as the Beta Israel. Perhaps Buber's assurance that Hasidism is the most important manifestation of the "soul-force of Judaism" also belongs to the museum. But I know that I have been immensely gripped by this investigation, and will never again think of Judaism as merely some kind of precursor to Christianity and Islam. What I have seen is a coherent religious universe quite unlike those religions or any other for that matter. I personally want to characterize what

Conclusions

I have seen as beautiful, but if the reader does not, then at least the reader must concede that Judaism – as we have seen it on film and have had it corroborated by Scholem, Buber, Steinberg and others – is *unique*.

It is unlikely that the reader will have got to this point at the first sitting and also seen all the films under discussion. I hope that the book will encourage viewing of at least the ten best films – granted, no more than a personal choice – as I have listed them in the Appendix. Better still, I hope that groups will view these films together and discuss them. I have found a film club kind of environment very rewarding for collectively exploring religion on film. Perhaps a university course could be based on the material here, or a study program in a yeshiva. What I do know is that it I found it a rather extraordinary journey of exploration. As I learned about key elements of the Jewish faith or small observances from one film, I found myself revisiting other films I had already seen, looking out for these details. Indeed I made many viewing iterations of some of the more important films, finding more previously undiscovered yet significant details. I hope that my presentation of these films will help viewers see the very real value of the films first time round.

Although this was a project I had in mind for many years, once I started it in earnest, I discovered many more films than I had realized with a bearing on the subject. Within them I found many more correlations than I had expected. But the biggest surprise must have been watching and re-watching *The Dybbuk*. One wouldn't guess that a ghost story of that vintage could embody such a profound and sustained Judaic piety, or provide such interesting correlations with the other films on such topics as the Kabbalah, the Sukkot, the role of the Hasidic rebbe, the matter of excommunication and exorcism, and the intensely religious community in which both the living and the dead might act out their dramas.

The ensemble effect of all the films I examined, including some not mentioned in the text, and including even the weaker offerings – alongside the texts I studied to clarify what I saw on screen – was both incremental and monumental. At the very least I can say that prior to this exercise – despite a lifetime examining the world's major and minor religions – I had been profoundly ignorant of the true contours of the Judaic faith.

My search for religious beauty was amply rewarded, but, whether we prefer this or another term for what is religiously profound, this form of investigation has opened up new religious vistas for me, and, I hope, for the reader. Are they vistas belonging to a museum? Have we only encountered religious antiques in this exploration? If so, let us treasure them.

If not, let us live them.

Appendix: Glossary of Judaic Terms

agunah	This is the *halachic* term for a Jewish woman who is "chained" to her marriage because her husband is missing or unable to grant her an official bill of divorce, known as a *get*.
bar mitzvah	Jewish coming of age ritual for boys, *bat mitzvah* for girls.
basherte	In an arranged marriage, ideal woman, destiny. *Bashert*, male equivalent.
bima	The podium used in synagogues for Torah reading during services.
challah	Braided bread used to begin the Friday night meal and the two meals eaten during Shabbat.
chazan	(Also hazzan) cantor, a Jewish musician trained in the vocal arts who helps lead the congregation in songful prayer.
dybbuk	A possessing spirit (possibly malicious) believed to be the dislocated soul of a dead person, ghost.
Ein Sof	G-d in the Kabbalistic tradition.
etrog	Citron, a lemon-like fruit used in the Sukkot celebration
Gemara	The component of the Talmud comprising rabbinical analysis of and commentary on the Mishnah.
get	A divorce document which, according to Jewish Law, must be presented by a husband to his wife to effect their divorce
Gilgul	Transmigration of souls (reincarnation)
Halakha	The collective body of Jewish religious laws derived from the Written and Oral Torah. Adjective: *halachic*.
halukka	The organized collection and distribution of funds for the Orthodox Jews the Holy Land, mostly in Jerusalem.
Hanukkah	Also known as the Festival of Lights, or Feast of Dedication, it is an eight-day Jewish holiday

Glossary

	commemorating the rededication of the Temple in Jerusalem.
Haredi	Ultra-Orthodox Jews
Ha'Shem	G-d
Haskalah	The Jewish Enlightenment
Hava Nagila	Meaning "Let us rejoice", a Jewish traditional folk song in Hebrew, typically played at Jewish weddings and Bar/Bat Mitzvahs
Hoshana Rabbah	The seventh day of the Jewish holiday of Sukkot, in which seven circuits are made by the worshippers with their *lulav* and *etrog*.
Kaddish	Prayer in general, or the Prayer for the Dead "The Mourner's Kaddish".
keriah	Tearing of a piece of clothing over the heart, usually a lapel, to indicate bereavement.
kibitz	To chat; to gossip; to make small talk or idle chatter.
Kiddush	Prayer recited before the Shabbat meal.
Kol Nidre	Aramaic declaration sung in the synagogue before the beginning of the evening service on Yom Kippur, the Day of Atonement.
kvetch	To whine or complain, often needlessly.
lulav	Closed frond of the date palm tree. It is one of the Four Species used during the Jewish holiday of Sukkot. The other Species are the hadass (myrtle), aravah (willow), and etrog (citron). When bound together, the lulav, hadass, and aravah are commonly referred to as "the lulav".
menorah	Ceremonial seven-branched candlestick.
mezuzah	Small box fixed to the doorframe containing a sacred scroll.
minion	Ten male Jews, the minimum for various observances.
mikveh	Ritual bath.
Mishnah	First part of the Talmud.
mitzvah	Religious duty, plural *mitzvot* (or *mitzvoth*).
mazel tov	expression of good luck, lucky you!, congratulations
Musar	A Jewish ethical movement in the nineteenth century
netilat yadayim	Ritual washing of the hands with a cup.
payot	Sidecurls.
rebbetzin	Wife of a rabbi.
Rosh Hashanah	Jewish New Year.
Seder	Passover meal.

Glossary

Shabbat	Jewish version of the Sabbath, beginning shortly before sundown on Friday and ending Saturday evening.
shadchan	The traditional Jewish matchmaker.
Shekinah	English spelling of a grammatically feminine Hebrew name of G-d in Judaism. The original word means the dwelling or settling, and denotes the dwelling or settling of the Divine Presence of G-d, especially in the Temple in Jerusalem.
shofar	Ram's horn, blown on religious festivals.
shtreimel	fur hat worn by many married Haredi Jewish men, particularly (although not exclusively) members of Hasidic groups, on Shabbat and Jewish holidays and other festive occasions.
shul	Yiddish term for synagogue.
Sukkot	Feast of Booths or Feast of Tabernacles is a pilgrimage festival lasting seven days. *Sukkah* in the singular refers to the booth itself.
tallit	Jewish prayer shawl.
Talmud	Contains the teachings and opinions of thousands of rabbis from before Christ to the 5th century CE. Has two parts, the first of which is the *Mishnah* and the second the *Gemara*, an elucidation of the Mishnah. The term Talmud can be used to mean either the *Gemara* alone, or the *Mishnah* and *Gemara* as printed together.
Tashlikh	Jewish practice usually performed on the afternoon of Rosh Hashanah, the Jewish New Year, where the previous year's sins are symbolically "cast off" by reciting a section from Micah that makes allusions to the symbolic casting off of sins, into a body of water such as a river or lake.
tefillin	Set of small black leather boxes containing scrolls of parchment inscribed with verses from the Torah, which are worn by observant Jews during weekday morning prayers.
Torah	The first five books of the Hebrew Bible, or this plus the rabbinic commentaries on it, or even the totality of Jewish teaching and practice.
Torah ark	A receptacle, or ornamental closet, which contains each synagogue's Torah scrolls. When possible the ark is located on the wall of the synagogue closest to Jerusalem.

Glossary

Tikkun Olam	Repairing or healing the world.
tsuris	Problems or troubles, borrowed from Yiddish.
tzeniyut	Modesty laws.
tzitzit	Knotted ritual fringes or tassels worn by observant Jews
tzaddik	In Hasidism: a righteous man, a saint.
ushpizin	Guest at the Sukkot festival
yarmulke	Skullcap
Yom Kippur	Day of Atonement, is the holiest day of the year for the Jewish people. Its central themes are atonement and repentance, traditionally observed with an approximate 25-hour period of fasting and intensive prayer,

Appendix: Ten Best Judaism Films

The Chosen	Widely regarded as one of the best Judaism films, it introduces us to debates within the faith and between Judaism and the modern world.
Ushpizin	A light-hearted story of a religious Jew in a Jerusalem setting celebrating the festival of Sukkot with his wife and two criminals.
The Quarrel	Two Holocaust survivors meet in Montreal and argue over their diametrically opposed reactions to their personal tragedies.
The Dybbuk	A remarkable Jewish ghost story, an early film of the "talkies" with subtitles and magnificent singing, taking in the Kabbalah, the Sukkot, excommunication and exorcism.
A Stranger Among Us	A woman police officer investigating a murder in a Brooklyn Hasidic community becomes entranced with a religious way of life she could not imagine.
Live and Become	The story of a non-Jewish Ethiopian boy who is adopted into Israeli society, becomes a Jew, and gives us many glimpses into alternative forms of Judaism.
Bee Season	A story of Kabbalistic mysticism pursued by a modern family in California.
Trembling Before G-d	A documentary featuring interviews with gay and lesbian Jews struggling to gain legitimacy within their own faith.
Little Jerusalem	A glimpse into a French Sephardic family where one sister is committed to her faith while the other is drawn to philosophy and secularism
The Believer	A difficult but rewarding film about a New York Jew who becomes a neo-Nazi, but undergoes a slow realization via the story of Abraham and Isaac that his path is not, after all, the right one.

Filmography

Adam Resurrected	2008	Paul Schrader
Agnes of G-d	1985	Norman Jewison
Arranged	2007	Diane Crespo, Stefan C. Schaefer
Atonement	2007	Joe Wright
Bee Season	2005	Scott McGehee, David Siegel
Believer, The	2001	Henry Bean
Big Lebowski, The	1998	Joel Coen
Black Narcissus	1947	Michael Powell, Emeric Pressburger
Body, The	2001	Jonas McCord
Bridget Jones's Diary	2001	Sharon Maguire
Cabinet of Dr Caligari, The	1920	Robert Wiene
Chosen, The	1981	Jeremy Kagan
Crimes and Misdemeanors	1989	Woody Allen
Deconstructing Harry	1997	Woody Allen
Der Golem	1920	Carl Boese, Paul Wegener
Devils Arithmetic, The	1999	Donna Deitch
Diary of Anne Frank, The	1959	George Stevens
Dybbuk, The	1937	Michal Waszynski
Everything is Illuminated	2005	Liev Schreiber
Exodus	1960	Otto Preminger
Eyes Wide Open	2009	Haim Tabakman
Fiddler on the Roof	1971	Norman Jewison
Hannah and her Sisters	1986	Woody Allen
Hannah Arendt	2012	Margarethe von Trotta
Holy Rollers	2010	Kevin Asch
Inglourious Basterds	2009	Quentin Tarantino, Eli Roth
Jazz Singer, The	1927	Alan Crosland
Jazz Singer, The	1980	Richard Fleischer
Kadosh	1999	Amos Gitai
Kippur	2000	Amos Gitai
Left Behind	2000	Vic Sarin
Left Behind II: Tribulation Force	2002	Bill Corcoran
Left Behind III: World at War	2005	Craig R. Baxley
Left Luggage	1998	Jeroen Krabbé
Little Jerusalem	2005	Karin Albou
Live and Become	2005	Radu Mihaileanu
Masada (The Antagonists)	1981	Boris Sagal
Matrix Reloaded, The	2003	Andy Wachowski, Lana Wachowski
Matrix, The	1999	Andy Wachowski, Lana Wachowski
Matter of Life and Death, A	1946	Michael Powell, Emeric Pressburger

Filmography

Title	Year	Director
My Father My Lord	2007	David Volach
Omega Code 1, The	1999	Robert Marcarelli
Omega Code 2 (Megiddo:) The,	2001	Brian Trenchard-Smith
Pawnbroker, The	1964	Sidney Lumet
Pi	1998	Darren Aronofsky
Pianist, The	2002	Roman Polanski
Possession, The	2012	Ole Bornedal
Price Above Rubies, A	1998	Boaz Yakin
Quarrel, The	1991	Eli Cohen
Schindler's List	1993	Steven Spielberg
Serious Man, A	2009	Ethan Coen, Joel Coen
Shadows and Fog	1992	Woody Allen
Shadows and Fog	1991	Woody Allen
Simon Magus	1999	Ben Hopkins
Sixth Sense, The	1999	M. Night Shyamalan
Song of Songs	2005	Josh Appignanesi
Stranger Among Us, A	1992	Sidney Lumet
Sunshine	1999	István Szabó
Time Of Favor	2000	Joseph Cedar
Trembling Before G-d	2001	Sandi Simcha Dubowski
Ushpizin	2004	Giddi Dar
Waltz with Bashir	2008	Ari Folman
Yankles, The	2009	David R. Brooks
Yentl	1983	Barbra Streisand
Zelig	1983	Woody Allen

Bibliography

Abrams, Nathan, *The New Jew in Film: Exploring Jewishness and Judaism in Contemporary Cinema*, London: I.B.Taurus, 2012

Arendt, Hannah, *The Human Condition*, Chicago: University of Chicago Press, 1998

Armstrong, Karen, *A History of G-d*, London: Mandarin, 1994

Bartov, Omer, *The "Jew" in Cinema: From "The Golem" to "Don't Touch My Holocaust"*, Bloomington: Indiana University Press, 2005

Bernheimer, Kathryn, *The 50 Greatest Jewish Movies: A Critic's Ranking of the Very Best*, Secaucus: Birch Lane Press, 1998

Buber, Martin, *Hasidism and Modern Man*, New Jersey: Humanities Press, 1988

Cohen, Rich, *Israel Is Real: An Obsessive Quest to Understand the Jewish Nation and Its History*, New York: Farrar, Straus and Giroux, 2009

Elon, Amos, *A Blood-Dimmed Tide: Dispatches from the Middle East*, London: Penguin, 2000

Gertel, Elliot B., *Over the Top Judaism: Precedents and Trends in the Depiction of Jewish Beliefs and Observances in Film and Television*, Lanham: University Press of America, 2003

Jacobson, Howard, *The Finkler Question*, London: Bloomsbury, 2010

Karmi, Ghada, *Married to Another Man: Israel's Dilemma in Palestine*, London: Pluto Press, 2007

Katz, Steven, (Ed.), *Mysticism and Language*, Oxford University Press 1992

Kierkegaard, Søren, *The Essential Kierkegaard*, Princeton, New Jersey: Princeton University Press, 1990

Kierkegaard, Soren, *Fear and Trembling: Dialectical Lyric by Johannes De Silentio*, London: Penguin, 1985

King, Mike, *Luminous: The Spiritual Life on Film*, Jefferson, North Carolina and London: McFarland, 2013

King, Mike, *Secularism: The Hidden Origins of Disbelief*, Cambridge: James Clarke & Co., 2007

King, Mike, *Postsecularism: The Hidden Challenge to Extremism*, Cambridge: James Clarke & Co., 2009

King, Mike, *The American Cinema of Excess: Extremes of the National Mind on Film*, Jefferson, North Carolina and London: McFarland, 2009

Kramnick, Isaac, (Ed.) *The Portable Enlightenment Reader*, London: Penguin, 1995

Bibliography

Lipsey, Roger, *An Art of Our Own: The Spiritual in Twentieth-Century Art*, Boston and Shaftesbury: Shambhala, 1988

Mantle, Burns (Ed.), *The Best Plays Of 1925-26 And The Year Book Of The Drama In America*, New York, Dodd, Mead & Company, 1926

Marienberg, Evyatar, 'Jews Have the Best Sex: The Hollywood Adventures of a Peculiar Medieval Jewish Text on Sexuality', *Journal of Religion and Film*, Vol. 14, No. 2 October 2010

Martin, David, *On Secularization: Towards a Revised General Theory*, Aldershot: Ashgate, 2005

Mazur, Eric Michael (Ed.) *Encyclopedia of Religion and Film*, ABC-CLIO, Santa Barbara: 2011

Medved, Michael, *Hollywood vs. America*, New York: HarperCollins Publishers, 1993

Miles, Margaret, *Seeing and Believing: Religion and Values in the Movies*, Boston: Beacon Press, 1996

Petsche, Johanna, 'Religion, G-d and the Meaninglessness of it all in Woody Allen's Thought and Films' in Hartney, Christopher Humphrey (Ed.) *Eternal Sunshine of the Academic Mind: Essays on Religion and Film*, Sydney : Dept. of Studies in Religion, the University of Sydney, 2009

Plotinus, *The Enneads*, (Trans. Stephen MacKenna), London: Penguin Books, 1991

Rudolf, Kurt, *Gnosis: The Nature and History of Gnosticism*, New York: HarperSanFrancisco, 1980

Sand, Shlomo, *The Invention of the Jewish People*, London: Verso, 2009

Scholem, Gershom, *Major Trends in Jewish Mysticism*, New York: Schocken Books, 1995

Steinberg, Milton, *Basic Judaism*, New York: Harvest Books, 1947

Watson, Peter, *A Terrible Beauty: The People and Ideas that Shaped the Modern Mind*, London: Phoenix, 2000

References

[1] Kramnick, Isaac, (Ed.) *The Portable Enlightenment Reader*, London: Penguin, 1995, p. 138
[2] Steinberg, Milton, *Basic Judaism*, New York: Harvest Books, 1947, p. 15
[3] Steinberg, Milton, *Basic Judaism*, New York: Harvest Books, 1947, p. 19
[4] Armstrong, Karen, *A History of God*, London: Mandarin, 1994, p. 226
[5] King, Mike, *Luminous: The Spiritual Life on Film*, Jefferson, North Carolina and London: McFarland, 2013, p. 237
[6] Medved, Michael, *Hollywood vs. America*, New York: HarperCollins Publishers, 1993, p. 61
[7] Abrams, Nathan, *The New Jew in Film: Exploring Jewishness and Judaism in Contemporary Cinema*, London: I.B.Taurus, 2012, p.24
[8] Abrams, Nathan, *The New Jew in Film: Exploring Jewishness and Judaism in Contemporary Cinema*, London: I.B.Taurus, 2012, p. 134
[9] Martin, David, *On Secularization: Towards a Revised General Theory*, Aldershot: Ashgate, 2005, p. 173
[10] King, Mike, *Luminous: The Spiritual Life on Film*, Jefferson, North Carolina and London: McFarland, 2013, p. 207
[11] http://en.wikipedia.org/wiki/Powell_and_Pressburger, accessed 18 May 2014
[12] Scholem, Gershom, *Major Trends in Jewish Mysticism*, New York: Schocken Books, 1995, p. 6
[13] Scholem, Gershom, *Major Trends in Jewish Mysticism*, New York: Schocken Books, 1995, p. 8
[14] Steinberg, Milton, *Basic Judaism*, New York: Harvest Books, 1947, p. 116
[15] Idel, Moshe, 'Reification of Language in Jewish Mysticism' *in* Katz, Steven, (Ed.), *Mysticism and Language*, Oxford University Press 1992, p. 43
[16] Scholem, Gershom, *Major Trends in Jewish Mysticism*, New York: Schocken Books, 1995, p. 7-8
[17] Medved, Michael, *Hollywood vs. America*, New York: HarperCollins Publishers, 1993, p. 62
[18] Scholem, Gershom, *Major Trends in Jewish Mysticism*, New York: Schocken Books, 1995, p. 36
[19] Scholem, Gershom, *Major Trends in Jewish Mysticism*, New York: Schocken Books, 1995, p. 37
[20] Steinberg, Milton, *Basic Judaism*, New York: Harvest Books, 1947, p. 47

References

[21] Buber, Martin, *Hasidism and Modern Man*, New Jersey: Humanities Press, 1988, p. 2

[22] Buber, Martin, *Hasidism and Modern Man*, New Jersey: Humanities Press, 1988, p. 41

[23] Scholem, Gershom, *Major Trends in Jewish Mysticism*, New York: Schocken Books, 1995, p. 13

[24] Plotinus, *The Enneads*, (Trans. Stephen MacKenna), London: Penguin Books, 1991, p. 47

[25] Plotinus, *The Enneads*, (Trans. Stephen MacKenna), London: Penguin Books, 1991, p. 49

[26] Plotinus, *The Enneads*, (Trans. Stephen MacKenna), London: Penguin Books, 1991, p. 49

[27] Kierkegaard, Søren, *The Essential Kierkegaard*, Princeton, New Jersey: Princeton University Press, 1990, p. 279

[28] Steinberg, Milton, *Basic Judaism*, New York: Harvest Books, 1947, p. 12

[29] Scholem, Gershom, *Major Trends in Jewish Mysticism*, New York: Schocken Books, 1995, p. 55

[30] Kierkegaard, Søren, *The Essential Kierkegaard*, Princeton, New Jersey: Princeton University Press, 1990, 284

[31] Kierkegaard, Søren, *The Essential Kierkegaard*, Princeton, New Jersey: Princeton University Press, 1990, p. 182

[32] Kierkegaard, Soren, *Fear and Trembling: Dialectical Lyric by Johannes De Silentio*, London: Penguin, 1985, p. 59

[33] Miles, Margaret, *Seeing and Believing: Religion and Values in the Movies*, Boston: Beacon Press, 1996, p. 88

[34] King, Mike, *Luminous: The Spiritual Life on Film*, Jefferson, North Carolina and London: McFarland, 2013, p. 238

[35] Medved, Michael, *Hollywood vs. America*, New York: HarperCollins Publishers, 1993, p. 63

[36] Bernheimer, Kathryn, *The 50 Greatest Jewish Movies: A Critic's Ranking of the Very Best*, Secaucus: Birch Lane Press, 1998, p. 3

[37] Miles, Margaret, *Seeing and Believing: Religion and Values in the Movies*, Boston: Beacon Press, 1996, p. 85

[38] Scholem, Gershom, *Major Trends in Jewish Mysticism*, New York: Schocken Books, 1995, p. 244

[39] Buber, Martin, *Hasidism and Modern Man*, New Jersey: Humanities Press, 1988, p. 40

[40] Scholem, Gershom, *Major Trends in Jewish Mysticism*, New York: Schocken Books, 1995, p. 344

[41] Plotinus, *The Enneads*, (Trans. Stephen MacKenna), London: Penguin Books, 1991, p. 47

References

[42] Armstrong, Karen, *A History of God*, London: Mandarin, 1994, p. 66

[43] Steinberg, Milton, *Basic Judaism*, New York: Harvest Books, 1947, p. 66

[44] Rudolf, Kurt, *Gnosis: The Nature and History of Gnosticism*, New York: HarperSanFrancisco, 1980, p. 15

[45] Steinberg, Milton, *Basic Judaism*, New York: Harvest Books, 1947, p. 88

[46] King, Mike, *Luminous: The Spiritual Life on Film*, Jefferson, North Carolina and London: McFarland, 2013, p. 181

[47] Bartov, Omer, *The "Jew" in Cinema: From "The Golem" to "Don't Touch My Holocaust"*, Bloomington: Indiana University Press, 2005, p. 240

[48] Scholem, Gershom, *Major Trends in Jewish Mysticism*, New York: Schocken Books, 1995, p. 340

[49] Bernheimer, Kathryn, *The 50 Greatest Jewish Movies: A Critic's Ranking of the Very Best*, Secaucus: Birch Lane Press, 1998, p. 183

[50] Medved, Michael, *Hollywood vs. America*, New York: HarperCollins Publishers, 1993, p. 63

[51] Marienberg, Evyatar, 'Jews Have the Best Sex: The Hollywood Adventures of a Peculiar Medieval Jewish Text on Sexuality', *Journal of Religion and Film*, Vol. 14, No. 2 October 2010, [2] http://www.unomaha.edu/jrf/vol14.no2/Marienberg_JewishText.html , accessed 10 May 2014

[52] Bernheimer, Kathryn, *The 50 Greatest Jewish Movies: A Critic's Ranking of the Very Best*, Secaucus: Birch Lane Press, 1998, p. 7

[53] Bernheimer, Kathryn, *The 50 Greatest Jewish Movies: A Critic's Ranking of the Very Best*, Secaucus: Birch Lane Press, 1998, p. 26

[54] Lipsey, Roger, *An Art of Our Own: The Spiritual in Twentieth-Century Art*, Boston and Shaftesbury: Shambhala, 1988, p. 236.

[55] Scholem, Gershom, *Major Trends in Jewish Mysticism*, New York: Schocken Books, p.17

[56] Scholem, Gershom, *Major Trends in Jewish Mysticism*, New York: Schocken Books, 1995, p. 285

[57] Scholem, Gershom, *Major Trends in Jewish Mysticism*, New York: Schocken Books, 1995, p. 124

[58] Scholem, Gershom, *Major Trends in Jewish Mysticism*, New York: Schocken Books, 1995, p. 133

[59] Wilson, Eric G., *Secret Cinema: Gnostic Vision in Film*, London: Continuum, 2006, p. 4

[60] Gertel, Elliot B., *Over the Top Judaism: Precedents and Trends in the Depiction of Jewish Beliefs and Observances in Film and Television*, Lanham: University Press of America, 2003, p. 232

References

61. Gertel, Elliot B., *Over the Top Judaism: Precedents and Trends in the Depiction of Jewish Beliefs and Observances in Film and Television*, Lanham: University Press of America, 2003, p. 234
62. Buber, Martin, *Hasidism and Modern Man*, New Jersey: Humanities Press, 1988, p. 45
63. Scholem, Gershom, *Major Trends in Jewish Mysticism*, New York: Schocken Books, 1995, p. 281
64. Marienberg, Evyatar, 'Jews Have the Best Sex: The Hollywood Adventures of a Peculiar Medieval Jewish Text on Sexuality', *Journal of Religion and Film*, Vol. 14, No. 2 October 2010, [23] http://www.unomaha.edu/jrf/vol14.no2/Marienberg_JewishText.html , accessed 10 May 2014
65. Gertel, Elliot B., *Over the Top Judaism: Precedents and Trends in the Depiction of Jewish Beliefs and Observances in Film and Television*, Lanham: University Press of America, 2003, p. 233
66. King, Mike, *Luminous: The Spiritual Life on Film*, Jefferson, North Carolina and London: McFarland, 2013, p. 208
67. Linnitt, Carol, 'Film Review: A Serious Man', *Journal of Religion and Film*, Vol. 13, No. 2 October 2009, [10] http://www.unomaha.edu/jrf/vol13.no2/reviews/SeriousMan.html, accessed 09/May/2014
68. King, Mike, *Luminous: The Spiritual Life on Film*, Jefferson, North Carolina and London: McFarland, 2013, p. 85
69. Marienberg, Evyatar, 'Jews Have the Best Sex: The Hollywood Adventures of a Peculiar Medieval Jewish Text on Sexuality', *Journal of Religion and Film*, Vol. 14, No. 2 October 2010, p. 283
70. http://en.wikipedia.org/wiki/Chaitanya_Mahaprabhu, accessed 26 May 2014
71. Mantle, Burns (Ed.), *The Best Plays Of 1925-26 And The Year Book Of The Drama In America*, New York, Dodd, Mead & Company, 1926, p. 176
72. Scholem, Gershom, *Major Trends in Jewish Mysticism*, New York: Schocken Books, 1995, p. 282
73. Scholem, Gershom, *Major Trends in Jewish Mysticism*, New York: Schocken Books, 1995, p. 291
74. Abrams, Nathan, *The New Jew in Film: Exploring Jewishness and Judaism in Contemporary Cinema*, London: I.B.Taurus, 2012, p. 153-154
75. Cohen, Rich, *Israel Is Real: An Obsessive Quest to Understand the Jewish Nation and Its History*, New York: Farrar, Straus and Giroux, 2009, p. 52
76. http://www.imdb.com/title/tt0247199/reviews?ref_=tt_urv, accessed May 20 2014

References

[77] Jacobson, Howard, *The Finkler Question*, London: Bloomsbury, 2010

[78] Bernheimer, Kathryn, *The 50 Greatest Jewish Movies: A Critic's Ranking of the Very Best*, Secaucus: Birch Lane Press, 1998, p. 56

[79] Scholem, Gershom, *Major Trends in Jewish Mysticism*, New York: Schocken Books, 1995, p. 99

[80] Steinberg, Milton, *Basic Judaism*, New York: Harvest Books, 1947, p. 91

[81] Steinberg, Milton, *Basic Judaism*, New York: Harvest Books, 1947, p. 93

[82] King, Mike, *The American Cinema of Excess: Extremes of the National Mind on Film*, Jefferson, North Carolina and London: McFarland, 2009, p. 127

[83] King, Mike, *Luminous: The Spiritual Life on Film*, Jefferson, North Carolina and London: McFarland, 2013, p. 72

[84] Allen, Woody, with Stig Björkman (interviewer), 'Woody Allen on Woody Allen' in Mitchell, Jolyon, and Plate, S. Brent, (Eds.) *The Religion and Film Reader*, New York and London: Routledge, 2007, p. 241

[85] Gertel, Elliot B., *Over the Top Judaism: Precedents and Trends in the Depiction of Jewish Beliefs and Observances in Film and Television*, Lanham: University Press of America, 2003, p. 92

[86] Petsche, Johanna, 'Religion, God and the Meaninglessness of it all in Woody Allen's Thought and Films' in Hartney, Christopher Humphrey (Ed.) *Eternal Sunshine of the Academic Mind: Essays on Religion and Film*, Sydney : Dept. of Studies in Religion, the University of Sydney, 2009, p. 27

[87] Bloom, Allan, *The Closing of the American Mind : How higher education has failed democracy and impoverished the souls of today's students*, London: Penguin, 1987, p. 155

[88] Lasch, Christopher, *The Culture of Narcissism: American Life in an Age of Diminishing Expectations*, New York and London: W. W. Norton and Company, 1991, p. 19

[89] Nathanson, Paul, 'Between Time and Eternity: Theological Notes on *Shadows and Fog*', in Plate, S. Brent (Ed.), *Representing Religion in World Cinema: Filmmaking, Mythmaking, Culture Making*, New York, Basingstoke: Palgrave MacMillan, 2003, p. 103

[90] Allen, Woody, with Stig Björkman (interviewer), 'Woody Allen on Woody Allen' in Mitchell, Jolyon, and Plate, S. Brent, (Eds.) *The Religion and Film Reader*, New York and London: Routledge, 2007, p. 242

[91] Allen, Woody, with Stig Björkman (interviewer), 'Woody Allen on Woody Allen' in Mitchell, Jolyon, and Plate, S. Brent, (Eds.) *The*

References

      Religion and Film Reader, New York and London: Routledge, 2007, p. 243

[92] Bernheimer, Kathryn, *The 50 Greatest Jewish Movies: A Critic's Ranking of the Very Best*, Secaucus: Birch Lane Press, 1998, p.102

[93] King, Mike, *Luminous: The Spiritual Life on Film*, Jefferson, North Carolina and London: McFarland, 2013, p. 208

[94] Mazur, Eric Michael (Ed.) *Encyclopedia of Religion and Film*, ABC-CLIO, Santa Barbara: 2011, p. 247

[95] Steinberg, Milton, *Basic Judaism*, New York: Harvest Books, 1947, p. 56

[96] King, Mike, *Secularism: The Hidden Origins of Disbelief*, Cambridge: James Clarke & Co., 2007, p. 103

[97] Bernheimer, Kathryn, *The 50 Greatest Jewish Movies: A Critic's Ranking of the Very Best*, Secaucus: Birch Lane Press, 1998, p. 173

[98] Abrams, Nathan, *The New Jew in Film: Exploring Jewishness and Judaism in Contemporary Cinema*, London: I.B.Taurus, 2012, p. 5

[99] Bernheimer, Kathryn, *The 50 Greatest Jewish Movies: A Critic's Ranking of the Very Best*, Secaucus: Birch Lane Press, 1998, p. 173

[100] Bartov, Omer, *The "Jew" in Cinema: From "The Golem" to "Don't Touch My Holocaust"*, Bloomington: Indiana University Press, 2005, p. 246

[101] Bernheimer, Kathryn, *The 50 Greatest Jewish Movies: A Critic's Ranking of the Very Best*, Secaucus: Birch Lane Press, 1998, p. 87

[102] Bartov, Omer, *The "Jew" in Cinema: From "The Golem" to "Don't Touch My Holocaust"*, Bloomington: Indiana University Press, 2005, p. 242

[103] King, Mike, *The American Cinema of Excess: Extremes of the National Mind on Film*, Jefferson, North Carolina and London: McFarland, 2009, p. 204

[104] Bartov, Omer, *The "Jew" in Cinema: From "The Golem" to "Don't Touch My Holocaust"*, Bloomington: Indiana University Press, 2005, p. 188

[105] Bernheimer, Kathryn, *The 50 Greatest Jewish Movies: A Critic's Ranking of the Very Best*, Secaucus: Birch Lane Press, 1998, p. 42

[106] Karmi, Ghada, *Married to Another Man: Israel's Dilemma in Palestine*, London: Pluto Press, 2007, p. 2

[107] Karmi, Ghada, *Married to Another Man: Israel's Dilemma in Palestine*, London: Pluto Press, 2007, p. 3

[108] http://en.wikipedia.org/wiki/Jerusalem_syndrome accessed 08 May 2014

[109] Buber, Martin, *Hasidism and Modern Man*, New Jersey: Humanities Press, 1988, p. 165

[110] Arendt, Hannah, *The Human Condition*, Chicago: University of Chicago Press, 1998, p. 104

References

[111] Buber, Martin, *Hasidism and Modern Man*, New Jersey: Humanities Press, 1988, p. 20

[112] Steinberg, Milton, *Basic Judaism*, New York: Harvest Books, 1947, 19

[113] Cohen, Rich, *Israel Is Real: An Obsessive Quest to Understand the Jewish Nation and Its History*, New York: Farrar, Straus and Giroux, 2009, p. 48

[114] Cohen, Rich, *Israel Is Real: An Obsessive Quest to Understand the Jewish Nation and Its History*, New York: Farrar, Straus and Giroux, 2009, p. 75

[115] Sand, Shlomo, *The Invention of the Jewish People*, London: Verso, 2009, p. 158

[116] Elon, Amos, *A Blood-Dimmed Tide: Dispatches from the Middle East*, London: Penguin, 2000, p. 104

[117] Steinberg, Milton, *Basic Judaism*, New York: Harvest Books, 1947, p. 122

[118] Watson, Peter, *A Terrible Beauty: The People and Ideas that Shaped the Modern Mind*, London: Phoenix, 2000

[119] Miles, Margaret, *Seeing and Believing: Religion and Values in the Movies*, Boston: Beacon Press, 1996, p. 88

[120] Steinberg, Milton, *Basic Judaism*, New York: Harvest Books, 1947, p. 131

[121] Sand, Shlomo, *The Invention of the Jewish People*, London: Verso, 2009, p. 155

[122] Miles, Margaret, *Seeing and Believing: Religion and Values in the Movies*, Boston: Beacon Press, 1996, p. 86

[123] Scholem, Gershom, *Major Trends in Jewish Mysticism*, New York: Schocken Books, p. 106

[124] Steinberg, Milton, *Basic Judaism*, New York: Harvest Books, 1947, p. 71

[125] Steinberg, Milton, *Basic Judaism*, New York: Harvest Books, 1947, p. 73

[126] Steinberg, Milton, *Basic Judaism*, New York: Harvest Books, 1947, p. 75

[127] Marienberg, Evyatar, 'Jews Have the Best Sex: The Hollywood Adventures of a Peculiar Medieval Jewish Text on Sexuality', *Journal of Religion and Film*, Vol. 14, No. 2 October 2010, [4]

[128] Steinberg, Milton, *Basic Judaism*, New York: Harvest Books, 1947, p. 130

References

Made in the USA
Charleston, SC
04 March 2017